Nothing Has to Make Sense

Muslim International
Sohail Daulatzai and Junaid Rana, Series Editors

With Stones in Our Hands: Writings on Muslims, Racism, and Empire
Sohail Daulatzai and Junaid Rana, Editors
Foucault in Iran: Islamic Revolution after the Enlightenment
Behrooz Ghamari-Tabrizi
Arc of the Journeyman: Afghan Migrants in England
Nichola Khan
Tolerance and Risk: How U.S. Liberalism Racializes Muslims
Mitra Rastegar
Nothing Has to Make Sense: Upholding White Supremacy through Anti-Muslim Racism
Sherene H. Razack

Nothing Has to Make Sense
UPHOLDING WHITE SUPREMACY THROUGH ANTI-MUSLIM RACISM

Sherene H. Razack

Muslim International

University of Minnesota Press
Minneapolis | London

Portions of chapter 2 are adapted from "A Site/Sight We Cannot Bear: The Racial/Spatial Politics of Banning the Muslim Woman's Niqab," *Canadian Journal of Women and the Law* 30, no. 1 (2018): 167–87; doi: 10.3138/cjwl.30.1.169; reprinted with permission from University of Toronto Press, https://utpjournals.press. Portions of chapter 2 are adapted from "The Racial/Spatial Politics of Banning the Muslim Women's Niqab: A Site/Sight We Cannot Bear," in *Law, Cultural Studies, and the "Burqa Ban" Trend: An Interdisciplinary Handbook*, ed. Anja Matwijkiw and Anna Oriolo (Cambridge, UK: Intersentia, 2021). Portions of chapter 3 are adapted from "'A Catastrophically Damaged Gene Pool': Law, White Supremacy, and the Muslim Psyche," in *With Stones in Our Hands: Writings on Muslims, Racism, and Empire*, ed. Sohail Daulatzai and Junaid Rana, 183–200 (Minneapolis: University of Minnesota Press, 2018). Portions of chapter 4 are adapted from "'We Didn't Kill 'em, We Didn't Cut Their Head Off': Abu Ghraib Revisited," in *Racial Formation in the Twenty-First Century*, ed. Daniel Martinez HoSang, Oneka LaBennett, and Laura Pulido, 217–45 (Berkeley: University of California Press, 2012).

Copyright 2022 by the Regents of the University of Minnesota

All rights reserved. No part of this publication may be reproduced, stored in a retrieval system, or transmitted, in any form or by any means, electronic, mechanical, photocopying, recording, or otherwise, without the prior written permission of the publisher.

Published by the University of Minnesota Press
111 Third Avenue South, Suite 290
Minneapolis, MN 55401-2520
http://www.upress.umn.edu

ISBN 978-1-5179-1234-5 (hc)
ISBN 978-1-5179-1235-2 (pb)

Library of Congress record available at https://lccn.loc.gov/2021061591.

The University of Minnesota is an equal-opportunity educator and employer.

UMP LSI

For my brother Zai

Contents

Introduction Anti-Muslim Racism, Whiteness,   1
White Supremacy, and Law

1 "A New Phase of a Very Old War": Islam and   51
White Conservative Christian Aggrievement

2 "I Can Never Tell If You're Responding to My Smile":   85
Desiring Muslim Women

3 "Terrorism in Their Genes": Racial Science   115
and the Muslim Terrorist

4 "We Didn't Kill 'em, We Didn't Cut Their Heads Off":   145
Torture and the Making of American Innocence

Conclusion Arriving as Muslim   177

Acknowledgments   199

Notes   203

Index   251

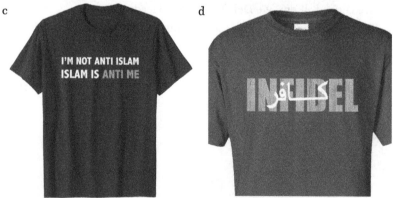

Figure 1. *(a)* "Allah Is Not God" T-shirt by TeeChip. *(b)* Anti-Muslim protestors at free speech rally (Screenshot/Fox10). *(c)* "I'm Not Anti Islam, Islam Is Anti Me" T-shirt by Anti Terror Designs. *(d)* "Infidel" T-shirt by Gadsden and Culpeper American Heritage Shoppe.

INTRODUCTION
Anti-Muslim Racism, Whiteness, White Supremacy, and Law

Once they are all in our heads, it is difficult to distinguish between
ghosts, demons, and dream figures.

—RENÉE L. BERGLAND, *THE NATIONAL UNCANNY:*
INDIAN GHOSTS AND AMERICAN SUBJECTS

In 2020, the year of Black Lives Matter protests worldwide and a global
pandemic, anti-Muslim T-shirts were in fashion. Sold everywhere, they
adorned protestors at freedom of speech rallies in Europe and North
America and were worn by political constituents of both the right and the
left, an indication of the political capital to be gained from denigrating
Muslims. The slogans ranged from in-your-face declarations that "Allah
Is Not God, Mohammed Is Not His Prophet" (Figure 1a) and "F**k Islam"
(Figure 1b) to cartoons from the French magazine *Charlie Hebdo* depict-
ing Muslim men and boys as rapists,[1] to a more restrained "I'm Not Anti
Islam, Islam Is Anti Me" (Figure 1c) expressing a liberal feminist position
about Islam's misogyny. The T-shirts are pedagogical sites that circulate
an anti-Muslim affect and provide a window into contemporary attitudes
to Islam and to Muslims. Through this window we see that Muslims remain entrenched in popular culture as a culturally backward, uncivilized
people of a religion that is antithetical to Christian and Western traditions. Muslims are cast as historical enemies and imagined as murderous
avengers invading and polluting white, Christian nations. Over time the
details of political imaginaries shift. The Muslim of the military expedi-
tions and wars of the Middle Ages and the barbarous occupiers of the

2 Introduction

Holy Land folds into refugees at the border of Europe, bearded patriarchs controlling women, and ultimately morphs into al-Qaeda and ISIS. Throughout, Muslims are figures of a global politics proclaiming the civilizational superiority of Europeans and of white Christendom.

What links the overtly ideological T-shirt to the one that trades on ideas of freedom and the rights of women is the structure of feeling to which they are both connected: a shared emotional investment in whiteness achieved through the Muslim as racial Other. When we analyze the work that T-shirts do—their circulation of an anti-Muslim affect—and refuse the distinction between "extremists" and liberals, we are able to see their joint contributions to the material project of white supremacy. We see how anti-Muslim feeling rides in on ideas of democracy, human rights, and women's rights and how overt expressions of white power derive from and are sustained by an edifice of white entitlement. The T-shirts offer clues about the affective worlds of the anti-Muslim subject, worlds in which whiteness must be protected. As emotions travel between individuals and feed into both a liberal and a far-right politics that urges bans on including Islam in the school curriculum, a denial of protection for Muslim children subjected to racist bullying, bans on the wearing of hijabs and niqabs in public settings, surveillance, indefinite detention, and torture of Muslims, we can see the formation of a powerful anti-Muslim affect and the racial violence it underwrites in law and society across the West.

This book is about how racial feelings and emotions form a deeply sedimented anti-Muslim affect. Traveling through law and society, an anti-Muslim affect forges a global whiteness as it moves. In considering the Muslim's importance for various anti-Muslim constituencies, the people for whom whiteness, Christianity, and the Muslim as archetypical enemy come together to provide a deep sense of purpose, selfhood, and national belonging, the book is particularly attentive to the legal and political projects initiated by white political actors. Given the level of racial animus they express, anti-Muslim T-shirts may give the impression that anti-Muslim racists are a part of a rising white nationalist politics in ascendance throughout the West over the past decade. The anti-Muslim animus in which they trade, however, has a much wider and older provenance in the making of white Western hegemony. Whether wearers of anti-Muslim T-shirts or not, anti-Muslim political actors range from those expressing an open white nationalism to others maintaining that Muslims threaten Western liberal values of democracy, secularism, and gender equality. For each end of the continuum, however, the Muslim is a figure who requires discipline that can take the form of lethal force, evictions from political community, imprisonment, surveillance, and stigmatization. Regardless of the level of force they endorse, anti-Muslim political actors all consider the Muslim as anathema to white Western civilization and turn to the state to authorize disciplinary measures against Muslims who are imagined as posing a specific *racial* threat to white entitlement. In this book I begin with one end of the continuum, the anti-Muslim subject who shares the sentiments of the far-right T-shirt wearers, and end with those on the other end who may not display their views as openly as those on the far right but who enact their anti-Muslim views as commitments to Western values of democracy, secularism, and women's rights. I argue that a profound anti-Muslim animus anchors both ends of the continuum and reveals that the Muslim is important to the making of whiteness and to the project of white hegemony.

Law is the field where anti-Muslim actors, liberal and far right, meet. Whether demanding bans on Islam in the school curriculum, bans on Muslim clothing and practices, or the authorization of indefinite detention and torture, anti-Muslim actors confine Muslims to a space of raciality in law where Muslims and other racialized figures are understood as racialized threat. I offer the argument that law's emotional discourses, places where one finds an abundance of Muslim phantoms, the ghosts, dream figures, and demons in our head that Renée Bergland refers to in the epigraph to this Introduction, reveal how law undertakes the affective work that shapes the state as a place where whiteness is protected through the figure of the Muslim. Powerful anti-Muslim emotions circulate through law and society, driving the politics considered in this book. If home is a place where Allah is not God and where Islam should not be a part of modern life, the anti-Muslim subject is often someone who feels aggrievement and rage that home is being invaded and must be defended. The Muslim is a phantom, an imaginary figure of the political unconscious who installs the European as modern and who haunts the white imagination as Europe's atavistic Other. If the European self

4 Introduction

emerges psychically through the Muslim Other, however, the act is one of "self-constitution, projection and imperial strategy."[2] Whether citizen, migrant, refugee, or wartime enemy, the Muslim is a live target of extreme and ordinary state violence.[3]

The legal and political dramas in which Muslims take center stage as Europe's antonym feature three allegorical figures I described earlier in *Casting Out: The Eviction of Muslims from Western Law and Politics*: the dangerous Muslim man, the imperiled Muslim woman, and the civilized European.[4] More than a decade later, each of these figures appears in bolder relief as wars, occupations, targeted assassinations, concentration camps, and bombs dropped by drones on Muslim populations proliferate. With the intensification of discourses of Muslims as global "terrorists," the Muslim man has become the "universal enemy" and is considered even more dangerous and deserving of annihilation.[5] The Muslim woman who once merited saving from her barbaric culture is increasingly resented as "in your face" and needing to be sanctioned for refusing offers of assistance into modernity.[6] On this landscape of heightened racial animus and intensified violence, the European engages in an aggressive white politics, evident not only in white nationalist movements but also in anti-refugee, anti-immigrant, and free-speech rallies, all of which target Muslims, among other racialized groups. As scholars such as Sohail Daulatzai and Junaid Rana maintain, to be a Muslim as either a faith figure or a racial figure is to live a dangerous existence.[7]

Although the racial aspect of the violence and terror directed at Muslims has always been clear—Muslims are evicted from political community and humanity and understood as deserving of considerable violence—anti-Muslim racism comes more fully into view *as a racism* when we consider white supremacy. Through violence directed at Muslims, white nations are able to secure white property interests, and through racial violence directed at Muslims, white and white-aspiring subjects are able to know themselves as superior and deserving. Muslims are not the only racialized group that is important to white imperial projects, but they feature in specific ways when the Christian core of whiteness is touched, as it is when white societies make the case for a superior civilizational status in contradistinction to Muslims and when Muslim bodies and lands are targets for violence and appropriation. Islam is made distinct as a racial object of white supremacy, Daulatzai and Rana propose, when we take colonialism, imperialism, and empire making into account.[8] In such a framework, anti-Muslim racism must be understood as a transnational phenomenon and one that contributes to the making of a global white supremacy. The Muslim today activates fear of an ungovernable Other, but crucially it is a fear accompanied by another: the fear that Europe is losing its grip over those it has historically dominated. More than a phobia, and a distinct form of racism, anti-Muslim racism should be understood as a crisis of colonial governmentality.[9] Confronted with the prospect of failing to maintain order in Muslim parts of the world, the West finds itself challenged in its supremacist endeavors and engaged in a showdown with those it has scripted as subordinate and disposable.

The making of whiteness through the figure of the Muslim proceeds differently in white settler societies such as the United States and Canada than it does in Europe (and, as I mention in the Conclusion to this book, different still in places such as India and China). In these diverse contexts, one nevertheless finds a classic pantheon of phantom Muslims— "terrorists," pedophiles, misogynists, monsters and the Antichrist along with oppressed and veiled Muslim women, testimony to the Muslim's importance in the making of the supremacist subject. As Sophia Arjana has shown, Muslims monsters represent "old anxieties" about the constitution of Europeans as superior, centuries-old projections that can be found "on the pages of manuscripts, and canvasses of paintings, in works of great drama, poetry and fiction, within travel diaries and government documents, and on screens of movie theatres."[10] Notwithstanding the Muslim's importance to European self-constitution, whiteness, a condition that is the product of systems of white supremacy, is not wholly fixated on the Muslim, even though Christianity has always given content to whiteness.[11] Muslims especially haunt the white imagination, however, in those places where ordinary, living Muslims stand in the way of capitalist accumulation and where by their presence in the Holy Land they interrupt dreams of the Rapture and the end times when living and dead believers will ascend to heaven to meet Jesus at the Second Coming.[12] The Palestinian question becomes the Muslim question in Christian eschatological scenarios, as Edward Said saw.[13] Muslims are in the line of fire when their lands attract imperial and colonial ventures and when they

6 Introduction

challenge white hegemony as Indigenous people, citizens, immigrants, and refugees. Muslims who do none of these things sometimes manage to stay out of the line of fire and may even participate in anti-Muslim projects themselves, as is the case with the Kingdom of Saudi Arabia, a key player in wars against Muslims. Anti-Muslim racism, like all racisms, develops not from any kind of primordial antipathy between Europeans and Muslims (the so-called clash of civilizations) but instead from racial projects of territorial expansion and capitalist accumulation. I propose that these various racial projects are linked in an international system of racial governance and that it is possible to identify an anti-Muslim racism that knits together white and nonwhite nations into a global white supremacy anchored in imperialism, colonialism, and racial capitalism.

White race making that mobilizes religion, where Christianity is a defining attribute of European civilization and Islam is the antonym, is a gendered, sexualized, and classed project, and we can trace the making of white masculinities and femininities through anti-Muslim racism in the legal projects that this book discusses. From the white men who go on shooting rampages against Muslims and the white men and women (and occasionally people of color) who rip the veils and niqabs off the heads of Muslim women to those following a more orderly pursuit of Muslims through legal bans on their practices, anti-Muslim actors display strong racial feeling and emotion that travels swiftly along virtual pathways, and through legal and political systems. Traveling from presidents, prime ministers, and political and social elites to everyday citizens, an anti-Muslim affect infects the globe and is deposited in legal systems as authorized military occupations, bans on Muslim practices, permissible torture and punishment, and a host of other evictions from political community. If we follow emotions as they form a coordinated response of anti-Muslim affect, we are able to see how whiteness is made through anti-Muslim racism and to consider the structures of power that whiteness consolidates.

To understand how anti-Muslim racism produces whiteness and makes contributions to a global white supremacy requires the convergence of three tenets. First, that it is necessary to see racism as a register that spans far-right and liberal positions and that the register is animated by emotions that coalesce to form an affect. Second, that the origins of white supremacy and white subjectivity can be traced to Christianity and imperialism and that its contemporary expression is inextricably linked with liberalism. White supremacy shifts and morphs according to the specifics of geopolitics and socioeconomic class, but a global white supremacy nevertheless persists. And third, that the law is where white supremacy and racial violence get legitimized.

This Introduction delineates the framework for these tenets in three sections. I begin in "Emotional/Affective Registers of Anti-Muslim Racism" by arguing that there are different affective routes into the story of white Western superiority through the figure of the Muslim. I propose as methodology that we take seriously the work that anti-Muslim emotions do, producing and sustaining entitled white subjects and generating an affect that powers anti-Muslim political projects in law and society. The bulk of my framework is outlined in "Whiteness, White Supremacy, and the Muslim," where I discuss the origins of race in the Christian imagination and the connections between whiteness, colonization, and imperialism. I consider the historical role that Muslims play in liberalism and emphasize the racial affect that the Muslim delivers and the transnational white politics it powers. In the third section, "Nothing Has to Make Sense: Maintaining Whiteness in Western Law," I discuss subjects who stand at the limit point of justice and in negative relation to the law, a place where claims for justice become illegible. I consider how the Muslim enters this crowded legal field. The white (and aspiring) subjects who display anti-Muslim feeling and whose emotions find legal expression reveal a racism that is not only related to other racisms but resides in the same legal home, a place of white race making where nothing has to make sense and where "Allah is not God" is a reasonable statement and "I'm not anti Islam, Islam is anti me" offers room for Muslim phantoms and demons who threaten white life.

Emotional/Affective Registers of Anti-Muslim Racism

In an important article, Barnor Hesse outlines the consequences of understanding racism as an exceptional event associated with fascism, the common meaning we give it when we consider the Jewish Holocaust. When we grant to racism "an ideological exceptionality" we uncouple it from Western imperialism. Hesse's singular contribution is his urging us to

8 Introduction

think about the relationship between the ideologically exceptional and routine racial governance. Specifically, we should not think of two varieties of racism, one exceptional and the other routine, but rather we should recognize that racism has imprints in both, a situation he describes as racism's conceptual double bind.[14] Racism's conceptual double bind is the problem that immediately presents itself when considering today's anti-Muslim T-shirts. When they draw the eye to a profoundly heightened racial animus toward Muslims and to the fascist politics they signpost, they appear to be unrelated to a liberal politics in which Muslims are separated into good and bad Muslims, with the former worth saving and considered for inclusion in the universal, and the latter slated for annihilation. Liberals remain the arbiters of Muslim fate; deciding whether or not Muslims should be assisted into modernity or annihilated keeps in place their status as a group that has not yet entered the modern. A liberal position lies at the heart of racial governance where white subjects and white nations appoint themselves as keepers of the universal, authorizing who can and cannot gain entry. The challenge, then, when making sense of contemporary anti-Muslim racism, a racism that is clearly all around us and not just on T-shirts, is to see how far-right and liberal positions reinforce each other, anchoring a global white supremacy in which Muslims have now acquired the status of a universal enemy. As Hesse invites us to do, how do we see both racial ideology and racial governance at the same time? I propose that we can keep both in mind when we consider how whiteness is made through the Muslim.

I begin this Introduction with anti-Muslim T-shirts because they illustrate the mutual imbrication of ideologies and governance in popular culture. If anti-Muslim T-shirts create a powerful anti-Muslim affect with the protection of whiteness at its core, they do so in different registers. The T-shirt "Allah is not God" arranges the world in a hierarchy of two kinds of people: believers of a Christian God and those who serve Allah. The T-shirt commodifies the arrangement and operates pedagogically in service of a specific politics. At a Republican political event in 2018, for instance, we see that the T-shirt is worn by James J. Stachowiak, whom the Southern Poverty Law Center identifies as a former police officer and owner of the antigovernment propagandist *Freedom Fighter Radio.* In a photograph taken at the event, Stachowiak's arms encircle the

Introduction **9**

candidate for Republican governor of Georgia, Brian Kemp, who gives him the thumbs-up sign. Stachowiak wears his heart on his sleeve; his cap announces that he is a supporter of President Trump, and a button on the T-shirt confirms his loyalty to Kemp. The caption of the photograph identifies Stachowiak as an anti-Muslim and a gun-rights activist, and the article it accompanies makes clear his Christian evangelical and white-supremacist politics, a politics shared by the gubernatorial candidate, whose politics Stachowiak endorses and whose subsequent election as governor of the state of Georgia is an example of the increasing support for white-supremacist political projects in the United States.[15] Militant white Christian nationalists, for instance, were among the groups attacking the U.S. Capitol on January 6, 2021, seeking to reclaim the nation for Christ.[16] If the wearers of the T-shirt "F**k Islam" (Figure 1b) ended up having a change of heart after speaking with local Muslims, a vigorous anti-Muslim animus continues apace in white politics that is explicitly Christian.[17]

While the T-shirts bearing the phrases "Allah is not God" and "F**k Islam" express strong sentiments at the heart of a specific version of American white politics, they are among a plethora of anti-Muslim T-shirts popular in Europe, shirts that announce a world divided into two religions, with Christianity ranked as the only authentic religion and people of European origin installed as an enlightened Christian people who must do battle with Muslims. The popular T-shirt with the word "Infidel" in English and in Arabic (Figure 1d) is visible on the bodies of white men at far-right demonstrations throughout the West and flags a similar structure of feeling of white Christians under siege from Muslims. It provocatively expresses that the wearer is a person who relishes the title of infidel, given that it positions him (it is nearly always men who wear these T-shirts) on the Christian side of European history and in an apocryphal time of Islamic armies invading Europe. Such T-shirts instruct us in a far-right politics that is openly white supremacist. It is tempting to consider this brand of anti-Muslim politics as exceptional, viewing it, in Hesse's words, as an "aberrant ideological affront,"[18] but when we take stock of the protection of whiteness that T-shirt wearers seek we see that the politics they express is connected to white entitlement and to a system of white supremacy that is the basis of colonialism and Western

10 Introduction

imperialism. As Rana and Daulatzai advise, we should not see this brand of white politics as exceptional but instead as "extensions of a racist architecture of control to define the white world."[19]

T-shirts that carry the same civilizational message of an enlightened, Christian Europe and a barbaric, premodern Islam, but conveyed simply as a feminist message about Islam as uniquely misogynist, are also a part of the stock-in-trade of anti-Muslim slogans. They offer a pronounced liberal inflection conveying anti-Muslim racism through ideas about freedom, human rights, and women's rights, ideas that are structurally supported through various UN agencies and are a part of the architecture that consolidates whiteness globally through the Muslim. The T-shirt emblazoned with the slogan "I am not anti Islam, Islam is anti me" (Figure 1c), for example, echoes the words of Ayaan Hirsi Ali, a Dutch-Somali and American anti-Muslim ideologue and former politician who rejects Islam on the basis that it oppresses women.[20] Casting Muslims as über-patriarchs and Europeans as uniquely given to gender equality, democracy and secularism, Hirsi Ali's position finds wide favor among the right and the left, allowing all to luxuriate in the story of Europe's emergence into modernity and Islam's failure to enter it. The story underwrites the regulation of Muslims as a part of progress, a logic that authorizes evictions from citizenship and wars and occupations in Muslim lands.

Notably, Hirsi Ali is herself a former Muslim, and her books reveal her aspirations to celebrate European civilization and to denigrate Muslims as unable and unwilling to integrate into Europe.[21] Popular memoirs by Muslim women who denounce Islam are best sellers in the West, as I and others have shown, and are a staple in the "global war on terror."[22] A part of a broader message about choice, freedom, and secular values that pits Western ideas about freedom against women's imprisonment by Islam, memoirists such as Hirsi Ali contribute to the circulation of anti-Islamic emotions that constitute Europeans as uniquely given to rationality, a history in which Christianity is deemed rational and not irrational religion.[23] Tellingly, such messages of civilizational superiority rely on the abstraction of women from their histories, on the attribution of their suffering to Islam and not to the social, economic, and political contexts of their lives.[24] Drawing on a language of women's rights and human rights and invoking Western ideals of a universal liberal political culture, they do not initially appear to be of the same emotional register as those who claim that Allah is not God. They serve nonetheless as a powerful call to whiteness and sustain an infrastructure in which war making and occupations can proceed on the pretext of saving Muslim women, a claim made by the Bush administration in its invasion of Afghanistan in 2002. As chapter 2 will show, campaigns to ban the hijab and the niqab in Europe and Canada proceed similarly and paradoxically as a forced unveiling in order to protect Muslim women from the patriarchs that oppress them. The affective charge generated by the claim to save Muslim women and offer them assistance into modernity installs a virtuous white subject who feels racial superiority as a capacity for goodness, an emotional state that fuels political projects of empire as surely as do the messages of overt hate and repugnance.

The most striking aspect of how Muslims are taken up in law and politics is the intense negative emotions that anti-Muslim legal and political actors regularly display, an indication that a strenuous self-making is in progress. These emotions range from desire and disgust, to rage and aggrievement that white Christians are culturally and materially imperiled and denied their due. These emotions are all the more striking because of the assumed rationality of the scenes where they are displayed. Western legal traditions are supposed to represent the apotheosis of Western culture, shaped above all by the idea that the law is autonomous and objective and is not a party to violence. Law students are taught that lawyering entails rising above emotional reactions and engaging in dispassionate scientific analysis. Even critical scholars who note that lawyering requires a willful disregard for social context still sometimes maintain that law cannot be transparently reducible to issues of power and that objective law exists.[25]

This book advances the idea that we know that we are in the presence of white race making from those places in law where nothing has to make sense, places where racial and imperial fantasies take root and the dream figures in our heads take over, inviting us to feel rather than to think about the place of Muslims in white, Christian life. Feelings and emotions often crowd out rationality, establishing subjects who believe in their own superiority and are prepared to make it true on the ground.

12 Introduction

The T-shirt wearer proclaiming that Allah is not God, for instance, strikes up an alliance with a politician, and as this book shows, such alliances are a part of legal efforts to expel Muslims from citizenship and to declare white Christians as the only legitimate citizens. The insistence that "Allah is not God," an antonym to "Jesus is God," succinctly expresses both the religious and, as I argue below, the racial boundaries of the nation. At the same time, the statement "Allah is not God" operates in the same emotional and cognitive register as the earth is flat and viruses don't kill. As most will grant, Allah is simply another name for God. It is tempting to dismiss the T-shirt's claim by noting its incoherence, but it is more important to consider the dimensions of the world that the T-shirt wearer is anxious to promote. Without a logic but capable of calling Christians into community, the statement "Allah is not God" is effective in building a politics. The same is true of the slogan "I'm not anti Islam, Islam is anti me," a slogan that calls into community those whose selfhood is shaped by a fantasy of Western civilizational superiority that is always implicitly white and Christian and not Islamic.

The anti-Muslim T-shirt shares its affective reach with law where the Muslim dwells in a place where nothing has to make sense. A sentencing hearing at Guantánamo with secret evidence, laws banning Muslim head coverings, a Muslim travel ban, a ban on Arabic calligraphy in art classes: none of it has to be defended on the terms of rationality or conventional law. Prisoners become enemy combatants and are not covered under the Geneva Conventions; the accused is not even accused but suspected, and no right of *habeas corpus* exists. Instead, as the chapters of this book explore, the most extravagant emotions hold sway in legal, political, and social settings where it can be declared that Muslims have a damaged gene pool; that seeing someone's face is a fundamental value in a secular society; that we are dealing with a culturally different enemy who requires torture; and that Allah is not God. The validity of any of these statements cannot be arrived at unless one accepts the premise of Muslim inferiority and European superiority, a premise sustained by racial feeling. When we are confronted with an incoherence that is obvious (Isn't Allah just another name for God? Is there really a gene for violence? Does anyone require torture? Is seeing a full face necessary for social interaction?), it is necessary to ask what the incoherence does, rather than search for a logic that is not there. The incoherence observable in anti-Muslim politics makes white community and protects it in law.

For Sara Ahmed, the key question in considering emotions (understood here as referring to mental and physical states) as social and cultural practice is to ask what emotions do. Subjects become "*invested* in particular structures such that their demise is felt as a kind of living death."[26] These emotions circulate and produce identities, traveling between bodies and coalescing to form social and national affect. We construct ourselves in imagination and affect.[27] The wearers of anti-Muslim T-shirts learn to think of themselves as a different and superior order of humanity than are Muslims. Collectively, they form a political community dedicated to protecting white life through disciplining Muslims. In the expression and enactment of an anti-Muslim racism, a white political community is born. As Shona Hunter explains, emotions form an affect when "anxieties become collectively owned and enacted to form institutional topography," binding people within a social order.[28] Rage, dread, aggrievement, and desire become a part of a larger affective economy. Drawing on Ghassan Hage's exploration of paranoid nationalism in Australia, where national subjects imagine that they are daily at risk from migrants, asylum seekers, and fellow citizens of color,[29] Hunter emphasizes that "whiteness ascends as the cultural manifestation of governmental power through a delusional fantasy structure enacted through paranoid forms of belonging via feelings of persecution, jealousy, and exaggerated self-importance which relate to the illusionary nature of governing omnipotence."[30] The insight that "whiteness is a fantasy position which comes through material, symbolic and affective work"[31] is relevant to law, where such emotions and fantasies are mobilized to install white citizens who must be protected from foreign threats, among them Muslims.

Whiteness is an emotional place to dwell, a place peopled by threatening Muslim phantoms as well as other ghostly figures, and notably, the ghosts of slavery and Indigenous dispossession. Spectral Muslims, like the Indian ghosts in Renée Bergland's canonical text *The National Uncanny: Indian Ghosts and American Subjects*, are manifestations of an internalized psychic struggle over the settler's legitimacy.[32] To believe in and enact one's own racial superiority and entitlement, it is necessary to banish from one's consciousness anyone whose existence undermines

14   Introduction

such claims. Muslims are evicted from consciousness whenever they can be transformed into monsters: Satan incarnate, pedophiles, aggressive wearers of the veil, "terrorists," and children who carry a propensity for violence in their blood ensure that European superiority is intact, even as the superior subject is forever haunted by the racial threats that constitute it.

It is useful to recall the relationship between ghosts, nationalisms, and hegemonies that Bergland analyzes. Native American and African American ghosts establish American nationhood (through the idea that all the Indians are dead and that slavery is over) and simultaneously call the nation's legitimacy into question. The American national subject is obsessed with Indian and African ghosts, an obsession that arouses dread and conceals a profound ambivalence about the triumph of America. In the same way, I propose that Muslim phantoms haunt white Christian consciousness. Phantom Muslims both establish and challenge the uniqueness of white Christian claims; while they call a triumphalist white Christian community into existence, they raise the disturbing possibility that Allah *is* God and that no God-given entitlement exists for white Christians. If the colonial mind-set is an obsessional one, causing colonizers to return again and again to those who haunt them, and if the land is haunted because it is stolen, Muslims join Indigenous and Black peoples as well as poor people and foreigners, all cast as "uncivil, irrational, and even spectral."[33] Black Muslims pose a unique double threat in this configuration, an entanglement that has profoundly shaped Black freedom struggles in the United States.[34] If each of these groups activates white fears in distinct ways, all Muslims do so symbolically and materially through the Christian core of whiteness and through their standing in the way of specific projects of capitalist accumulation.

Whiteness, White Supremacy, and the Muslim

Anti-Muslim racism has been called "an imaginary racism" used as a weapon to silence legitimate criticism of Islam as a religion that is fanatical, given to violence, and impervious to change.[35] Western supremacist literature with Islam as its target is an ever-expanding genre. As Pankaj Mishra notes of this genre, "Sympathy for nonwhite victims of imperialism and slavery, and struggling postcolonial peoples in general, [comes]

Introduction **15**

to be stigmatized as a sign of excessive sentimentality and guilt."[36] Remarking on the illegibility of anti-Muslim racism even among critical race scholars, Junaid Rana and Diane Fugino suggest that scholars are more prepared to grant that an anti-Arab racism exists (notwithstanding the denial of this racism by those who cite that Arabs have been racially classified as white in American law).[37] As they point out, connecting racism to a specific group, Arabs, naturalizes race as real, making racism a phenomenon of natural antipathy to a group other than one's own, rather than a system designed to protect white interests. When Muslims are regarded as a religious group to whom one might feel a natural cultural antipathy, they are not seen as the targets of racism. Further, as Namira Islam points out, the tendency to demote Islam from a religion to a culture has the effect of making a distinction between good Muslims, those who do not practice their faith, and bad Muslims, those who practice their faith and are "too Muslim."[38] The tendency to regard racism as due to prejudice and to regard religion as separate from race and culture has prompted critical scholars to prefer the term "anti-Muslim racism" (a preference I share) rather than its more popular cousin "Islamophobia" in the hope that the structural aspects of anti-Muslim racism and its contributions to the making of whiteness and white supremacy become more salient. "Islamophobia" is a term that often leaves white supremacy outside the frame of analysis.[39]

In spite of the long-standing connections between whiteness, colonialism, imperialism, and Christianity, it is often presumed that anti-Muslim sentiments emanating from white Christians have a straightforwardly religious rather than a racial basis and that contemporary white Christian aggrievement directed at Muslims springs from anxiety over increasing secularization,[40] or from a legitimate sense of loss over the culture wars,[41] or from economic loss. This analysis separates religious identity from racial identity and serves to naturalize white aggrievement as something that surfaces only when whites have lost ground or are confronted by non-Christian or non-religious peoples. These presumptions fundamentally miss how a population comes to understand white entitlement through religion and, crucially, obscures the basket of fears, aggrievement, and desires, the stuff of which hegemonies are made and that collect in and operate to power white supremacy. Anti-Muslim

16 Introduction

animus, a part of this basket of colonial emotions, easily develops into an affective politics where white Christians come to know themselves as a persecuted and vulnerable minority, denied their birthright as Anglo-Saxon and obliged to confront what is imagined to be a profoundly anti-Christian state that is seen as refusing to secure white interests. Colonial and racial impulses die hard in a system that is predicated on them. As the African American writer James Baldwin feared, whites have been in this emotional state of entitlement too long to abandon it.[42] Taking his cue from Baldwin, Robert P. Jones reminds us in *White Too Long* that "in survey after survey white Christians stand out in negative attitudes to racial, ethnic and religious minorities *(especially Muslims)*, the unequal treatment of African Americans by police and the criminal justice system, their anxieties about the changing face of the country, and their longing for a past when white Protestantism was the undisputed cultural power."[43]

Whiteness organized along this Christian line, whether subliminally or not, provides comfort and reassurance and a way of being in the world that offers white Christians access to political power domestically and to imperial power more broadly. There has been much hand-wringing about the racism that seems to have spread through American society riding in on a wave of intensified religious feeling. Typically, Christian evangelicals get blamed for a rising mean-spiritedness, but some soul searching has occurred over the state of mainline Protestantism as well. For instance, John Compton has written about "the end of empathy"[44] among non-evangelical Protestants. He offers an argument that white Protestants once believed in a just society and in "kindness" toward their fellow men but that without the leadership of their churches and the social direction toward a more collectivist orientation they have now succumbed to a more individualist life full of racial anxieties and resentments. Mindful of the rising influence of white evangelical Christianity, Compton argues that without direction from their churches, mainline Protestants have "stopped loving their neighbors," abandoning the progressive path they once trod and moving in the political direction of Christian evangelicals. While it is certain that white Christianity has always been composed of both conservative and progressive strains, and commitments to racial justice ebb and flow, Compton's account ignores the enduring link between white entitlement and Christianity and the way in which race making proceeds through religion not just for white evangelicals but for white Christians generally, and sometimes for Zionists, effects that become visible when we examine more closely the making of whiteness through the figure of the Muslim.

The link between whiteness and Christianity, and the implications this has for Muslims, remain unacknowledged in many quarters. The elision produces denial that Muslims are constituted as a race and consequently that anti-Muslim feelings and emotions and the practices they underwrite amount to race making. Significantly, Muslims become illegible as subjects of racial harm. To cut through what is often an emotional morass concerning the relationship between race and religion, one has to begin with the nature of whiteness and the project that is white supremacy. In 2020, reporting on the year of massive protests against anti-Black police violence, the *New York Times* endeavored to explain to its readers the increasingly widespread use of the term "white supremacy." The newspaper remarked that the phrase no longer refers only to card-carrying white supremacists of the KKK variety but instead to a social system in which all white people enjoy structural advantage. The phrase makes people uncomfortable, the *Times* lamented; it lumps all white people into one group and makes them feel accused. Every white person becomes David Duke, Grand Wizard of the KKK.[45] The worries expressed by the *Times* announce that a system, white supremacy, should not be connected to those whose interests are protected by it. Indeed, the *Times*' position may even be a sly denial that white supremacy exists at all, the problem of police violence put down instead to prejudice and a few bad cops. In contrast, Black scholars (among others) and the Black Lives Matter movement insist that a system based on protecting white interests remains in place, one built on Indigenous dispossession, Black enslavement, and vigorous American imperial expansion beginning with Mexico, the Philippines, Hawai'i, and continuing today with unceasing imperial wars and occupations. The system vests profit in white hands, although it is certain that not all whites benefit equally. Significantly, the system of white supremacy relies on an intense, violent, and organized subjugation of Indigenous, Black, and Brown life, the constitutive racial terror required to make the white nation-state and empire.[46]

Obscured in the *Times*' ruminations on the structural is the critical

18 Introduction

role played by whiteness, defined variously by scholars as a social relation, an identity, an ideology and crucially, as property. As Cheryl Harris brilliantly argues, *being* white ensures economic returns, a positional superiority that gives whiteness something in common with property: the right to exclude.[47] An acquired competence, whiteness is constructed dominance over those who do not possess it. Whites therefore have "a possessive investment in whiteness," the historian George Lipsitz argues.[48] To the extent that one can accumulate it, whiteness offers privilege. It is something that has to be protected, and there is no better way to protect it than to maintain the line between those entitled to it by virtue of skin color and other visible differences and those who must be kept out. As Kalpana Seshadri-Crooks observes, "Whiteness is a structuring principle of racial meaning; as a linguistic construct, it also subjects individuals to a phantasmatic [unconscious] identification that the body's surface seems to literalize."[49] To inhabit whiteness is to know oneself as entitled to the fruits of earth and to merit its bounty. It is to be committed to a system in which the earth's bounty is not shared with those imagined as undeserving of it. Whiteness is both an aspiration and a location in a social hierarchy (or a set of locations).[50] It is also a state of mind. Whiteness requires strong emotions about the entitlement of whites and the unfitness of others. It is the site of complicated feelings and emotions of which anxiety is a hallmark. As Saidiya Hartman discusses, the denial of Black sentience, the slave's status as object of property, and the slave's suffering block white responsibility for Black suffering. Hartman shows how whites often assume a too easy identification with Black suffering, refusing to acknowledge their implication in it.[51] The result is that empathy is compromised. White supremacy's animus, Dylan Rodríguez argues, drives the multiple forms of violence and terror that white supremacy requires.[52] The Christian cast to this animus brings unique attention to the Muslim and the Jew (though in different ways), aspects that often receive less attention among critical scholars than the racial animus that is anti-Blackness. Noting that whiteness is a phenomenon that is well beyond the notion of prejudice, William Pinar asks: "What is the psychosexual structure and historical character of whiteness that renders it so aggressive, so tortured, so interested in subjugation?"[53] Scholars have pursued answers to this question theologically and across a range of disciplines.

Tracing the origins of race in the Christian imagination and emphasizing its theological roots, Willie Jennings argues persuasively that when Christians first imagined themselves as replacing Jews as the chosen people, they saw salvation as possible only through faith in Christ. Christian identity became positioned as white and fully outside the identities of Jews and Muslims, a worldview that is imperialist at its core, since it is the white subject who will determine who is salvageable and who is not. In the aggressive "desacralization of the world" that is colonialism, the disruption and destruction of people's identities bound to specific lands, whiteness becomes a global vision, a world organized by proximity to whiteness and premised on the universal idea that the earth belongs not to those who dwell on it but to those who own and develop it and who deserve it.[54] For Jennings, whiteness is above all a spatial performance of imperial mastery. Christian identity, imagined as "floating above land, landscape, animals, place and space, leaving such realities to the machinations of capitalistic calculations and the commodity chains of private property," requires even as it produces a racially ordered world.[55] The whiteness that Jennings describes as coming more fully into its own through the transatlantic slave trade and Indigenous dispossession is born of and depends on an intense embodied encounter with the racial Other. Jennings pays no attention to the Muslim as one of Christianity's racial Others, emphasizing instead the anti-Blackness and the commodification of Black bodies that are sustained by a Christian worldview anchored in property. Black Muslims are also rendered invisible in this otherwise insightful analysis, coming into view only as Black and not as Muslim or as both.

One hundred years earlier, the African American sociologist W. E. B. Du Bois sought to describe the affect of whiteness in "The Souls of White Folk," an essay that is less cited than his book *The Souls of Black Folk*. Offering what continues to be a rare and penetrating analysis of whiteness as demanding the abjection of racialized others, the essay strikes a personal note of fury and despair.[56] For Du Bois, whiteness was an embodied condition characterized by "a great mass of hatred" principally directed at Black people who would lay claim to an equal humanity. (As with others, Du Bois did not consider racial animus directed at Muslims and even subscribed to it himself, seeing "the Mohammedan religion" as

20   Introduction

making Palestinians despotic, antidemocratic, and standing in the way of Jewish homeland in Palestine.)[57] Linking American whiteness to colonial aggrandizement the world over, Du Bois put the connection between whiteness and property bluntly: "It is the duty of Europe to divide up the darker world and administer it for Europe's good."[58] Remarking here on whiteness as a condition produced in projects of imperial aggression, Du Bois notes the emotional foundations upon which projects of territorial expansion and capitalist accumulation are built. Whiteness is an emotional condition marked by aggrievement and hostility, and it is given over to racial fantasy. White "orgy, cruelty, barbarism, and murder done to men and women of Negro descent" were driven by everyday rages that take white people to "the bottom of the world."[59] Du Bois offers examples of such everyday rages, examples that are arresting when we think of the quotidian emotions that might underpin the T-shirt wearers' impulses above and the aggressive racial politics such emotions generate:

> I have seen a man—an educated gentleman—grow livid with anger because a little, silent black woman was sitting by herself in a Pullman car. He was a white man. I've seen a great, grown man curse a little child who had wandered into the wrong waiting-room, searching for its mother: "Here, you damned black—" He was white. In Central Park I have seen the upper lip of a quiet, peaceful man curl back in a tigerish snarl of rage because black folk rode by in a motor car. He was a white man.[60]

"I see these souls undressed and from the back and side,"[61] Du Bois writes, considering what it is about whiteness that it should be so maniacally desired and so violently secured. His answer, "that whiteness is the ownership of the earth forever and ever,"[62] alerts us to the material and affective project of white supremacy, a racial project of accumulation created and sustained by "tigerish snarls of rage"[63] directed at little Black girls and Black folk riding in a motor car. Similarly, bell hooks writes of the emotions directed at Black women who are regarded as icons of deviant sexuality, emotions that led Harriet Jacobs in *Incidents in the Life of a Slave Girl* to describe the psychosexual dynamics of slavery as "a peculiar institution" and white people as "a cage of obscene birds."[64]

For Du Bois, Christianity gives content to whiteness, endowing co-

Introduction 21

lonialism and imperialism with a moral base and its cultural character.[65] Beginning with his observation that in the settler colony whiteness is conflated with godliness, several scholars make the case that Christianity plays a prominent role in how white identity emerges in the United States.[66] Edward Blum, a scholar of Du Bois, suggests that the role of religion in race making may go unnoticed because religion is often understood as superstructural and not, as Du Bois saw, central to how subjects come to understand themselves as white.[67] "Creating, defining, and defending whiteness," Blum shows, "played a significant role in biblical debates over slavery."[68] Seeking divine sanction for slavery early on, whites relied on the Bible to promote white power, unity, and "national whiteness" for a long time after the abolition of slavery. White people acted on their colonial impulses *as Christians,* imagining that their superiority mandated the occupation of Indigenous lands and domination of racialized Others.[69] The conjoining of white entitlement to the land with Christianity gives whiteness its Christian hue, as chapter 1 shows, discussing white parents' objections to the covering of Islam in the school curriculum. Whiteness, a frontier aesthetic with its emphasis on an aggressive gun-toting masculinity, combines with religious fervor to produce "a conjunction of the sacred and violence," a whiteness in evidence at political protests over a threatened and lost white world, events where an aggressive white masculinity is on full display.[70]

Theologically articulated and inescapably colonial and imperial, whiteness depends on even as it produces a powerful racial affect in which Muslims have a specific role to play as white Christianity's racial Other. Scholars who recognize that race, as David Goldberg put it, is "knotted with religious resonance" emphasize that the European is born as a racial category up against the figures of the Muslim and the Black, arrangements that predate the arrival of Europeans in the Americas.[71] As Nasar Meer writes, resurrecting this older genealogy of racism more fully "implicates the formation of race within the racialization of religious subjects" and underscores why it is important to understand culture and religion as never outside of race.[72] The conventional chronology of modern racism proposed by Michael Omi and Howard Winant, for instance,[73] where European antipathy toward Muslims is seen as a dress rehearsal for modern racism, is easily refuted when one examines the

22 Introduction

racial contours of the Moor and the Jew in Elizabethan England, as Nabil Matar does for the Moor and James Shapiro for the Jew.[74]

We are all Moors now, Anouar Majid declares, making the claim that "the ultimate horror of the Holocaust would not have been conceived without the tradition of racism initiated by [fifteenth-century] Spain."[75] Undoubtedly, early colonial histories leave residues that continue to shape race making both in the Americas and Europe, as evidenced not only by the cry from the far right that the Crusades are upon us again and a caliphate threatens to invade white Europe and the Americas, but also by the uncanny similarities between the anti-Muslim bans of today and the fifteenth-century royal edicts of Iberian Spain prohibiting Islamic dress, Friday prayers, and the speaking of Arabic.[76] Bans of this kind in Europe are discussed in chapter 2 and in the Conclusion in China, where the Muslim Uyghur population is under extraordinary surveillance for signs of the presence of Islam in their lives.[77] As Meer compellingly argues, Europe's premodern Christian character contained the framework for the making of Muslims as a race against which a superior whiteness is made.

When we connect the Moor of fifteenth-century Catholic Spain or sixteenth-century England to today's imaginary Muslims, we risk forgetting important aspects of the genealogies of contemporary racisms and may be led to overemphasize cultural memories of the historical clash between Christianity and Islam at the expense of the ongoing imperatives of colonialism, imperialism, and racial capitalism that inspire them. If Europeans of both the Old World and the New forged a common white identity with Christianity as its core and the Muslim as enemy, it is important to remember that white identity is in service of a material project, one with a permanent war-making structure. Muslims inhabit the American and European landscapes of primitive accumulation as Moors, as obstacles to white Christian property interests, as colonized peoples, and as imperial enemies. The Turks and Moors of the Spanish and English imaginaries of the sixteenth and seventeenth centuries are the ancestors of today's Muslim "folk devils," but as Pnina Werbner advises, we must remember that folk devils are not born of an irrational hatred but rather of the metanarratives of Western modernity and the economic arrangements it underwrites.[78]

Modern race is "the secularization of the religious," Goldberg suggests, explaining that religion does not disappear into race so much as race "takes up some of religion's driving terms."[79] If, as Goldberg maintains, race offers religious affect, we might also note that religion offers racial affect. The God-given right to colonize racial Others becomes race, the knowing with religious certitude one's assigned place for self and others and turning oneself into a sovereign power, a condition Goldberg describes as "deific."[80] As Jennings underscores, the ability to universalize the earth and to "free it from the strictures of particular ways of life," as Christians did when Jewish identity was severed from the historical origins of Christianity, opens a path for legitimizing colonial conquest by enabling Christians to imagine themselves as possessing the earth.[81] The movement toward the universal requires constitutive racial Others who form its outside, those who do not merit inclusion in it.

Liberalism and the Muslim

Relying on the metaphor of the fishbowl to describe the liberal imagination, Ratna Kapur notes that in liberalism "freedom remains defined as a liberal, external pursuit, involving the accumulation of further rights by a rational, finite and individual subject."[82] Freedom is not available to Muslims, who are defined as an irrational people held in thrall to religion and unable to become the rational, finite, and individual subject of the liberal imagination. Muslims reside outside the fishbowl and reinforce its boundaries. Overwhelmingly Western and Eurocentric, liberal freedom excludes those who hold divergent notions of freedom and defines them as "inherently alien." Notably, liberalism already incorporates what we might call a race line, excluding those who do meet the requirements of the human. Liberalism contains an exclusionary dynamic that prompts the liberal subject to engage in an endless eviction of the insufficiently modern from the category of the human in order to maintain the liberal boundaries of personhood. In this regard, rights are "techniques of governance which discipline and regulate the subject of human rights, and where practices of self-discipline and self-governance become normalized and experienced as freedom."[83] As Kapur notes, even the minimalist claims of human-rights advocates are dogged by the need to install the proper subject of rights against those who exist outside of it. In her

24 Introduction

example, in liberalism an unveiled, sexualized, and autonomous subject is deemed the proper subject of human rights, a subject who achieves definition through her non-autonomous veiled sister, a dynamic we see referenced in the T-shirt "I'm not anti Islam, Islam is anti me" and in arguments banning the Muslim woman's niqab and hijab, as chapter 2 discusses. "A self-referential schema of entitlement" underpins rights claims, where an authentic subject of rights wrestles with those imagined as undeserving of rights, a battle that is constitutive of the liberal subject.[84] When we consider Islam's foundational role in the crafting of European identity, we come to understand the Muslim's importance to liberalism and can appreciate why anti-Muslim racism remains so critical to the production of whiteness and to white supremacy. There is much anxiety and fear, Kapur comments, when the human-rights project is critiqued, emotions I suggest have historically circulated often around the figure of the Muslim.[85]

In laying out a compelling argument for Islam's foundational role in liberalism, Joseph Massad shows how Christianity came to be constituted as the self and origin of democracy through the idea of Islam as its antonym.[86] Recalling Said, he notes liberalism's foundational fiction: Oriental cultures produce despotism; occidental cultures produce democracy. Democracy, secularism, and, later, gender equality become developments that are seen to begin with the Greeks and the Romans, the people to whom modern Europeans are linked in a historical line unbroken by the presence of Muslims. This historical fiction that develops with the decline of Ottoman political power and European territorial expansion captures both the left and the right as Europeans come to know themselves as a superior race up against Muslims who are deemed as culturally and sometimes biologically unable to progress into modernity. It is important to consider what the liberal imaginary leaves out. Requiring a monolithic Islam without its own traditions of reasoning[87] and Christendom as a unitary community, the project of thinking about Islam as Europe's Other must forget Islamic traditions and history in the bid to define them as inimical to modern life. We cannot, then, remember that Muslim women gained property rights before their European sisters, for example.

The story of Europe's emergence into modernity is also the story of its

Introduction **25**

historical journey into secularism, imagined as an achievement internal to Europe and to its Christian populations and unavailable to Muslims. Tracking the shadow of Islam in the European liberal project, Massad shows that Christianity itself, and later a new hyphenated connection between Judaism and Catholicism as a Judeo-Christian alliance, comes to be associated with rationalism, science, and reason, and Protestantism with capitalist economy and political democracy, developments foregrounded by the idea of Muslim despotism and an inferior Orient. Always imagined as a definitive break with religion, the Enlightenment instead inaugurates Christianity as reason and Islam as the antithesis of everything rational. As Irfan Ahmad notes, Enlightenment philosophers from Kant to Voltaire typically saw Muhammad as a zealot and the Arab or Mongol as opposing Protestant hard work.[88] In the postwar period of the twentieth century, hostile Orientalists would be able to convincingly argue that Muslims were likely to be communists who oppose individualism and human rights.[89]

The racial fault line that separates the culturally democratic from the undemocratic confines good (salvageable) Muslims to those who must be assisted into modernity, while it maintains bad Muslims as requiring force.[90] The missionary impulse to convert Muslims to the ways of Western democracy is haunted by the prospect that Muslims may not in the end be salvageable, although it does not curtail efforts to "find" and "nurture" a moderate Islam as evidence of Europe's tolerance. As in colonial law, which reserved two systems of law, one for the colonizer and one for the colonized, democratic law, as I discuss below, maintains spaces for the despot. Freedom in the liberal imagination, Kapur reminds us, comes with a governance structure: those thought to be incapable of choice have to be assisted into modernity by force if necessary: "The paradigm excludes those subjects who are constituted as either unassimilable or incommensurate, and thus fail to conform to the dominant normative arrangements that constitute part of the liberal scaffolding of freedom."[91] In liberalism, Muslims are often positioned as despots who fail to conform to normative arrangements and must therefore be disciplined.

The argument that "democracy and despotism come to be both posited as civilizational, religious, and cultural achievements and failures respectively" turns on the idea of culture, religiously shaped, as unchangeable.[92]

26 Introduction

It is this cultural racism that anchors the treatment of Muslims suspected of involvement in terrorism today. As chapter 3 details, Muslim detainees are indefinitely detained on the premise that we cannot know when the Muslim propensity for violence would emerge. Given this innate cultural flaw, it is necessary to suspend the right of *habeas corpus,* the right to know of what one is accused. Muslim culture is also the reason given to pursue saving Muslim women both from themselves and from Muslim men, as the bans on Muslim women's clothing discussed in chapter 2 reveal. The meaning of gender itself becomes the ground on which races are made. As feminist scholars have long shown, Western women have for some time defined their freedom against the idea of the oppressed third-world woman and have pursued projects to save Muslim women armed not only with a sense of the superiority of their own cultural and Christian sensibilities but also with the power of their own states behind them. Muslim women have not been the only targets of such civilizing projects, but they take center stage when political conditions bring special attention to Muslims.[93]

An International Whiteness/Global White Supremacy

In *Drawing the Global Colour Line: White Men's Countries and the International Challenge of Racial Equality,* Marilyn Lake and Henry Reynolds chart the spread of whiteness as a transnational form of racial identification in the twentieth century when whiteness became the basis of geopolitical alliances. United in their alarm over a rising tide of color, white nations constituted themselves as an international imagined community of white men, all pursuing segregation and immigration restrictions. As Lake and Reynolds write, "White men's countries rested on the premise that multiracial democracies were an impossibility."[94] "Glorious manhood" was the basis of white men's countries, gendered racial discourses that traveled across the British empire establishing an affective community of white men anxious to draw distinctions between white and nonwhite nations.[95] The "global ascendancy of the politics of whiteness" cast imperial nations such as Japan on the nonwhite side of things, something that Japan vigorously protested.[96] The evictions from a white international began early in the century with the Paris Peace Conference in 1919, when Japan's bid to have a racial equality clause in the Covenant of the League of Nations was soundly defeated.[97] The eviction of non-white nations from the club was cemented following World War II when the prospect of international agreement on the concept of the equality of nations and races gave way to the Universal Declaration of Human Rights with its principle of nondiscrimination between individuals and not collectivities. As we saw with liberalism and the figure of the Muslim above, such rights regimes are techniques of governance, drawing a color line between the subjects of human rights and those evicted from it.

The intersecting colonial and imperial histories of the Americas and Europe incubate a contemporary transnational response to Muslims that contributes in significant ways to the global whiteness named by scholars as a spatial imaginary that organizes the world as a space over which the European stands as highest on an evolutionary scale. Whiteness extends over space itself "layered with each generation of landowner [and] enacting a racialized spatial geography."[98] Each event, from imperial wars to the occupation of lands and the "global war on terror," further collapses over there and over here, linking all those imagined to be Muslim as enemies and, importantly, suturing white identities under one global frame as civilized peoples menaced by an Islamic racial Other. White citizens who imagine themselves as entitled to the bounties of the earth come to feel that they are besieged by Muslims and that an anti-Muslim politics expresses what is worth protecting. These feelings and emotions contribute to a global politics of being white. They amount to an affective racial economy with an economic, political, and social infrastructure and a permanent war-making structure dedicated to the protection of white interests. Wars and military violence are the contexts in which a global whiteness is made, and a global white supremacy is installed.[99] On this landscape "the racialized Muslim is a planetary figure,"[100] a situation that has only intensified in the past few decades.

The "global war on terror" sometimes merits an abbreviation (GWOT) in a wide number of scholarly texts where it is assumed to need little explanation. Its phantom figures are now so normalized that the words "religious extremist/extremism," "terrorism/terrorist," "radical/radicalism," "jihad/jihadist," and "fundamentalist/fundamentalism" must all be placed within quotation marks in this book to alert the reader that they are phantasms, conjured figures from a pantheon of imaginary Muslims who do

28 Introduction

the work of installing a civilizational divide between Muslims and others. The meaning of these terms is so taken for granted and naturalized as having a transparent meaning that we do not see the miniature industries dedicated to their creation and circulation in the name of an anti-Muslim racism. Meant to install the figure of the premodern and violent Muslim, the terms work hard and nowhere more so than in law, where they automatically confine Muslims to the space of raciality, a space where nothing has to make sense and where such racialized subjects exist in a negative relation to law.

Installing a phantasmic global Islamic enemy marked by "religious extremism," the "global war on terror" has enabled states to label Muslim constituencies with whom they are in conflict as "terrorists" and "extremists." As Sean Roberts has shown for China's internal campaign against a Muslim minority, a struggle that is one of an indigenous Uyghur population fighting for self-determination is handily transformed by the People's Republic of China (PRC) into what it labels a campaign against "Islamic extremism." The designation of Uyghurs as "Islamic terrorists" and "extremists" enables what some observers have called a cultural genocide against the Uyghur inhabitants of the semi-autonomous region of western China known as Xinjiang.[101] Under the aegis of counterterrorism, the Chinese state is able to target Uyghurs for mass internment and coerced and segregated residential labor, including family separation and population transfers. Operating with impunity, the PRC secures the collaboration of the United States on a geopolitical landscape where there is increasing consensus about a global Islamic enemy against whom all force is authorized. All roads lead to the bazaar, as Said put it some time ago.[102]

Describing the contemporary world order as an era of American empire, Darryl Li notes that since the 1991 war on Iraq, the United States has been free to pursue military intervention without significant contestation, force it has directed overwhelmingly at the Arab world.[103] In this world order of American empire, "there have been two primary ways of characterizing armed conflicts: localized ethnic wars and a globally threatening militant Islam."[104] Appointing itself as "referee or policeman committed only to lofty values such as humanitarianism," the United States produces the Muslim terrorist "as the one the world must band together to defeat."[105] Offering an illustration of how the racialized Muslim

Introduction **29**

becomes central to international governance regimes, Tendayi Achiume and Aslı Bâli show that humanitarian intervention, counterterrorism, and migration control converge in the case of Libya starting in 2011. The racialization of Muslims as "terrorists" enabled the framing of Libya as an Arab (and not an African) state "awash in jihadis" and thus requiring "unilateral applications of force in the territory at the discretion of First World militaries wielding counter-terrorism doctrine."[106] Licensing an armed insurrection against Libya on the pretext of needing to protect the civilian population, the UN Security Council authorized a massive bombing campaign in 2011, in which thousands of civilians were killed and the Libyan dictator Muammar Gaddafi deposed. The bombing campaign and the ensuing destruction were followed by a freezing of Libyan state assets and new imperatives around counterterrorism and migrant management. In a very short time, Libya was "unmade" as a state and recast as a country beset by Muslim "terrorist" actors and migrants, a place requiring bombings in the name of humanitarian intervention. American foreign policy, which emphasizes military force, restructures Muslim societies by offering support for proxy wars from Syria to Yemen. In so doing, the United States disregards humanitarian crises in Syria, Yemen, and Gaza and promotes an international order fractured by a reduced commitment to the rule of law; these actions sustain the Muslim as the quintessential enemy of the West in the making of a global white supremacy.[107] American exceptionalism, America as the power appointed to keep the world safe from the threat of Islam and the Muslim, is consolidated through the Islamic figure, "suffusing U.S. policy with a moral righteousness and a benevolent flair."[108]

The Muslim as racialized Other and "terrorist" comes to matter within the United States when the Muslim is the figure "signifying imperial enmity."[109] Keith Feldman shows that American national security infrastructure is often routed through the "case" of Israel and Palestine. That is, Israel, as a crucial reference point for U.S. imperial culture, binding two settler societies under the banner of settler colonialism, sustains the "durability of whiteness as a privileged category of national existence."[110] A domestic anti-Muslim racism is invigorated by these international developments. Nadine Suleiman Naber charts how anti-Muslim racism became central to the making of American imperial power producing and

30 Introduction

sustaining an external Muslim enemy and a domestic one at the same time. From the 1967 Arab-Israeli War to American pursuit of economic expansion in the Middle East from the 1970s to the 1990s, the first Gulf War, bombings in Sudan and Afghanistan, the sanctions against Iraq, and ultimately to the occupation in 2003, an anti-Arab racism melded into an anti-Muslim racism travels the world. Scholars of Orientalism and anti-Arab racism in the United States point to the impact of American support for the occupation of Palestine, which, as Said noted some time ago, requires and produces the idea of the Arab as "Islamic terrorist," a representation that cemented itself in American consciousness well before the events of 9/11.[111] With the collapsing of the category Muslim with Arab, Arab Americans who might have previously enjoyed a "proximity to whiteness" lose their place in the racial hierarchies of the nation, quickly becoming "Islamic terrorists" in the nation's imaginary during times of war making and imperial occupations. Anti-Muslim racism traverses these transnational routes as when the 1979 Islamic Revolution in Iran dislodged earlier Orientalist frames in the West of a romantic Persia, replacing it with the Muslim as "fundamentalist, traditional, backward and fanatically religious."[112] Importantly, such cultural developments justify military interventions in the Muslim world even as military interventions require them.

An "international system of legal Apartheid" provides the infrastructure for global white supremacy.[113] "Anti-terrorism" laws and an entire apparatus of security laws targeting Muslims now dot the globe, casting their shadow on every aspect of how nations draw their racial boundaries. The present postcolonial migrant "crisis" in Europe, Nicholas De Genova argues, should be understood not as crisis but as part of a global racial formation (which De Genova labels anti-Blackness), one that continuously produces mass death. Notably, the deadly crossing of the Mediterranean by asylum seekers is often narrated as an invasion of Muslims. Unleashing a full-blown racial panic, asylum seekers are seen as dangerous, unassimilable potential *Muslim* rapists and criminals.[114] De Genova notes that even three-year-old Aylan Kurdi, who drowned in the Mediterranean along with his mother as they attempted the dangerous crossing, was depicted in the French magazine *Charlie Hebdo* as a Muslim sexual predator in the making. Imagined as "fundamentalist," sexually perverse, and irredeemably patriarchal, it becomes possible to evict Muslims from law and society in the name of secularism and gender equality—and, significantly, in the name of national security. The idea of a fatal cultural incompatibility between Muslims and white Europeans, an incompatibility that is premised on the paradox of European culture as both Christian and secular, easily generates anti-Muslim violence and absolves Europe of its role in producing the refugee bodies that wash up on the shores of the Mediterranean.

Significantly, the global South joins the global North in enacting laws that rival the laws of their former colonial masters in the drawing of the civilizational line between Muslims and citizens. As Malinda Smith argues, when all conflicts get reduced to 'America versus Islam' in the global South, the narrow frame condenses Africa into stereotype, painting the continent as rogue, a place where "terrorism" is incubated and where "terrorist Muslims" abound.[115] There is no room in the frame to consider imperial legacies and ongoing imperial aggressions. Indeed, as Smith observes, imperialism itself becomes a story of the good old days when imperialist masters kept Africa safe. When Ethiopia provides the United States with its African Guantánamo and in return is helped by the United States in its efforts to intervene in Somalia, and when a global network of rendition sites hosts prisons and black sites devoted to the imprisonment and torture of Muslims accused of involvement in "terrorism," we see white supremacy on a global scale and an imperial whiteness formed against the figure of the Muslim; the players, however, are not all white.

Cracks in the Color Line

In this book I devote almost no time to the anti-Muslim subject who is nonwhite, whether this be the Christian evangelicals of color who attend seminars organized by their churches about Muslims as "terrorists," or African American Christians who have at times supported Zionism and aligned themselves with the anti-Muslim agendas of their white counterparts, or Christians of color who pursue assimilationist agendas or paths to whiteness through anti-Muslimness. Indulging in anti-Muslim racism can provide access to imperial power, as Judy Han suggests it does for Korean evangelical Christians both in the United States and Korea.[116]

32 Introduction

Whiteness is interpreted and translated into a status in multiple ways by those who seek to access to its benefits. We can perhaps rephrase Fanon's "You're white because you're rich and you're rich because you're white" into "you're rich because you can access whiteness." Whiteness, Rana observes, is the racial infrastructure of accumulation, the thing on which the process depends.[117]

Exploring the paths to whiteness that nonwhites and those who are white-aspiring take, hoping to translate class and money into race privilege, Sedef Arat-Koç suggests that there are cracks in the color line Du Bois identified as the problem of the twentieth century. As whiteness becomes more conditional on class in an intensified global capitalism, whites who face socioeconomic threats are urgently invited into whiteness as compensation for their losses. White nations offer white belonging for the price of economic suffering and the dismantling of the welfare state, a phenomenon confirmed in the rise of white populist movements around the globe that are instigated and fostered by white states. The invitation into whiteness offers those positioned too closely to "Muslimness" and to Islam a chance to escape the "Orientalist judgments" that proximity to Muslims brings and to access white privilege more easily.[118] If all ethnic groups must Orientalize the Other and occidentalize themselves, moving toward whiteness through anti-Muslim racism, as Arat-Koç asserts, those who are not considered white enough—for example, Eastern Europeans—negotiate European belonging through an aggressive Christianity and an intense anti-Muslim animus that, Arat-Koç suggests, is deeply internalized. To the near white Europeans Arat-Koç discusses who access whiteness through a distancing from Muslims we can add Jews of European origin for whom whiteness provides shelter from anti-Semitism, and Christians who are deemed insufficiently white, as were Mormons who were once seen as "Oriental" threats on U.S. soil:[119] all can reap the benefits of whiteness and stave off their eviction from it through anti-Muslim racism.

How might we understand these anti-Muslim processes in the global South or the East? The Muslim is an important figure to supremacists of all stripes, and indeed to anyone or any nation attempting to locate themselves in the schema of an international whiteness. In China, India, Myanmar, and other parts of the global South where Muslims have been marked as disposable, race making is certainly more complicated than an expanding white supremacy in Europe and North America would suggest. Histories and patterns of racialization differ. Anti-Muslim movements draw upon racial hierarchies forged through religion in different ways, although always in lockstep with the specific neoliberal imperatives of capitalism. In India, for example, Hindu nationalists come to understand their superiority through Hinduism instead of through Christianity, whereas in Myanmar, the supremacy of the Buddhist majority over the Rohingyas incorporates a kind of race making through religion. The economic stakes of race making are high. The middle classes of such countries become part of a global elite constituted as white, anxious to secure the financial benefits of whiteness. The stigmatization of Muslims and their expulsion from political community yields land and resources. *White* supremacist may not be the appropriate descriptor to apply to such diverse political leaders as Narendra Modi in India, or Xi Jinping in China, or Aung San Suu Kyi in Myanmar, but what is clear of all such figures is the globalized anti-Muslim racial discourse in which they traffic and its economic underpinnings, even as these leaders are certain to inflect anti-Muslim projects with a local patina.

From a cache of leaked Chinese government memos instructing authorities to round up Muslim minorities in Xinjiang and to "show absolutely no mercy" to the local Uyghur population,[120] to the Indian government's revoking of the semi-autonomous status of Kashmir and the imposition of martial law on its predominantly Muslim population,[121] and to Myanmar's ethnic cleansing of the Rohingya Muslim minority,[122] Muslim is even more synonymous than a decade ago with bans, detention camps, torture, extrajudicial killings, and war. On this global landscape, one that is pockmarked by mass detention centers, aerial bombardments of Muslim populations, and cultural genocides in progress, it is imperative to consider how the multiple sites of anti-Muslim racism are related. At the core of each anti-Muslim project in the global South is a nucleus of racial feeling, a place where Muslims are imagined as subhumanity and where their disposability vests power in the hands of elites who traffic in racial mythologies. Borne along these currents of racial feeling, anti-Muslim subjects arrive at a place of coherence, coming into their own as superior, emplaced, and national subjects as well as members of a global

34 Introduction

imaginary that is anchored in racial capitalism and the politics of empire. The twin processes of capitalist accumulation and race making operate through each other. Tracing the Muslim in these arrangements offers an opportunity to understand how they do so.

The designation of a global Islamic enemy as a race takes us on a long road, one that involves torture, war, occupations, and genocide. The "jihad" fighter, especially the one who travels across national boundaries, has been declared a universal enemy, Darryl Li argues. While mujahideen are seen as foreign fighters, we do not regard American soldiers fighting imperial wars as foreign fighters, that is, as fighters intervening in disputes in nations to which they don't belong.[123] We are unable to contemplate the politics of the jihad fighters as anything but "terrorism" and American soldiers as anything else but representatives of the international community with the authority to protect the world from Muslims. Locked in this imperial frame, one driven by racial animus against Muslims, we are unable to "to have serious conversations about political violence" on either side of the divide.[124]

Muslims are hardly the only group to endure the things discussed here. One has only to compare the hundreds of cribs in a Uyghur mass detention camp to the migrant children in the United States who are kept in cages and are separated from their parents, or the bodies of refugee children washing up on the shores of the Mediterranean, to recognize a broader phenomenon of disposable populations. In tracing the figure of the Muslim in these deadly arrangements, both in their ordinary and extreme forms, I hope to open a window into how such arrangements are a part of race making in global capitalism. When Hindu teenagers learn in the military training camps of the Hindu national right that the nation must be defended from Muslim rapists and "terrorists," fear and hate are mobilized to sustain the idea of Hindu supremacy as a racial formation.[125] Powerful emotions are channeled into a political project that has as its root the eviction of Muslims from political community. In the same way, the idea that Chinese Uyghur Muslims are confined to concentration camps on the basis that they are "terrorists" who require reeducation transforms Uyghurs into racial threats, and the Han Chinese majority into a superior race.[126] These anti-Muslim projects of the global South are linked to those in the global North through shared technologies and neoliberal economies, discourses that are distinctly civilizational and racial. Law has a central part to play in racial governance.

Nothing Has to Make Sense: Maintaining Whiteness in Western Law

In his book *Enemy Aliens,* law professor David Cole surveys torture at Abu Ghraib, the U.S. Supreme Court's enemy combatant decisions of 2004 that declared "terror" suspects as persons who do not merit the status of full personhood in law, and the continuing anomalous status in law of prisoners detained at Guantánamo, and concludes: "The brutality we have visited upon suspects in the war on terror is possible in large part because we have portrayed 'the enemy' as less than human."[127] Others have reached the same conclusion when analyzing the legality of drone-executed bomb attacks that result in large-scale civilian casualties, targeted assassinations, indefinite detention, and wars fought on the strength of rumors about weapons of mass destruction. Raciality, Denise Ferreira da Silva writes, the condition of being raced as an inferior being, lies at the basis of the state's decision to kill certain persons: "Such killings do not unleash an ethical crisis because these persons' bodies and the territories they inhabit always-already signify violence."[128] How do bodies and territories come to acquire the status of those "not comprehended by universality" and not included in the ranks of the human, bodies declared to be "nobodies" who, in the case of Muslims, are believed to carry the seeds of violence in their blood? On what philosophical arguments do hierarchies of the human depend?

Ferreira da Silva offers an argument in three steps about the emergence of the Western concept of Man, a category from which Muslims are routinely evicted. First, social scientific accounts of human difference, "the onto-epistemological arsenal constituted by the concepts of the racial and the cultural, and their signifiers . . . produce persons (ethical-juridical) entities not comprehended by universality."[129] Second, states deploy this arsenal to declare who stands in a negative relation to law and whose annihilation preserves the security of the state. Third, whoever endangers the state cannot be construed as legitimate. Thus, on the terrain of the racial there is no distinction between the law (as legality) and the state (as authority). Violence is authorized against those evicted from the

36 Introduction

universal. Ferreira da Silva takes us back to Enlightenment thought from the seventeenth century onward, noting that for Locke, reason emanates from the mind, a mind that has triumphed over body (a mind that owns itself) and works always to constrain, regulate, or limit body. If in this way universal reason is always already violent and engaged in recovering man from the state of nature, law is the scene of violence where the subjugation of all that would threaten reason takes place on behalf of the state. Clarifying that she is not arguing that racial subalterns figure outside the domain of rights, but instead are continuously evicted from it in the name of the state's self-preservation, Ferreira da Silva emphasizes that those configured as "the other side of universality" cannot be included in the nation except as that which must be suppressed and repressed, a continual process that I describe as race making. When raciality is in play, when we find "the human body as inscribed by the arsenal of scientific reason," we find two fundamentally different types of minds, the one self-determining, the other outer-determined.[130] Law protects the former and reserves for the latter the force that enables the state to preserve itself. To stand in a negative relationship to law is to occupy the space reserved for outer-determined others and to be the target of law's violence, as Muslims have been in the "war on terror" and earlier.

Incoherence marks the spot where threatening racial phantoms and outer-determined others reside, the place in our heads where ghosts, demons, and dream figures become indistinguishable. Incoherence signals the presence of a haunted rationalism, one where "ghosts within the mind are more powerful and more significant than many of the beings that walk abroad."[131] Ghosts have long been linked to law and justice, appearing to decry not only their own murders but also stolen kingdoms.[132] Native and African Americans play a spectral role in American politics, as "simultaneously there and not there" and existing at the limits of justice, as Ferreira da Silva notes.[133] If they disturb and haunt the Constitution, they also introduce confusion and anxiety.[134] Emotions do the work of reconciling ideas about universal rights with the eviction of the racialized subject from equal consideration in law. If the Muslim is always apprehended through the prism of the "terrorist," and the prisoner through the prism of the slave, law that preserves a space for subpersons depends on the emotions that these phantom figures elicit. As Toni Morrison suggests, when we see incoherence, contradiction, and emotional disorder, we know that the legal subject is "black."[135] Morrison's comment is offered in the context of three American examples: O. J. Simpson's portrayal at his trial for the murder of his white wife, Nicole Brown, as someone who is simultaneously mindless and a "thoughtful, meditating murderer"; Rodney King, who was seen as a major threat to the *twelve* rioting police who beat him and who were all declared innocent of attempted murder; and a "beaten up, sexually assaulted black girl [who] wakes up in a hospital room and is 'convicted' of raping and defiling herself." We need not reconcile these contradictions or ponder their implausibility, Morrison writes: "Difficult explanations are folded into the general miasma of black incoherence."[136] Miasma, something unpleasant that circulates like a bad smell around the Black subject, conveys that we are in the presence of a subject we already understand, one who penetrates our senses as dread, disgust, and threat.

A miasma of incoherence similarly surrounds the Muslim, the miasma that is a feature of those spaces in law where whiteness is protected. We become reconciled to the implausibility of the statements pronounced about Muslims in legal settings when we rely on our senses, feeling the violence and deep misogyny of bearded Muslim patriarchs and duped but intransigent wearers of hijabs and niqabs of our imaginaries well before any words about them penetrate our consciousness. What is declared true of Muslims slams into the stomach with all the force of racial insult and injury and is doubly shocking because of the official settings in which it occurs. What to make of judges insisting on an assaulted Muslim woman's uncovering in order to properly judge her credibility? Who believes that Muslims have a catastrophically damaged gene pool? When the latter statement comes from an avowed white supremacist and yet is taken to be expert knowledge about Muslims in a sentencing hearing, racism has displaced logic. Courts are able to believe in the racial science of the expert because the subject being discussed is already deeply *emotionally* known. To those momentarily disturbed by the incoherence, the gap between cognition and feeling is closed when we remember *where* the statements are being uttered and by whom. We are often persuaded that statements such as "Muslims have a catastrophically damaged gene pool" are true because they are uttered in a court of law.

38   Introduction

Ideas about Muslims possessing a genetic predisposition for violence ride in on racial feeling and although law's fictions are daunting, as Colin Dayan observes, we readily believe in them. For Dayan, the miasma of Black incoherence is known to law but unknown to the naked eye and to common sense. The ghosts of slavery envelop law in the miasma of the slave. For this reason, law is not to be mistaken for logic and it is not to be interpreted literally but reasonably. Yet we must ask, as Dayan does, what kind of reason defies logic?[137] The answer: the reason of a colonial and slave-owning state, a reason that persists long after the initial acts of dispossession and the formal abolition of the slave trade. In the capacity of law to make the obscene lawful (slavery, torture, rape, indefinite solitary confinement, preventive detention), America transitions from a colonial and slave nation to a democracy by preserving those spaces where the mass incarceration of Black, Brown, and Indigenous people and their unmaking as persons in law continues apace. These are formal spaces that proliferate where the miasma of Black incoherence has work to do to protect whiteness.

The Muslim emerges in law as an effect of the legal groundwork laid by colonialism and slavery in the Americas and by its antecedents in Europe, an outcome we see in the treatment of Muslim prisoners. Dayan describes this groundwork with respect to prisoners in American law. The slave nation continues in the Thirteenth Amendment, where slavery is abolished but can continue as a form of punishment for prisoners, the change benefiting the white employers of prison labor. The slave morphs into the prisoner, and the slave's miasma forever clings to the prisoner, who remains a being against whom all violence is authorized. Similarly, in the Eighth Amendment, prohibiting cruel and unusual punishment, the cruelty that is prohibited is excessive; cruelty itself, however, is assumed to be legitimate for the prisoner, who is always already imagined as slave. Thus, as Dayan observes, "In this juridical calculation, what is harsh, brutal, or excessive turns into what is constitutional, customary or just bearable."[138] Judges spend their time adjudicating where the limit lies between excessive cruelty and permissible cruelty, law and policy particularly in evidence when the Bush administration defended its use of torture against Muslim "terror" suspects in the "war on terror." Engaging in a series of debates—for example, whether waterboarding was merely

Introduction **39**

an enhanced interrogation technique and not torture—permissible cruelty won the day. As many pointed out, some of the practices being defended were already practiced in America's prisons.[139] There is permissible cruelty at the limits of justice, the place where the slave's aura as a being with a negative relationship to law is strongest and where we find the Muslim.

Nothing has to make sense in a framework that already sets aside a space for the slave, a being not comprehended by universality. In this space, a sexually assaulted Black girl can be convicted of raping herself. The space she occupies is one where language "constructs a legal person who stands in a negative relation to the law, who has no rights, and whose fundamental status thus remains distinct from all others."[140] What happens in the places in law where what is reasonable takes the place of what is logical or true? Dayan writes that "captives are human in form, but dead in spirit"; legal rituals establish prisoners as civilly dead, as the enslaved were. The prisoner comes to lack the right to themselves, becoming instead "a human who is no longer granted the moral sensibility and conscience necessary for personhood."[141] Evicted from personhood, the prisoner is stripped of the right to experience suffering, an outcome we see in the prisoners at Abu Ghraib prison during the American occupation of Iraq, where the torture of prisoners became known as enhanced interrogations methods. From the everyday, such as prisoner limitations on reading, to the extraordinary, such as torture and solitary confinement without an end, the ritual repetition of the slave's status reenacts slavery and preserves intact the racial project of accumulation based on the inherent superiority of Europeans.

If the slave persists in American law and clears a path for the phantom Muslim as "terrorist" who can be tortured or killed with impunity, the place that law maintains for the slave is intrinsic to Western modernity. Subpersons have a distinct legal status, one that authorizes violence against them. As Samera Esmeir discusses for colonial Egypt and as we saw with liberalism, the human becomes an effect of law itself; it is the law that "decided on the empirical meanings of the human and all that seemed to threaten it."[142] If the law decides who is human and who is not, the slave is everywhere, as Anna Agathangelou reminds us, drawing on Fanon to emphasize the visual register of race through which we

40 Introduction

apprehend imperial power.[143] If capital always imagines a slave's body from which it can forcefully extract value, and indulges in dreams of land to be appropriated, it remains able to do so because the figure of the slave haunts the colonial and capitalist imagination as the raw material from which a material and psychic whiteness is made. Racial fantasies summon power as a "technology that severs being from existence, thereby rendering it flesh."[144] These fantasies, Fanon suggested, make visible and proclaim invisible the lawless privilege of whiteness. Notably, as Agathangelou observes discussing the fantasy of Osama bin Laden and its connection to imperial power, "the less cohesive the logic the more productive Orientalism becomes."[145] We are ushered into Orientalist fantasy through miasma and incoherence. If, as she shows in a popular representation of a turban-wearing and bearded bin Laden featured as the "Before" picture next to a turbaned O. J. Simpson as the "After," we must ask, along with Fanon, "What kind of affect does the Black body deliver?," we must also consider what kind of affect the Muslim body delivers.[146] The shared terrain of subpersonhood is formed by the idea that their lands are available for consumption and their bodies are slated for disposability.

Returning to the question "What kind of affect does the Muslim body deliver?," we can conclude that Muslims are never far from the surface of white fears, an affect connected to the foundational role that Islam plays when imagined as the antithesis to European modernity. The Muslim may well be the postmodern "folk devil par excellence," Werbner suggests, emphasizing the psychoanalytic terrain on which media images of "terror," war, and violence augment existing racial imaginaries. Unleashing "the fear of physicality unbound," the Muslim as "terrorist" is received as "upfront, morally superior, openly aggressive, denying the promiscuous society and the validity of other cultures—in short, a different kind of folk devil altogether."[147] While scholars dispute the genealogy of the Muslim folk devil, the strong emotions the phantasmic Muslim provokes are unmistakable. Meer comments, for example, on the visceral cultural response to the prospect of Turkish accession to the European Union and suggests that its intensity resembles Matar's description of how the relationship between Ottoman and Hapsburg empires was transformed, in Matar's words, into "a cosmic conflict of Christianity against Islam, of the Christian cross versus the Muslim crescent."[148] As chapter 1 describes, the Crusades enter the imaginary of today's white supremacists with all the emotional force of a cosmic event. Upon entering the website *Gates of Vienna,* one of several small blogs of the Christian right, users encounter a painting of the siege of Vienna in 1683 and are reminded that this was a time when Islam was poised to overrun Christian Europe, a moment once again upon us. Hage offers another possibility for the Muslim's prominence as racial enemy. Studying the relation between racism and speciesism, he proposes that in this contemporary era's globalization of the "Islamic other," the dominant racist classificatory metaphor for Muslims has changed from cockroach to wolf. Remarking that the metaphor tells us about racists themselves, orienting the racist person toward a particular action, Hage suggests that whereas the cockroach is a nuisance, the wolf is perceived as dangerous, ungovernable, and exterminable.[149] Ungovernability, he further reminds us, is not an intrinsic quality but rather a relation.

Claims to modernity and the necessity of law-preserving violence in keeping the unreasonable at bay reach us through the senses as an affect, no less in law than in politics. The incoherence and miasma that surrounds the Muslim and the Black are above all a contradictory tangle of emotions drawing us inexorably toward the conclusion that racial violence and terror are authorized processes of white states and a global racial order. Hage reminds us that "vagueness, empirical 'all over the placeness' contradiction, blocking-of-the-obvious, and even sometimes a totally surrealist grasp of reality are the very conditions of possibility of the maximal efficiency of racist practices."[150] Achille Mbembe uses the phrase "Black reason" to describe the performance of incoherence in social, legal, and political forums, places where nothing has to make sense and where violence is authorized.[151] Mbembe rightly emphasizes that "Black reason," a colonial and slave logic ("occupation and extraction" and "capture and predation"), is a "psycho-oneiric complex" and that race and racism are a fundamental process of the unconscious.[152] He calls attention to delirium, describing racism as "a form of psychic derangement, the mechanism through which the repressed suddenly surface." As something that "manifests through the senses," racism is about desire,

42 Introduction

one that is always infected with dread and worry.[153] The racial Other cannot be included, only repressed.

Considering both the North American and European contexts, Mbembe describes "Black reason" as "a kind of giant cage" with "race as its chassis." Reason rests on race, "a perverse complex, a generator of fears and torments, of disturbed thoughts and terror, but especially of infinite sufferings, and ultimately, catastrophe." Race is "phobic, obsessive, at times hysterical." It deploys dread and practices "altruicide: the constitution of the Other not as similar to oneself but as a menacing object from which one must be protected or escape, or which must simply be destroyed if it cannot be subdued."[154] We see all of these features in play when the law considers Muslims. In the majority decision of the U.S. Supreme Court approving the executive order banning foreign nationals from select Muslim majority countries from entering the United States, the infamous "Muslim travel ban," we witness a court relying on the specter of dangerous, unassimilable Muslims to justify the travel ban as a national security measure. No more than a specter is needed. Dread is deployed, and the law can do its work to install white Christians as normative citizens menaced by "terrorist Muslims."[155]

To speak of Muslim phantoms is to pay attention to the operation of desire, fear, and dread and to consider law as an emotional discourse that sustains race making in individuals and nations. It is to encounter souls that are undressed, to recall Du Bois. Mapping law's incoherence when the subject is Muslim takes us through a continuum of rage, desire, dreams of blood purity, and appeasements made to a vengeful Christian God. The hooded prisoner with blacked-out goggles, the Muslim youth thought to carry the seeds of violence in his blood, the niqab wearer who is imagined by judges and politicians as refusing reciprocity with her face covering, and the school textbook Muslim whose five pillars of religious belief described in the school curriculum call forth a deep rage and fear in white Christian parents—all are seemingly indispensable phantoms of modern life. Phantom Muslims bring into the light of day white men and women as entitled to all, as possessors of Muslim women's bodies, as the jailors of imagined "rock star teenage imams," as torturers who subdue and cage, as shooters protecting white communities from racial threats, and as keepers of racial knowledge about genetics and passed-

Introduction **43**

down traits. The figure of the Muslim works affectively in law to ignite fears of the loss of white Christian entitlement and to invite force. The white subjects who appear on the following pages exhibit aggrievement, vengeance, ressentiment, frustrated imperial ambition, repugnance, dread, and disgust toward Muslims, emotions that begin as a fear of engulfment by Muslims both phantasmatic and real. Agathangelou insightfully observes: "The anxious subject trembles in fear that the fundamental source, the raw material, the flesh that constitutes it as coherent and powerful, may violently expose its cynegetic extermination."[156]

A tortured subject who is perpetually anxiety ridden, the white anti-Muslim subject is an obsessed and conflicted subject, a condition long theorized by scholars as colonial fantasy. As Meyda Yeğenoğlu powerfully argued some years ago in her book *Colonial Fantasies,* the hijab and the niqab are the sites of an enduring colonial fantasy (understood here as both the conscious and unconscious mind), the place where discourses of sexual and colonial difference are powerfully mapped onto each other. Fascination, anger, and frustration coalesce around the idea that the veiled woman is refusing to yield herself to the Western gaze. Unavailable, she is an enigma who is simultaneously feared and desired. Without her unveiling, the Western man and the Western woman cannot know himself or herself as being in control, sovereign, and desired. In Yeğenoğlu's words, "the metaphysical will to know gains a sexual overtone. Troubled with this mask, the Western subject is threatened and seduced at the same time."[157] The rending of the veil enables access and possession. Possession, the dictionary reminds us, is about having, owning, controlling. It is about an item of property, something that belongs to one. The erotics of possession shed light on the psychic and sexualized underpinnings of anti-Muslim racism and of bans on the hijab and niqab in general. If desire marks the colonial encounter, the bid to know and possess the Other can only be accomplished through violence: the rending of the veil.

We must also take note of the obsessions anti-Muslim racists display with the idea of Muhammad as a pedophile and with the ways in which anti-queerness is frequently yoked to anti-Muslimness in the white-supremacist imagination even as anti-Muslim racists also sometimes embrace white queerness as a marker of their own modernity.[158] As Jasbir

44 Introduction

Puar's pathbreaking analysis in *Terrorist Assemblages: Homonationalism in Queer Times* makes clear, anti-queerness in "terrorism" discourses, as exemplified by bin Laden's portrayal as monstrous by association with sexual and bodily perversity, operates to entrench heterosexuality as the mandatory term of patriotism. At the same time, such sexualized national discourses offer white queers inclusion in the nation via whiteness. The always tentative inclusionary gesture extended toward white queers solidifies the United States as gay-friendly and feminist, an exceptionalism premised on the idea that Muslim societies are neither.[159] The Muslim as sexually perverse, a perennial figure in racial science, remains important to the making of whiteness. The marking of Muslim men as full of rage and sexual frustration, dysfunctions seen as originating in their families and leading to a commitment to "terrorism," continues unchanged in the sentencing of Muslim men suspected of involvement in terrorism, as chapter 3 discusses.

Whether expressing masculine imperial frustration that veiled women refuse to uncover, or white feminist insistence that covered women must enjoy the right to be seductive, or a lethal rage that a threatening homosexual Otherness penetrates and endangers all that is rightfully theirs, the anti-Muslim subject maintains the boundary between self and racial Other through force. Writing of the masculine fascist fear of engulfment by the mass (Jews, communists, and women in the context of pre–World War II Germany), the German scholar Klaus Theweleit proposes that it is only through dominance over women and the racial Other that the ego can avoid breakdown.[160] Through violence enacted against women and racial Others, fascist men remain hard, organized, phallic bodies and male egos defending themselves against the flood. It is the injuring body that has to express these racial arrangements. Theweleit observes that the fascist man escapes his own fears by "mashing others to the pulp he himself threatens to become."[161] Rey Chow and a host of feminist scholars, myself included, discuss how acts of violence toward the racialized woman entail Western women becoming sovereign subjects through the forceful unveiling of the Muslim woman, binding her to a system of receiving feminist assistance into modernity through violence.[162] Such racial fantasies are in evidence, as chapter 2 shows, when bans on Muslim women's clothing are defended as feminist protection of Muslim women.

In the West, an anti-Muslim movement in law and politics is borne along these currents of racial feeling and colonial fantasy, an emotional and psychosexual structure that is foundational to white life and imperial culture. An amalgam of fears and desires attached to a range of racial Others, anti-Muslim affect powers a liberal politics that emphasizes nationalism, secularism, and a monocultural white nation as well as a right-wing politics in which specific political goals include unqualified support for Israel, bans on abortions, gun rights, and immigration clampdowns, a politics inextricably linked to racial and imperial power. The white supremacy that structures modernity, Rodríguez reminds us, displays a capacity for endless permutations:

> To attempt to define and describe white supremacy in an absolutist, ironclad, transhistorical manner is not a useful exercise: its matrices of institutional mobilization, conceptual apparatuses of civilizational, national and subject ordering, and grammars of articulation (both as a rhetoric of power and commonsense arrangement of everyday rule) too quickly flex and change in response to the political expediencies and social crises composing certain historical conjunctures.[163]

White-supremacist animus, to use Rodríguez's term, has a changing comportment, disguising itself in liberal regimes as improvement, as I have argued of white settler-colonialism's legal responses to Indigenous peoples,[164] and positioning itself as in the best interests of the formerly enslaved and the colonized. Revising and elaborating the violence white supremacy requires, moving from a slave-owning state to one in which anti-Blackness remains constitutive and where Black bodies are "regularly subjected to violent white will," white-supremacist animus can assume the form of a liberal state intent on an always differential inclusion of the racially subordinate. In the liberal framework, racism is exceptionalized and the state transforms white racial terror into something only a few bad whites pursue and some always deserve. It is this endless flexibility that we see in law with respect to racialized groups, Muslims among them.

Nothing Has to Make Sense discusses several legal sites in the West over the past two decades, places where dread, phobia, hysteria, and desire reign

46 Introduction

free and a global whiteness is made through the figure of the Muslim. In following phantom Muslims across these legal and political landscapes, we encounter the *frenzied* making of white nations, masculinities, and femininities. The Muslim man, variously imagined as snake, wolf, Satan incarnate, and "terrorist" evildoer, and the Muslim woman, imagined as imperiled and in need of saving but also now as aggressive and in your face, inhabit those places in politics and law where nothing has to make sense, places where phantoms dwell and races are made through powerful emotions and where blatant injustice is justified.

As the chapters of this book show, strong feelings and emotions sustain and are sustained by the legal projects that are discussed here. As I discuss in chapter 1, for example, when the mother of a student assigned an exercise in Arabic calligraphy in art class announces that upon seeing the calligraphy "immediately I had a bad feeling come over me," we see the way that the mother's grievance against the school for exposing her child to anything associated with Islam is fueled by emotions of dread that sustain anti-Muslim political projects. Simultaneously, these political projects give rise to the mother's dread in the first place, providing her with a sense of self, a kind of dwelling place.[165] Chapter 1 considers the legal projects aimed at the banning of Islam in the curriculum in the United States. Largely the province of white evangelicals but joined by white-supremacist groups and some Zionist Jews, efforts to ban Islam in schools have until recently largely floundered in the courts and among policy makers. Significantly, when cases are lost, the Muslim as "terrorist" threat is nevertheless reified; the law is merely the arbiter of when Muslims can stay in the universal and when they are booted out. Sustained by key Christian organizations and conservative media, these local efforts circulate anti-Muslim emotions that are a part of a settler consciousness and provide a vocabulary through which white citizens come to know themselves as defenders of the borders of Christianity, race, and nation. Christian evangelical contributions to the making of a national anti-Muslim affect are considerable and have a disproportionate impact on American foreign policy in the Middle East. Revealing how anti-Muslim affect is made and how it circulates, these local conflicts also offer glimpses into those individuals who "experience the world Islamophobically,"[166] those for whom Islam and Muslims are a deeply threatening Otherness that reaches into the very core of everyday white, Christian life.

Chapter 2 discusses a series of legal initiatives in North America and Europe to ban the wearing of hijabs and niqabs by Muslim women. A part of a global focus on embodied citizenship designed to exclude Muslims, bans on Muslim women's attire and cultural practices are underwritten by phantasmic scenes in which lawmakers, among others, demand that Muslim women yield to white men and women, libidinal currents that flow through Western law. Legal scenes where bans on Muslim practices are imposed are punctuated with unwielded moments of desire. Trials and hearings are distinguished by emotional outbursts, exaggerated claims, and an openly sexualized discourse. Bans of this kind, I show, are dreams of imperial possession often enveloped in a liberal language of freedom. They require performances of whiteness where Europeans are installed as modern subjects uniquely given to democracy, secularism, and gender equality while Muslims are declared as standing outside of modern life.

In chapter 3, a sentencing hearing at Guantánamo in which Muslims were declared to have a "catastrophic gene pool" provides an example of sociobiological arguments resurrected to defend the incarceration and torture of Muslims suspected of involvement in "terrorism." Identified as a potential carrier of "extremist" sympathies and a proclivity for violence, Muslims may be incarcerated indefinitely. As it always has, racial science plays an important part not only in anti-Muslim racism but in the legally authorized disposability of Indigenous, Black, and racialized populations. Scientifically scripted as a subspecies, Muslims, among others, are marked for disposability, and the state's "terrorism" experts are conscripted to make the case for their eviction. Following the figure of the Muslim on the legal landscape illuminates the infrastructure of racial knowledge required to evict Muslims from political community and to mark them as outside the modern, atavistic holdouts whose communities remain tribal and given to violence. It reveals the global reach of anti-Muslim propagandists and scholars.

Chapter 4 examines the making of national memory in the post–Abu Ghraib period when Americans began to make sense of the sexualized torture of Iraqi prisoners conducted by U.S.-led coalition forces on an

48 Introduction

unprecedented scale in the early 2000s. How to explain it? How to think about the policy makers and the ordinary soldiers who went along with torture? How to believe that we are now post-torture and the darkness is over? Torture at Abu Ghraib and violated Muslim bodies have not penetrated the consciousness of the nation, encased as it is in a story of torturers as mere dupes of unscrupulous leaders. Muslims remain illegible as targets of racial harm, their communities deserving of the violence that is visited upon them. I offer that the politics of memory about Abu Ghraib in the two decades since 9/11 tell us about the making of the American subject as innocent—of torture, of racial violence, and of terror. Reviewing the much-lauded documentary *Standard Operating Procedure,* by Errol Morris, I find that Americans live with the story of torture at Abu Ghraib by extending sympathy and compassion to torturers. Race has an important role to play in the redemption of torturers: post-torture discourses create a moral community of Americans who were obliged to torture an innately barbaric enemy. The idea of Arab/Muslim savagery secures how torture comes to be remembered as an unfortunate by-product of poor leadership rather than racial violence carried out in the name of empire.

In the Conclusion, "Arriving as Muslim," I take stock of the geopolitics of the present moment when a globally organized fraternity of white *and* nonwhite nations agrees on the Muslim "terrorist" as the figure against whom supremacist regimes will be constituted and I consider that global white supremacy requires an oppositional response that thinks beyond the nation-state. The Muslim entered the scene of carnage in the New World as both a slave and a ghost, prompting the Spanish invaders to consider where in their own racial typologies of the Muslim and the Jew to fit Indigenous peoples. Indians became Moors, and Black Saracen was the label applied to Muslim slaves from West Africa.[167] Today, scripted as antimodern rather than premodern,[168] in Asia, the Middle East, North America, and Europe, the Muslim is imagined not so much as haunting the scene of capitalist accumulation as wreaking havoc and derailing it.

Standing amid the violence of the encounter between Muslims and those impelled to declare that Allah is not God and that Islam is their nemesis, it can seem that what is a needed is a retreat from religion altogether or a return to some purer version of it. Readers of this work have sometimes sought a redemptive route by suggesting that although the realm of science and reason are deeply contaminated with ideas of the civilizational Christian subject and already haunted by its Islamic opposite, a different version of Christianity is possible. While I have little to say about alternative ontologies and epistemologies, I hope that I have contributed to a critical conversation and emphasized the urgency we face as we imagine another world. I propose in this book that attention to the figure of the Muslim provides insight into the terrible violence of today's world by showing how white supremacy is globally organized in the West, the networks, affinities and ideas upon which it depends and, importantly, the white and white-aspiring subjects it produces and sustains.

Figure 2. *Gates of Vienna* website adapts Bernardo Bellotto's (il Canaletto) *Vienna Viewed from the Belvedere Palace*, 1761.

CHAPTER 1

"A New Phase of a Very Old War"

Islam and White Conservative Christian Aggrievement

Gates of Vienna, one of several small blogs of the Christian right, takes its name from the siege of Vienna by the Ottoman ruler Suleiman the Magnificent in 1529 and from a subsequent battle in 1683 when, according to the blog, "Islam seemed poised to overrun Christian Europe." Posting a count of the number of days without an attack carried out by "Islamic terrorists," the authors of the blog warn: "We are in a new phase of a very old war."[1] As the blog's defining image (see Figure 2) illustrates, the manicured gardens, fountains, and churches of European cities have long been imagined as requiring walls to keep out marauding Muslims. The Crusades may not have the widespread resonance that Christian right bloggers believe, but they are an increasingly circulated shorthand for a long-standing contestation between Christian Europe and the Islamic world. How much is this old episteme a part of contemporary anti-Muslim racism, a repurposed countermemory shaping how white Americans and Europeans practice their own whiteness as an intrinsically Christian whiteness that is forever menaced by an Islamic enemy?

This chapter discusses the anti-Muslim subject for whom whiteness and the defense of Christianity have required the banning of Islam in American high school textbooks and the elementary school curriculum. It asks: Who is the subject impelled to construct Islam and Muslims as an arch-enemy, and who is so easily roused to enact this antipathy in law? The conflicts discussed in this chapter span the two decades since 9/11, a period of intensifying anti-Muslim racism. They feature a variety of

52 "A New Phase of a Very Old War"

social actors who display anti-Islamic feelings and emotions about an imperiled America where white Christian children are imagined to be at risk from Islamic demons and "terrorists" alike in schools that are feared to be rapidly "Islamizing." Opposed and sometimes ridiculed by other parents for views deemed unsophisticated and parochial, anti-Islamic Christian actors maintain a deep conviction that when Islam is given space in the curriculum, their own God disappears. The vigorous pursuit of textbook Muslims and efforts to erase the presence of Islam in the school curriculum generate an anti-Muslim affect that keeps alive the idea that Muslims are a foreign threat and religious enemy over whom white communities must keep a close watch. In this way, the idea of the Crusades becomes tangible for many Americans.

Notwithstanding the ideological tenor of the anti-Muslim political discourses discussed in this chapter, it is important to note that far-right interventions in school politics occur in the context of a sanctioned multicultural approach to education. Specifically, the notion of liberal pluralism tolerates the presence of Islam in the curriculum, but it does so on condition that Muslims appear as the Orientalist figures of a medieval Islam. Rejecting outright the inclusion of Muslims as targets of racial harm or as colonized peoples, the multicultural curriculum that so angers the Christian right contributes to the racializing of Muslims as Other. As we find in the contestations below, while courts distance themselves from the overtly white politics of the Christian right, they simultaneously uphold the multicultural premises of inclusion of Muslims. While critics of Christian parents may believe themselves to be progressive and even antiracist, their tolerance of Muslims as exotic faith figures keeps in place a normative white Christianity and may even preserve a place for those who, in the name of their own faith, reject altogether the presence of Islam in the curriculum. Progressive and conservative views on Islam, then, are not so much antithetical as complementary. As Richard Slotkin observes about American national mythology, progressives and populists draw on "a common myth/ideological language in which there is substantial agreement on such central concerns as the exceptional character of American life and history, the necessity and desirability of economic development, the vitality of 'democratic' politics, and the relevance of something called 'the Frontier' as a way of explaining and rationalizing what is most distinctive and valuable in 'the American way.'"[2] These components of national mythology are visible in the discourses discussed below.

If anti-Islamic actors emphasize that they are acting out of a deep religiosity, their emotional responses have an intensely colonial and imperial character that amounts to an affect that is at once religious and racial. Those who propose to ban Islam do so from an affective position of "ressentiment, rancor, rage, reaction to humiliation and suffering," emotional states that, Wendy Brown reminds us, "are at play in right-wing populism and support for authoritarian leadership today."[3] However, the deep sense of being marginalized as Christians in a society seemingly too given over to secular pluralism gives rise to an economic, spiritual, and social distress about Muslims that takes the form of resentment and rage at being denied customary white entitlements. Religious feelings and emotions about Muslims coalesce to form a politics shaped by a *settler*-colonial consciousness of Muslims as foreigners who cannot be allowed to undermine white Christians' hold on national culture. Conservative, Christian, anti-Muslim actors are courted and supported by individuals and organizations who mobilize a similar politics of white settler protection. When they turn to law to protect their interests, parents find themselves directed and controlled by individuals and groups with a politics anchored in white, colonial, and Christian entitlement. Sometimes, Christian parents find support from Zionist interlocutors who are anxious to build support for Israel and who share interests born of a settler orientation and anti-Muslim animus.

Discourses of racial resentment do not emerge out of thin air, and if the figure of the Muslim has always simmered beneath the surface of white Christian identity, its emergence as a full-blown phantom on the American landscape is easily tracked to "the historical contingencies that shape mythic expression."[4] America's imperial activities in the Middle East, including military occupations in Afghanistan and Iraq as well as extensive support for the Israeli occupation of Palestine, engender visceral negative responses to Muslims, suturing imperial sentiments about the Muslim as a wartime enemy to those about Muslims as illegitimate residents of the Holy Land. For white evangelicals, the Muslim features as racial threat theologically and politically when Muslims appear to stand in the way of the Jews' return to Israel and the end-of-the-world scenario of the Rapture. Evangelical leaders who trumpet ideas of an "Islamic

54 "A New Phase of a Very Old War"

jihad" against Christianity foster strong anti-Muslim antipathies. It is difficult to say how much the idea of a Jewish homeland in Palestine and the role that this plays in the end of the world is the majority theology among Christian evangelical Americans, but support for Israel and anti-Muslim/Arab/Palestinian feeling remain important aspects of Christian whiteness. More salient, however, is the settler-colonial imaginary shared between white Americans and Jewish Zionists,[5] a bond of whiteness forged against the racialized Indigenous population. Sharing a frontier settler aesthetic where gun-toting white fathers and protective white mothers guard the schoolhouse gates, protecting white children from harm, white settlers readily identify with the "tough," militaristic Jewish settler of Israeli national mythology who is obliged to confront the "terrorist" indigenous population of Palestine, a racial, settler-colonial imaginary with which all North Americans are familiar.[6]

As religious/racial enemies, Muslims populate the news feeds of Fox News and far-right websites, creating a circuit board along which anti-Islamic affect travels. This coordinated anti-Muslim response brings together strange bedfellows. For instance, members of the Proud Boys, a far-right white-supremacist group (who gained notoriety when they attracted the support of President Trump for their disruptions of Black Lives Matter protests[7] and who were among those participating in the January 2021 insurrection at the U.S. Capitol),[8] rely on scripts about Muslims as members of Hamas, parroting Zionist and Christian evangelical narratives about Muslims as "terrorists" attacking Israel. Together these political constituencies form a key part of the Christian right, an unwieldy category, as several scholars note.[9] The Christian right has at times included politically conservative Catholics, Jews and Mormons and while overwhelmingly white, the bloc has also included people of color who are evangelical. Of special interest here, however, given the conflicts I explore, is the question of white evangelical Christians and their Catholic and Zionist allies who are interpellated into whiteness and anti-Islamic politics through religion and through a shared settler consciousness. In this politics, we see the seductions that whiteness holds, as Jews and some people of color seek to express their affinities to European identity by joining with the Christian right to warn of a Muslim/Arab/Palestinian propensity for violence.

In the first part of this chapter, in order to traverse the Christian evangelical and racial landscape of anti-Muslim emotions that fuel the school contestations, I examine the Christian settler subject's emotional investments by exploring how a religious claim hitches a ride on a colonial and imperial one. Amalgamating Manifest Destiny with theology, Muslims are scripted as religious, racialized enemies who stand in the way of the triumph of white, Christian civilization. This imperial structure of feeling joins with an Orientalism that for more than four centuries has traversed the West, preparing the ground for the contemporary attention to the Islamic enemy breaching the walls of America and Israel. The evangelical Christian worldview features an embattled community anxious to protect the white, biblical family from the Islamic enemy. Christian parents tread along gendered paths when they organize against the presence of Islam in the school curriculum, practicing a defensive politics that centers aggressive white men protecting their families from secular forces and racialized threats.

In the second part of the chapter I explore specific, highly gendered scenes of aggrieved Christian parents protesting curricula on Islam. Here, the school is imagined as a place where Christian children can be recruited to militant Islam and where white fathers use guns to protect their children, while white mothers engage in media battles to preserve Christian education. Although several of the legal challenges discussed in this chapter were dismissed in appellate courts, they paved the way for political and legal efforts that began bearing fruit in the climate of the intensified white nationalist politics of the Trump administration (2017–20). The anti-Muslim discourses that are circulated carry ideological weight and contribute to building a political constituency that grew increasingly nativist and racist even as protests mounted in 2020 proclaiming that Black Lives Matter. Anti-Muslim interests gained ground in the decades under review, and not only among conservative Christians and Zionists.

The Christian and Zionist Settler Subject and the Muslim

As discussed in the introduction to this book, Islam's foundational role in the formation of European identity as white traveled with European colonizers to the Americas. Christianity is central to white settler notions of entitlement to the land as a God-given right, a religiosity that

56 "A New Phase of a Very Old War"

inflects the aggrievement, fear, and threat whites feel from racial Others.[10] Describing the amalgam of fears and desires that make up the Christian settler subject in the Americas, Willie Jennings outlines the four developments that give birth to the settler subject in the Americas: land is stolen; people are stolen; people are stripped of their space and place amid a refashioning of bodies and places in which the European is architect; Europeans imagine themselves as racially superior against those bodies deemed to be beyond salvation.[11] A theological vision of the world in which Christianity has legitimate authority over all life is married to a colonial imaginary that drives the settler project in the Americas. Juridical logics structure the settlers' understanding of their place in the colonial world, inviting the settlers of both America and Palestine to regard themselves as God's chosen people.

"There are more than twenty towns in the United States named Canaan or New Canaan, and several Palestines," Steven Salaita observes in *The Holy Land in Transit: Colonialism and the Quest for Canaan*, pointing to the irony that in biblical times and in 1948 the lands of Canaan and Palestine "were eradicated in place of something new, only to reappear in the United States in place of something already there."[12] The settler societies of America and Israel share foundational narratives, a logic that shapes the claims made by Christian parents by infusing them with the mythology that Anglo-Saxon settlers are the original citizens justly entitled to insist on the hegemony of their own culture and beliefs.[13] Based on the idea that Indigenous peoples are disappearing and are unable to adapt to modern life, the settler master narrative installs Americans as "the chosen harbingers of a civilizing mission that must tame flora, fauna, and human life."[14] The same settler narrative that routes entitlement through religion is also foundational to Israel. As Edward Said pointed out in *The Question of Palestine*, the argument that turns colonial dispossession of a people into a story of an empty land awaiting European improvement draws on "the picture of a handful of European Jews hewing a civilization of sweetness and light out of the Black Islamic sea."[15] Colonization often proceeds in the guise of progress and rationality. Settler projects that erase Indigenous rights do so on the basis that the original inhabitants are not entitled to the land because they are unable to develop it. A religious claim of the settler's God-given right to the land is anchored in racial feeling, producing a colonial mind-set that easily accepts the rightness of all settler projects and understands them as civilizational battlegrounds between a modern and a premodern peoples.

Settler discourses that pay attention to the Muslim as racial and religious Other have a common logic and aesthetics that is born of anti-Islamic discourses evident in Christian evangelical teachings. Reviewing popular evangelical literature from 1991 to 2003, Richard Cimino found anti-Islamic discourses to be central to all strands of the Christian evangelical movement.[16] Among the evangelical apologetic movement, for instance, David Hunt and Robert Morey use the imagery and language of the Crusades and rely on texts such as Ergun and Emir Caner's popular book *Unveiling Islam* (2002), in which the twin claims are that Islam is inherently violent and that Muslims worship a false God.[17] Such texts are anchored in the idea that Christianity is distinct from all other faiths and is the only true religion. The texts emphasize that conservative Christians are daily undermined by secular, materialist, and pluralist forces of liberal America that promote the false ideal that all faiths are equal. Evangelicals of the biblical prophecy movement, who emphasize that the end of the world and the return of Christ cannot occur without Jews rebuilding the temple of the Mount in Jerusalem, view Muslims as standing in the way of the prophecy's fulfillment. For charismatic mission strategist George Otis, Islamic nations will wage the ultimate jihad against Israel, an eschatological scenario emphasized by several evangelical leaders and writers. Muslims, Otis points out, populate the lands closest to Israel.[18] The violent, marauding Muslims of Christian evangelical texts leave their readers with ready-made antipathies toward Muslims and harness those emotions to a Christian worldview that centers the protection of whiteness. The solid racial and imperial line that runs through Christian Zionism (whose adherents believe in the establishment of a Jewish state in Palestine) maintains a racial structure that comes into operation through patriarchy when vengeful masculine subjects imagine themselves as doing battle with their Islamic foes.

The protection of the biblical family that lies at the core of the evangelical belief system has always meant the white biblical family, as evangelical leaders such as Pete Peters openly averred. Ann Burlein, whose study of Peters and James Dobson shows the racial line that runs solidly

58 "A New Phase of a Very Old War"

through evangelical belief and politics, notes that the white biblical family is imagined as under siege from a host of "unruly bodies," including sexual minorities, immigrants, and African Americans.[19] In the communities around Peters and Dobson, Burlein finds the biblical story lines of embattled Anglo-Saxon and Anglo-Celtic peoples who consider themselves to be the ten of the original twelve Hebrew tribes of Israel—God's chosen people. Under siege by secular humanists and liberal multiculturalists, such Christians, although diverse in many ways, understand the bible-based family with its specific gender roles as key to the nation's white cultural heritage. Burlein shows that Peters was attempting to mainstream white supremacy through the Bible, a biblicization linking past and present, made visible with the use of language such as harlots and infidels.[20] This brand of defensive Christianity requires white militias and gun rights. Dobson focuses on the family as the bulwark against an urban and foreign takeover. Burlein concludes:

> Studying the Right, listening to the argument in these margins, is to hear mainstream America talk to itself, interpolate itself, reproduce itself anew: as white, as male, as middle-class, as Protestant, as straight, and as innocent.[21]

In the same vein, Sophie Bjork-James argues that in defense of a lost social order the sexual politics of Christian evangelicals are white sexual politics, where whiteness is defined via hostility to queer and trans bodies and opposition to their rights, a politics in which an aggressive white masculinity takes center stage.[22]

In her study of the rise of Christian Zionism over the last two decades, Victoria Clark describes the aggressive Christian masculine evangelical subject as deeply invested in the idea of Western white superiority.[23] Clark devotes a chapter in her book to "talking Texan," the term from the late reverend Jerry Falwell, who used it to refer to violent retaliation against anyone who attacks Christianity:

> Harking straight back to the Puritan ethos of Old Testament eye-for-an-eye justice of us and them, good and evil, black and white, the language Falwell imagined talking to Hezbollah is rooted in the culture of descendants of the Puritan Scots who subdued the Irish for Cromwell and then departed for the western extremity of the

New World in the early nineteenth century. The idiom of hard men engaged in wresting the Wild West frontier of the future United States, first from its indigenous American-Indian inhabitants and then from Mexicans, Texan is pithy to the point of callous, in-your-face, and frequently humorous.[24]

Texan speakers use phrases such as "God's foreign policy statement" and "Israel of the heart" all the while making frequent references to the coming apocalypse. Quoting from Genesis 12:3, that those who support Israel will be blessed while those who do not will be cursed, those who talk Texan advise Israelis that they must never give up land that God has ordained for them. Defense of the land requires combating the grand evil of Islamic "fundamentalism" through preemptive strikes against Muslim communities.[25] Clark maintains that for most Christian Zionists, belief in Armageddon, when Jesus returns to the earth, and specifically to Jerusalem, is not metaphoric. Christian Zionists deeply believe that they will survive the terrible destruction that is unleashed at the end times and be whisked away to heaven. The rest of the world, Clark advises, urgently needs to understand the power of such beliefs and its impact on American foreign policy in the Middle East.[26] Citing polls in 2006 that confirm that almost half of all Americans believe that Israel was given to the Jews by God and that 31 percent believe that this is so in order to facilitate the Second Coming,[27] Clark suggests that such a heightened quotidian relationship to the Rapture has not occurred since the Crusades.

The appeal of such beliefs surely lies in the work they do to install a superior Christian subject who is able to wrest both America and Israel from those who stand in the way of Christianity's triumph. The vengeful subject defending the world against Satanic enemies and usurpers is a subject drawn to the thunderous militaristic appeals of their pastors. Clark encountered such American Christian evangelical tourists on a tour of Jerusalem, subjects who were endlessly fascinated with the Israeli military and wanted the right to shoot one of their guns.[28] Easily imagining themselves in a story of the Crusades or, equally, on the supposed American frontier, these Christians possess an unquestionably racial fantasy that comes fully dressed as religious obligation. These racial/religious scripts produce subjects emboldened to protect white Christian life and to defend the biblical family from the phantom Muslims who are

60 "A New Phase of a Very Old War"

imagined as features of the school curriculum. Such anti-Muslim feelings and emotions are easily mobilized in white nationalist politics.

Harnessing Aggrievement and Dread in the Classroom

Battles over the proper place of religion in public education in the United States have a long history dating to the 1920s. They became especially intense when Supreme Court decisions in 1962 and 1963 banned the compulsory recitation of the Lord's Prayer and Bible study sessions in schools under the First Amendment's Establishment Clause. These legal events provoked vigorous pushback from Christian evangelical churches.[29] Religious studies scholars analyzing this historical moment explain rising Christian evangelical aggrievement over the decisions and over their declining political influence as a function of opposition to the secularization of the school curriculum. Rather than view school conflicts as simply a battle between religious and secular forces broadly, as many have proposed, I contend that when we do so we are apt to miss where Islam fits affectively in the overall framework of evangelical Christianity. In neglecting the racialization of Muslims, we fail to comprehend racial and colonial animus. As I suggested above, a Christian evangelical worldview installs a gendered, racial cast of characters, with Muslims assuming their role as the demonic Other who threatens Christendom and stands in the way of the end times. Muslims also activate colonial and imperial feelings when they threaten white entitlement. White Christian parents gird themselves for a racial battle, joining with other political constituencies on the Christian and Zionist right and the white-supremacist far right to organize collectively to target Islam in the school curriculum.

By the time the school battles discussed below occurred, school curricula had, in the spirit of liberal multicultural inclusion, already been crafted to reflect the belief that high school students should be exposed to all religions (rather than no religion).[30] In this context, teaching about Islam was on a par with learning about many diverse, non-Christian religions. The curriculum devoted less than 5 percent of the study of world religions to Islam. It also preserved room for critique of Islam and other religions, all the while striving to maintain a nondevotional, academic pedagogy. As the American Academy of Religion emphasized, religions were to be understood as internally diverse, dynamic, and embedded in culture.[31] The inclusive thrust of this approach reveals little about how curricular aspirations materialize on the ground, and still less about the limits of multicultural inclusion. As the school conflicts reveal, teaching Islam in the curriculum has meant emphasizing its foreignness. Establishing Christianity as normative, the curriculum casts Islam as a medieval religion and consigns Muslims to the premodern. Popular pedagogical approaches at the elementary school level such as role-playing further exoticize Muslims, preserving the binary of rational Christianity and irrational Islam that has for so long anchored the concept of Europeans as a modern, rational people.

Muslims have little to gain in the framework of liberal politics, since they are granted inclusion on the ground of tolerable difference, a status that depends on transforming Islam into something that whites will tolerate because it confirms Christianity's hegemony. Importantly, when Muslims remain in the space of foreignness, they do not enjoy full personhood in law. We can anticipate that law may at times grant tentative inclusion, but only on the basis that Muslims must not stray too far from the allotted spot of the incompletely modern. Muslims cannot remain in the curriculum, for instance, if they are represented as the colonized population of Israel, a limit made manifest when Palestinian struggles are excised from the school and university curriculum on the basis that a settler-colonial narrative of Israel is anti-Semitic and anti-Israeli.[32] Christian evangelical interests in restricting the presence of Islam in the curriculum are joined to a more liberal politics of inclusion; each is interested in restricting what can be taught about Muslims broadly and about Palestinians specifically.

Undoubtedly, a nondevotional approach and one that does not attend to Christianity exclusively (although it preserves Christianity as the majority religion) would have struck conservative Christian parents as evidence of their declining influence, but the responses to the teaching on Islam discussed below suggest a more specific objection and affect in play, and one that mirrors the civilizational divide that is preserved intact in the multicultural curriculum. In the examples below, the mere mention of Islam in a textbook or a parent's sight of Arabic calligraphy provoked bad feelings about a Satanic Islam, and any contact, however limited, that Christian children had with Islam was felt to be contaminating. Parents felt that Christian children could lose their own God and be put on the path to terrorism, an emotion fed by the belief that all

62 "A New Phase of a Very Old War"

Muslims are "terrorists." Legitimate Americans were imagined as losing their place to foreigners who do not share their religion and culture and who seek to undermine them. Such heightened responses and the racial phantoms they invoke reveal that those who live in fear of Muslims understand their place in the world to be under assault from an enemy imagined as dangerous. The mere recitation of an Islamic creed or the drawing of Arabic calligraphy must be rejected on the grounds that these activities bring Muslims too close into the bosom of the Christian family.

Mobilizing Resentment: From the Local to the National Stage

In the fall of 2001, a teacher in Contra Costa County, Northern California, in the small school district of Byron (fifteen hundred students), using an apparently standard instructional guide in world history (a curriculum resource that was developed in 1991),[33] taught a unit on Islam to a seventh grade class. The pedagogy of the unit emphasized simulation, and students were encouraged to adopt roles as Muslims for three weeks in order to help them understand what Muslims believe. As a part of the role-play it was suggested that students adopt Muslim names, recite Muslim prayers in class, memorize a passage from the Qur'an and give up something for a day in order to understand fasting during the month of Ramadan. The students were also asked to formulate a critique of elements of Muslim culture. If the timing of the event shortly after 9/11 and the role-play assignments and pedagogical approach were ill-advised, the exercise itself was modeled on a one-dimensional portrait of a medieval, conservative Islam (the manual emphasized A.D. 610–1100) that emphasized Islam's archaic foreignness. An Orientalist framing of Islam thus became the basis for inciting Christian resentment.

In 2001, with the heightened attention to Muslims that followed in the wake of the terrorist bombings of the World Trade Center and the Pentagon, the simulation exercise seemed guaranteed to attract attention. Christian conservatives in the rural school district sued the school district, arguing that the activities in question crossed a line from education to endorsement of a religious practice, and ultimately, to religious indoctrination. The plaintiffs in the suit, Jonas and Tiffany Eklund and their two children, particularly objected as Christians to the simulation

"A New Phase of a Very Old War" 63

exercise and to what they considered a too tolerant portrayal of Islam. They pointed out that only the unit on Islam required such role-play (ironically, role-play pedagogy is a consequence of the multicultural curriculum's emphasis on cultural and religious difference). A federal district court in San Francisco found no constitutional violation in the school's practice, a decision that prompted online observers to name the judge in question as a "Public Enemy," to condemn her support for the constitutional right to abortion, and to paint her as an al-Qaeda supporter.[34] The U.S. Court of Appeals for the Ninth Circuit agreed with the lower court's decision, and ultimately the Eklund family lost their case. The decision to dismiss the suit emphasized the school district's argument that schools need to be able to address religion in the curriculum without fear of reprisal. In 2006 the Ninth Circuit Court concluded that the unit on Islam did not attempt to indoctrinate.[35]

Law is the conduit through which anti-Muslim animus travels, forging whiteness as it does so even when legal challenges fail—perhaps especially when they fail, as then they contribute to grievance. Deposited in the legal record and ready for transport to the national stage, the story of whiteness that is achieved through anti-Muslim racism gains ground each time it is performed, filling white Christians with the warmth of entitled belonging and righteous rage. That the Eklunds failed in their suit does not alter the circulation of an anti-Muslim affect but instead revitalizes it. Law provides the stage on which the conflict is framed as one between normative white citizens and a foreign Muslim enemy. Legal players perform a Christian morality play even though the play's conclusion is that this time around, the enemy does not need to be engaged in battle. The script that is enacted provides the basis for a broader mobilization of Christian whiteness from the local to the national stage.

The Eklunds were not simply lone parents who disagreed with the teaching of Islam in the curriculum and decided to challenge it in court. They were supported in their activities by the Thomas More Law Center, an organization that describes itself as a nonprofit public-interest law firm based in Ann Arbor, Michigan. It is worthy of note that Thomas More, after whom the center is named, was a fifteenth-century Catholic lawyer who was executed for refusing to recognize the divorce of Henry the Eighth from Catherine of Aragon and the English church's break

64 "A New Phase of a Very Old War"

with Rome.[36] Signaling common ground with Jews, the Law Center lists the goals of its mission: "Preserve America's Judeo-Christian heritage; Defend the religious freedom of Christians; Restore time-honored moral and family values; Protect the sanctity of human life; Promote a strong national defense and a free and sovereign United States of America," a mission it accomplishes "through litigation, education, and related activities."[37] Firmly anchored in a politics of Christian, conservative values, the law firm has been involved in several lawsuits against school boards (discussed below). The Law Center has devoted a considerable part of its relatively small budget ($1.5 million) to cases involving banning curriculum on Islam in schools. Its founder, Richard Thompson, a prominent Christian evangelical lawyer, is heavily involved in the antiabortion movement and is a frequent media voice on Fox News among others.[38]

It is not hard to see that the Eklunds' lawsuit was one in a concerted longer-term strategy revolving around the teaching of Islam in schools, a strategy in which other conservative Christian groups, such as ACT for America (ACT), have actively participated for almost two decades.[39] For example, in 2011, ACT published *Education or Indoctrination: The Treatment of Islam in 6th through 12th Grade American Textbooks,* in which it took issue with the presentation of Islam as a religion of peace.[40] ACT, whose founder, Brigitte Gabriel, is a notable Lebanese American who is a Christian and an outspoken anti-Muslim activist, identifies five policy foci: Israel (and specifically efforts to change the definition of anti-Semitism to include criticism of Israel); immigration reform (and specifically an end to sanctuary cities, the building of the border wall, and greater policing of migrants); "anti-terrorism" (defined as confronting the violence of "radical Islam"); military and law enforcement (and notably advocating for increased policing); and constitutional freedoms (including textbook reform and campaigns against honor killings and FGM, both attributed to Islamic cultures).[41] Together, these commitments reveal ACT for America's interest in securing settler access to property, an entitlement defined against those seen as foreign threats, chief among them Muslims.

In 2019 the Thomas More Law Center published what was promoted as a special investigative report that claimed to have uncovered evidence that "Islamic propaganda was being forced on teachers in rural school

"A New Phase of a Very Old War" **65**

boards."[42] This report, primarily directed at school boards that hired a Muslim consultant, Huda Essa, to lead a two-day seminar on Islam, maintains the same positions as in the Eklund case above, including arguments about the lack of attention to Christianity and Judaism, the suppression of Islam's propensity to wage war, and discussion of its "terrorist" histories. Essa, the Law Center charged, "while quick to indict America as guilty of 'cultural genocide,'" was "silent on the 1400 years of actual genocides, also known as jihads, in which Muslims wiped out Jewish tribes on the Arabian Peninsula, and slaughtered millions of Christians throughout the Middle East, North Africa and the European Continent."[43] As with a meme, the story line of "Islamic jihad" as a genocidal project aimed at Christians and Jews circulates widely, ensuring its repeatability intact and fueling a broad white settler politics involving gun rights, immigration control, and settler rights over Indigenous peoples.

The Eklunds' lawsuit attracted the support of the Mountain States Legal Foundation, an organization that filed a friend-of-the-court brief supporting their position.[44] The foundation lists its budget at $2.1 million and describes its mission as "constitutional liberty, economic opportunity and the right to own and use property."[45] Involved in several gun-rights cases, such as opposition to efforts in Boulder, Colorado, to raise the minimum age for firearms possession to twenty-one, as well as opposing environmental and Indigenous rights and the tearing down of Christian war memorials, the foundation labels itself "the spirit of the American West" that commits itself to defending the frontier it imagines as one peopled by sheep farmers, ranchers, and miners—all white—under attack by the deep state promoting multicultural equality. Indeed, the defense of America and Israel from marauding Muslims is often understood on the unabashedly colonial terms expressed by the foundation, an affect that is also visible in the issues identified by ACT for America.

The Christian story line about Islam as a violent religion is also circulated by Middle East Forum, a think tank founded by Daniel Pipes, one of the most prolific Zionist ideologues writing on the threat of "radical Islam."[46] Pipes wrote that the Eklunds' lawsuit confirms that American children were being recruited for Islamic terrorism through schools. Suggesting that the students were forced to utter the words "Allahu akbar" (God is great) and were duped into believing that the words are merely a common salutation in the Islamic world rather than a "militant Islamic war-cry," Pipes even wondered whether John Walker Lindt, [47] the soldier known as "the American Taliban," might have been subjected to the same school curriculum as the Eklund children when Lindt was a child in California. As he wrote in the *Jerusalem Post*, referencing the Thomas More Law Center's and Richard Thompson's arguments in court, impressionable, white, Christian children are at risk of being recruited to terrorism if exposed to material such as the simulation exercises.[48] Interventions from Christian right organizations and Fox News repeat ad nauseum the logic that to teach about the Islamic world is to indulge in indoctrination, to engage in terrorism, and to denigrate Christianity and Judaism. In his masterful study based on big data analysis of the anti-Muslim messages circulated by 120 civil society organizations after 9/11, Christopher Bail found that through a vigorous circulation of condensed anti-Islamic scripts in press releases, newspaper articles, television transcripts, nonprofit tax forms, legislative documents, and social-media messages, these organizations were successful in mainstreaming an anti-Muslim message.[49] Using plagiarism detection software, Bail concluded that legislators proposing anti-Sharia bills, for instance, lifted verbatim phrases from anti-Muslim organizations in the texts for their legal projects.[50]

The national network of anti-Muslim interests that organize on curricula issues also brings their forces to bear against Muslim children. In 2016, Muslim parents and students reported extensive bullying to the San Diego School District Board of Education. At a July 26, 2016, meeting, after hearing testimony from Muslim students about bullying, the board unanimously voted to include in its broader anti-bullying program a response to the experiences of Muslim students. The board then consulted the Council on American-Islamic Relations (CAIR), which had launched a national anti-bullying program after a spike in hate crimes against Muslims in the wake of 9/11. The program adopted a multicultural approach that included plans to honor Muslim holidays, create safe spaces for Muslim students in schools where they are numerous, and increase awareness of Islamophobia and of Muslim beliefs and culture more generally. Many parents, both Muslim and non-Muslim, were supportive. However, a small group of outraged parents argued in a school

"A New Phase of a Very Old War" **67**

board meeting on May 16, 2017, that the plan favored Muslims over others, failed to educate students about the evils of Islam, and indoctrinated them in a religion bent on America's destruction. CAIR, they argued, was a "terrorist" organization, and in any event, Muslims were not bullied, as a report circulated by CAIR had claimed (CAIR noted that a survey showed that in California 55 percent of Muslim students reported being bullied.)[51]

Parents opposed to the anti-bullying program drew heavily on the support of a number of Christian organizations and allies prepared to frame their opposition to the anti-bullying measures in terms that invoked both liberal discourses about individual freedom and far-right discourses about Muslims as "terrorists." ACT had already circulated a narrative about CAIR as a "terrorist" organization nationally, and ACT Mission Viejo repeated the organization's line that Islamic "terrorism" was a worldwide pandemic that threatened the American way of life. (The strategy of casting any exposure to Islam in the curriculum as inciting "terrorism" dovetails with other anti-Muslim campaigns to label specific groups and individuals as terrorist.)[52] Two men of color feature in this conflict, each with connections to conservative Christian organizations devoted to the defense of family values. Jose Velazquez, describing himself as Hispanic and an aggrieved navy veteran, felt that no special measures were needed for Muslims. He himself had been bullied in school, and he simply went to the principal to complain. Velazquez decided to partner with the Freedom of Conscience Defense Fund (FCDF) to fight the anti-bullying program when he learned of CAIR's involvement. The FCDF, led by lawyer Charles LiMandri, describes itself as committed to halting "harassment and intimidation of people of conscience," including Catholics, Protestants, Jews, and Mormons.[53] An ally of other Christian organizations, and notably the Thomas More Law Center, the FCDF is involved in a number of cases, including defending the erection of crosses and opposing Planned Parenthood. It partnered in the lawsuit against the school board with the organization Citizens for Quality Education, describing in a brief that CAIR's ultimate mission was to change American society and advance "radical Islam." Frank Xu, a board member of San Diego Asian Americans for Equality, also protested, believing that Muslims did not face bullying and that there was no place

68 "A New Phase of a Very Old War"

for religion in schools. Presenting himself as a staunch secularist who was anxious to protect his own moral values, Xu invoked his Chinese origins to argue that he was not in favor of religion in schools. Opposed to sex education in schools, San Diego Asian Americans for Equality mostly concerns itself with promoting Asian Americans as successful and educated professionals and entrepreneurs.

The parties in the school bullying conflict reached a settlement in February 2019 in an agreement that specified how religion could be talked about in schools and how it could not. Retaining the commitment to covering the teachings of all religions in schools, the agreement places Muslims as secondary victims of bullying; any racial harm that might come their way would first have to be processed through the Jewish experience in order to be acknowledged. The Anti-Defamation League (ADL), an organization inspired by Jewish beliefs and active in condemning anyone critical of Israel, replaced CAIR as the organization that would be consulted on school bullying of Muslim students.[54] For the ADL, anyone critical of Israel is guilty of anti-Semitism, and the ADL frequently indicts Muslims on this charge. That the ADL should replace CAIR made it virtually conclusive that Muslims would not be seen as the targets of racial harm themselves, that spot being reserved for Jews. Ironically, in its replacement of CAIR with the ADL, the resolution of the school conflict draws from the demonization of Muslim organizations as "terrorist." CAIR is one of the principal organizations targeted in this way. A solution that apparently recognizes the targeting of Muslim children nevertheless ensures that the children's interests would be safeguarded by an organization that itself participates in the targeting of Muslims. As Bail has shown, anti-Muslim organizations have connections to mainstream civil society organizations such as the ADL.[55] If the outcome of the anti-bullying conflict rested on a premise of multicultural inclusion that understood Jews rather than Muslims as targets of racism, the process itself reveals that the school conflicts were not religious/secular contestations pure and simple, but complicated racial ones.

"Breitbart Live" and Aggressive White Masculinity

The May 16, 2017, meeting of the San Diego Unified School District Board of Education was a contentious one, and not only around the issue of the bullying of Muslim schoolchildren.[56] African American parents wanted to

"A New Phase of a Very Old War"   69

know why the superintendent blocked the hiring of an African American principal in a high school with a high level of racial minority and poor population, Latino parents spoke of the lack of services to such schools, and an array of speakers of all races, some representing LGBTQ organizations and programs, spoke in favor of the board's sex education programs while others (mainly white speakers) denounced its inclusion in the curriculum of education about contraception and premarital sex as antithetical to family values and as exposing children to pornography. Yet the anti-bullying program earned the long evening's most dramatic interventions. Summing up how she experienced these particular interventions, Aaryn Belfer, a parent and journalist covering the event for the *San Diego City Beat*, wrote: "It was Breitbart live. It was Richard Spencer. It was David Duke."[57]

For all her extravagant tone, Belfer's characterization was not far off the mark. The school board meeting at which the anti-bullying program was discussed was attended by well-known white supremacists whose political targets included but were not limited to Muslims. One such speaker, a leader of the group Patriot Fire, Roger Ogden, warned that Muhammad "engaged in sex slavery" and "had sex with children." (Ogden's group has long been known for protesting, virtually and in person, San Diego's Chicano Park, which they consider to be racist because it has "anti-American and Chicano supremacist murals.")[58] Kristopher Wyrick, another well-known local white supremacist and Proud Boy member, wearing a T-shirt with a prominent red cross, demanded that the board stop the anti-bullying program. Protesting angrily that he only had one minute to speak, Wyrick began by saying he was "a very, very proud American," declaring that "[I've held] many titles [over the years, but] one of them I will not accept is 'infidel.'"[59] He confronted the board about its decision to teach his child about Islam and offered statistics to show that Muslims were not the main people being bullied. The attention paid to Muslims was for him a contravention of the principle of no religion in schools. At the end of his one minute, Wyrick refused to leave the podium without addressing what he described as "CAIR's pro-Islam curriculum," its Hamas affiliations, and the brainwashing of the minds of the young. Notwithstanding his insistence on no religion in schools, the use of the word "infidel" places Wyrick's intervention in what Burlein has described as "biblical memories and plotlines,"[60] evoking as it does a tenth-century

70 "A New Phase of a Very Old War"

confrontation between Christians and Muslims and the designation of someone who is an unbeliever. Furnished with the anti-Muslim scripts of conservative Christian and Zionist organizations, Wyrick shared ground with Zionist Jews and an array of groups with deep commitment to a white Christian America.

Anti-Muslim positions staked out by aggressive white men such as Wyrick often turn violent.[61] What the school confrontations show is that an aggressive white masculinity is at the forefront of these confrontations, and when Islam is the target, white Christian men can imagine themselves as warriors for Christ or for free speech and country, armed and standing for the nation, engaged in wars without end against those who would call them infidels. The showdown is scripted as one against liberals who would insist on multiculturalism to the detriment of Christian values, principally those involving banning abortions and sex education, but it also expresses an openly white race politics. Not all who protest Islam's presence in schools exhibit the degree of organized white-supremacist engagement shown by Wyrick but many demonstrate an anger that is plainly Christian and territorial in affect even as their protestations are announced as a defense of freedom of speech and secular education.

Those who defend Christian values are often denounced by their opponents as unsophisticated hicks, reactions that only contribute to white grievance. When the journalist Aaryn Belfer called out Wyrick's wife, Kristy, for her comment that CAIR was Hamas and commented separately that a member of the audience had labeled the organization Planned Parenthood baby killers, Kristy responded in the comments section of Belfer's posting that she did indeed consider Planned Parenthood to be baby killers. Her comments provoked defenders and attackers, the latter anxious to point out her ignorance and lack of schooling.[62] In such virtual encounters we can just glimpse the confrontation between those who understand themselves to be Christian and deeply committed to their beliefs about abortion and about Islam, on the one hand, and those who style themselves as sophisticated, urban, and in support of a multicultural politics, on the other. Each side utilizes a shared vocabulary of freedom and rights. Muslims remain foreigners to be protected and included as a faith group or reviled as one.

Aggressive white masculinity and Christian rage were in full view in another school conflict when in a public school in Charles County, Mary-

"A New Phase of a Very Old War" **71**

land, in 2014, eleventh grade student Caleigh Wood came home and told her father about her homework assignment in her Advanced Placement world history course. In the year-long course covering the period 1500 to the present, approximately five days were devoted to the Muslim world, the smallest unit in the curriculum. The course described the unit's goal as studying empires of the Middle East and their relationship to Islam. It contrasted peaceful Islam with "fundamentalist" Islam and ended with slides of the destruction of the World Trade Center on 9/11 and earlier bombings in 1993. Of note is the way in which an ostensibly critical approach to teaching Islam immediately reifies a good Muslim/bad Muslim scenario that keeps the figure of the "terrorist" Muslim in play even as the overarching framework is one of tolerance. One of the teacher's slides on "fundamentalist" Islam included the controversial statement that a Muslim's faith is stronger than the average Christian's. As part of her homework assignment, Caleigh was required to do a worksheet in which she had to name the five pillars of Islam and the content of the Shahada, the Muslim creed that there is one God and that Muhammad is his messenger. Caleigh's father, John Wood, directed her to refuse to complete any assignment associated with Islam, which he understood as a promotion of Islam.

As he would claim in a later lawsuit, John Wood felt his family's God was being denied by the assignment. After telling his daughter not to complete her homework, Wood phoned the school, leaving a message complaining about the homework assignment. When he was contacted a day later, he asserted to the vice-principal, Shannon Morris, that he had contacted lawyers and was going to create "a shit storm" of controversy. He then told her "you can take that fucking Islam and shove it up your white fucking ass!"[63] Shaken by the aggression of the interaction, Morris then communicated with the principal, Evelyn Arnold, who soon after became aware of Facebook posts in which Mr. Wood declared that he "just about fucking lost it" and "My white ass is going into school on Monday and letting my feelings be known." Wood revealed that he became "fucking livid" when he learned that Caleigh's teacher (Mr. Bryden, a fellow Christian) was a Navy SEAL. As the court related:

> In response to a comment from a friend cautioning him not to get arrested, Mr. Wood responded that he would "try." In response to a

72 "A New Phase of a Very Old War"

> suggestion that he study Islam because he could not defeat what he could not understand, Mr. Wood stated that a "556 doesn't study Islam and it kills them fuckers every day." In a subsequent post, Mr. Wood states that he would use his daughter's study sheet as "confetti on Monday!" These interactions took place during the school's Homecoming week.[64]

Here, "556" refers to 5.56-millimeter ammunition used in the U.S. armed forces' standard-issue rifle. Principal Arnold then contacted her Central Office administrators in an email in which she wrote: "At this point I am happy to call Mr. Wood myself but he doesn't appear to want to listen and instead wants to curse and scream. His demeanor on the phone was so extreme that I do have concerns about him coming up to the school. Since he works at Ft. Belvoir and states that he is a Marine, I am assuming that he has access to weapons."[65] Soon after, the police issued a restraining order against Mr. Wood prohibiting him from entering school grounds, an action he did not contest with the school itself, but in the later lawsuit he claimed it was retaliation against his complaint.[66]

In his statement to the U.S. District Court for the District of Maryland on February 17, 2016, Wood explains that the homework assignment promoted Islam by representing it as a fact rather than a belief, that it denigrated Christianity (when the teacher noted that Muslims who were "fundamentalists" held stronger beliefs than Christian "fundamentalists"), and that it forced his daughter "to violate her faith" by writing the Shahada.[67] Wood emphasized that his strong responses were informed by his Christian faith and by his military experience with Muslims. After 9/11, which was significant to him, he became a first responder and firefighter, Wood explained, adding that he relied on his "Christian faith to get me through" such events.[68] While serving during Operation Desert Storm, two of his comrades were killed, leaving him "very angry, as I have seen so much death and destruction caused in the name of Islam and I was simply asking for an alternative assignment for my daughter."[69]

The courts were not sympathetic to these arguments. Agreeing with the lower court, the U.S. Court of Appeals for the Fourth Circuit concluded, "This is not a case in which students were being asked to participate in a daily religious exercise." The assignments "involved no more than having the class read, discuss, and think about Islam." Students were merely being asked to identify the tenets of Islam.[70] The comparative faith statement (admitted by the school board to be unfortunate) that had so caused offense "focused on Islamic fundamentalism as a political force." Indeed, stressing the need to examine single statements in context, the court advised that "academic freedom would not long survive in an environment in which courts micromanage school curricula and parse singular statements made by teachers."[71]

On May 13, 2019, the Thomas More Law Center filed a Petition for Writ of Certiorari in the Wood case, asking the U.S. Supreme Court to consider whether the First Amendment clause forbidding governments from establishing an official religion or unduly favoring one religion over another has been violated and whether a public school "may require a student to assert religious beliefs and recount a prayer that offends the student's religious convictions as part of a homework assignment."[72] The long-term strategy of opposing any curriculum discussing Islam may now bear fruit, as the United States, under the presidency of Donald Trump, gained a Supreme Court majority of conservative Christian justices.

Christian Mothers

Aggrievement has a gendered face in school conflicts, expressed above as an aggressive masculinity concerned to "kill them fuckers every day,"[73] but it also comes packaged as motherly concern that is differently aggressive and no less territorial. Here the sentimentalizing of parental authority that Burlein describes in *Lift High the Cross: Where White Supremacy and the Christian Right Converge* is more in evidence as a specifically feminine role. Burlein emphasizes the importance of children to white-supremacist discourse, noting that Virgil Griffin, Wizard of the Christian Knights of the KKK, was able to produce an empowering sense of agency by representing "white Christians as a victimized minority fighting for the survival of its endangered young."[74] Children are essential to conservative countermemories (alternative ways of remembering history) "as the crossing point by which to reverse the direction of people's affective investments."[75] The leaders of the Christian right, notably Pete Peters and James Dobson, emphasize the Bible-based family, whose enemies are sex education, multiculturalism, and pop culture and who are represented as a people suffering either a rural economic crisis (Peters) or a suburban

74 "A New Phase of a Very Old War"

one (Dobson). Countermemories, Burlein notes, help to form identity and subjectivity. For both Peters's and Dobson's constituencies, the Christian man "dreams of this land made holy by white Christian men who rise from the ashes of victimization like a phoenix, poised to take a stand and take this country back,"[76] a description that seems apt in the cases of Wyrick and Wood. The Christian woman, on the other hand, embodies the sacredness that is her gender and preserves "the family as a cultural strategy to Christianize the nation."[77] The women discussed below seem to inhabit these gender-constrained roles, although their interventions are so immediately absorbed in a larger politics that their own gender-specific affective responses are muted, at least in the public record.

In Augusta County, Virginia, in 2015, when Kimberly Herndon learned that her daughter's high school teacher assigned students to draw some Arabic calligraphy, she became deeply alarmed. "When I saw the language, the Arabic language, immediately I had a bad feeling come over me," Herndon told a reporter.[78] As she wrote in a Facebook post about the teacher who assigned the exercise, "She should be fired for that. She should be fired because she had them write an abomination to their faith and causes a little girl to cry herself to sleep because she was worried she had denounced her God."[79] The calligraphy in question upset Herndon not only because it was the Arabic language but also because it was the Shahada, the Muslim creed of faith in one God and in Muhammad as his servant and messenger. Echoing John Wood's claim that his daughter would violate her faith merely by writing out the Shahada, Herndon invests Islam with a demonic power to disturb young minds and to destroy Christianity. The sentiments she expresses about Islam's power reveal a faith marked by profound antipathy to Islam, a dread that is deeply felt and readily exploited. If one wonders in passing how Herndon had sufficient knowledge to identify the Shahada, it is clear that Christian parents such as Herndon are well acquainted with the scripts provided by conservative Christian organizations. For Herndon, in assigning the Arabic calligraphy the teacher "gave up the Lord's time" and "gave it to Mohammed."[80] Herndon understood the Shahada as "the chant that is shouted while beheading those of Christian faith, or people of the cross as being called by ISIS." She concluded her Facebook post by writing: "Blessed be the name of THE LORD. THE LORD OF LORDS AND

THE KING OF KINGS. THERE IS POWER IN HIS NAME AND HE IS WORTHY OF ALL PRAISE."

The calligraphy assignment was part of the same world cultures course in which students learned about Islam and other religions through interactive assignments in the school conflicts discussed earlier. As in the 2001 San Francisco school conflict discussed above, when the same interactive assignment prompted the Eklund family to object as Christians, Herndon, a mother of six, declared the assignment to be "Islamic indoctrination." As a Christian mother, she felt she had little choice. Her Facebook posts elaborated: "I am preparing to confront the county on this issue of the Muslim indoctrination taking place here in an Augusta County school. This evil has been cloaked in the form of multiculturalism." Vowing that "I will not have my children sit under a woman who indoctrinates them with the Islam religion when I am a Christian, and I'm going to stand behind Christ," Herndon announced that she would keep her high school–age son at home until the Supreme Court settled the issue. In a meeting Herndon subsequently organized at the Good News Ministries, dozens of parents expressed similar views and called for the teacher to be fired.[81] Others, however, posted their own objections to the meeting on Facebook, where they quickly outnumbered those protesting the assignment. In one such post critical of Herndon and others, a parent asked whether the outraged parents attending the meeting were actually concerned that their child might convert to Islam. As James Woods commented sarcastically:

> Is that the fear here? If you are far enough out of touch with your own child that you think their geography teacher might convert them to Islam against your will, then maybe it's time to turn off the TV and spend some time with your kids. Besides, if they don't learn about Islam at school, how will they know who to hate? Writing something on a piece of paper doesn't make it true. We're talking about Muslims, not witches.[82]

Suggesting a contempt for Christian parents such as Herndon, James Woods and others, while apparently more numerous, did not appear to have the external support Herndon and her supporters could marshal. The Augusta County school outlined its position in a press release, explaining

76 "A New Phase of a Very Old War"

that students learn about all religions in this way. The calligraphy exercise was about artistic complexity, and students were not being asked to profess belief in Islam when they were asked to copy it. The lessons, the press release insisted, were in line with the standards of the Virginia Board of Education. Confronted with a media storm and deluged by email, most of which was from outside the county, the school board soon found itself obliged to close Augusta County schools and administrative offices, based on the recommendations of law enforcement. Although the board members maintained that no specific threats had been received, they were alarmed by "the tone and content" of the email and phone calls they received and decided to err on the side of caution.[83] Ultimately, playing its role as the decider of when and where and how Islam would appear in the school curriculum, the board announced that while the Arabic calligraphy lessons would continue, it would use a nonreligious text instead.[84]

Fox News, conservative bloggers, and Christian right organizations and their Zionist supporters were quick to circulate both the protest and theories about the problem of Islam in schools. Indulging in conspiracy theories about the deep state, *Gates of Vienna* speculated that since the assignment was drawn from the state's own curriculum, it "almost certainly means it originated with the federal government. If that's the case, I can guarantee you that it was inserted in that form by members of the Muslim Brotherhood."[85] Dan Miller, writing for the Clarion Fund,[86] a nonprofit organization founded to educate the public about the threat of "radical Islam," and referencing what he learned from a Fox News interview with the founder of the Christian Action Network and from Breitbart News, suggested that during the Bush administration schools simply taught about the traditions and cultures of Islam, whereas under Obama, teaching about Islam took on a whole new patina, requiring children to be indoctrinated by Islam.[87] Campus Watch, the Middle East studies website of Daniel Pipes, circulated an article published in the *Christian Post* in which Stoyan Zaimov repeated Herndon's posts and advised that conservative groups and parents in other states had taken up the call to condemn "indoctrination" in schools. Zaimov reported that the American Center for Law and Justice (ACLJ), a prominent legal organization of the Christian right, had already received seven thousand calls from parents in Tennessee complaining of the same practices. The

ACLJ summarized the issue: "When public middle school students are required to recite Muslim prayers and statements of belief, to write those statements as though they are fact, and to memorize historically inaccurate information about the background of the Islamic religion, someone must cry foul."[88]

Christian women are an important part of crying foul, particularly on specific media platforms such as Fox News. Christian mothers draw on the resources of sympathetic media, attracting lesser-known bloggers as well as noted conservative Christian and anti-Muslim commentators such as Robert Spencer of Jihad Watch, Daniel Pipes of Campus Watch, and Tucker Carlson of Fox News. The school conflicts have the distinctive flavor of an orchestrated media intervention, and the intended environment in which they play out is not only the local but the national level. Such was the case when two professional women from Chatham, New Jersey, a small, wealthy suburb of New York City, complained about their children's assignments on Islam in the same course that has been the focus of all the school conflicts thus far: world cultures. In an email to the district leaders of the Chatham School Board and in person at a February school board meeting, Libby Hilsenrath complained that her seventh grade son was required to watch a five-minute-long "Intro to Islam" video that seeks to convert viewers to Islam. Her son was also forced to watch a cartoon video on the five pillars of Islam in which two cartoon boys, a Muslim and a non-Muslim, have a dialogue that ends with the Muslim cartoon figure inviting the non-Muslim to come and see how he prays. Both videos, a lawsuit would later claim, carried "doctrinal messages" calling for conversion to Islam. Other exercises were named as conversion exercises, including the writing of the Shahada in a homework assignment, the target of most of the lawsuits of the past decade.[89]

In a February newsletter, the school board defended its practices on the teaching of religion. On February 20, 2017, Libby Hilsenrath appeared on *Tucker Carlson Tonight* along with another parent, Nancy Mayer, and in this prominent Fox News media spot made the following claims: the school teaches about one religion and not others; Christianity could never be taught this way, and in fact one of their children was sanctioned for quoting the Bible in a school exercise; and curriculum meetings are held in secret. The women then reported that they had been treated as

78 "A New Phase of a Very Old War"

bigots by other parents, that they had been "stared down" in the grocery store, and that their requests for a meeting with the superintendent of education and for information on who picks the curriculum were rejected. Although invited to the school board meetings, Hilsenrath and Mayer maintained that the time allotted to parents at those meetings was simply too short and they could not adequately convey their concerns in such a forum. Feeding the women's sense of aggrievement, Tucker Carlson approvingly restated their messages, concluding, "The board blew you off." He was sure, he added, that special-interest groups were involved in preparing the unit on Islam in the curriculum, a likely reference to CAIR and an echo of the conspiracy bloggers of the far right.[90] The stage was thus set for the scenario of two embattled Christian mothers deeply worried about Islamic indoctrination in schools who had no option but to sue the school board, an action they then took with the help of the Thomas More Law Center and Fox News. In its heavily attended March 6 meeting, confronted with the power of the nationally staged messages on Fox News, the school board's president, Jill Critchley Weber, could only repeatedly insist that the claims made on Fox News by the two mothers were "patently false."[91] Neither Hilsenrath nor Mayer attended the meeting, although both maintained that they would continue the fight "regardless of the personal attacks." As Hilsenrath said in a statement posted by the Thomas More Law Center, "One of my fundamental obligations as a parent is to guide the religious and secular education of my children."[92]

All major religions are taught in state-approved lesson plans, the school board insisted, and anyone is free to come to both curriculum and school board meetings. The school board meeting, filmed and available for viewing on YouTube, nevertheless could not easily compete with Fox News and with the string of conservative Christian and anti-Muslim commentators who repeated verbatim the women's messages and Carlson's framing of it on Fox News.[93] All fanned the flames of aggrievement. The women's "crime," the Thomas More press release emphasized, was that they appeared on *Tucker Carlson Tonight*.[94] The women were "defamed as bigots, Islamophobes, and accused of being hateful, ignorant and intolerant," attacks that only got worse after the Fox News show, repeated the conservative Christian blog *Women of Grace*.[95] In a steady

"A New Phase of a Very Old War" **79**

stream of articles in 2018, repeating the talking points of Chief Counsel Richard Thompson of the Thomas More Center, Breitbart News,[96] the *Christian Post*,[97] and the *Jackson Press*[98] reposting Richard Spencer's article in Jihad Watch[99] and Church Militant,[100] conservative media alerted readers to the "crime" against the women and the details of "Islamic indoctrination." They also linked the women's complaint to those of other parents defended by the Thomas More Law Center, such as the lawsuit of Richard Penkoski,[101] an evangelist who hosts the online ministry "Warriors for Christ," concerning the same exercises on the Shahada.[102] Thompson emphasizes that school boards across the country are violating the Establishment Clause (which requires that schools must maintain neutrality against all religions) and that "Islamification" is a threat to national security. America, Thompson maintains, is a Christian nation under attack.

On June 13, 2018, U.S. District Judge Kevin McNulty (appointed by Obama and the brother-in-law of Senate Majority Leader Chuck Schumer) denied the motion of the School District of Chatham to dismiss the Hilsenrath and Mayer lawsuit. Judge McNulty noted that the lawsuit presents "controversial issues" and merits an opportunity to consider the substantive issues of the case.[103] Celebrated as a victory by Christian right organizations, it may well be that the ongoing school cases taken up or endorsed by the Thomas More Law Center,[104] the ACLJ,[105] the FCDF,[106] the Christian Action Network, and the Clarion Project,[107] among other Christian right organizations, may find the court a more hospitable place than at any other time in the previous two decades. School conflicts over textbooks and curricula on Islam now dot the landscape, from Florida[108] to Georgia,[109] Texas,[110] Wisconsin,[111] and Tennessee.[112] Described by David Horowitz, a notable anti-Muslim ideologue, as battles in *Dark Agenda: The War to Destroy Christian America*,[113] the increasingly tightly networked individuals and organizations working in defense of Christianity in schools have found powerful allies in government. Utilizing the same arguments, and even the same soundbites, the campaigns to protect children from Islam have now moved to universities, where they meet up with efforts to ban criticism of Israel and to define such criticism as anti-Semitic.

80 "A New Phase of a Very Old War"

Whereas the court in *Wood* (discussed above) declared that academic freedom would not long survive in circumstances where authorities attempted to micromanage curricula, in the fall of 2019, Secretary of Education Betsy DeVos ordered Duke University and the University of North Carolina at Chapel Hill to remake their Middle East Studies programs, on penalty of losing federal funding. The U.S. Department of Education deemed the program contrary to America's security interests and maintained that students were being offered a biased curriculum that criticized Israel and that did not contain enough "positive" imagery of Judaism and Christianity in the region.[114] For two decades, conservative Christians, aided by Zionist Jewish allies, have been working hard to ban Islam in schools. Their efforts are now bearing legal and policy fruit. By any measure a strong and organized political lobby, the Christian right's interventions into education circulate an anti-Muslim affect made up of white Christian aggrievement that offers an example of how race is made through religion.

It is a feature of all five scenes that nothing has to make sense. Fears about a Satanic Islam fill the void left by logic. The Shahada, a one-line prayer that is as quotidian in the Muslim world as Christians uttering the phrase "Praise the Lord," is tagged as a "terrorist" war cry. Writing the five pillars of Islam or drawing Arabic calligraphy converts children to Islam. A cartoon of a five-year-old Muslim boy inviting his non-Muslim friend to see how he prays carries hidden doctrinal messages. Muslim advocacy and organizations are "terrorist" if they send aid to the children of Gaza. State legislatures pursue anti-Sharia legislation even though there is no constitutional way for Sharia to become the law of the land. Thirty percent of Americans then believe that Muslims want to establish Sharia law in America.[115] In this strange place where nothing has to make sense, anti-Muslim violence grows, traveling along an infrastructure that is well established.

Conclusion: From White Christian Aggrievement to Murderous Rage

Aggrievement and rage have global reach. When an obscure pastor from Florida, Terry Jones, author of a little-known polemic titled *Islam Is of the Devil*, burns a Qur'an, protests erupt throughout the Muslim world,

"A New Phase of a Very Old War"   81

resulting in scores of those Muslim protestors being killed at the hands of their governments.[116] A young white man in Norway, Anders Breivik, kills seventy-seven Norwegian teenagers he imagines as an obstacle to the ethnic cleansing of Muslims from Europe. Breivik, who describes himself as inspired by noted American and European anti-Muslim ideologues, sees himself as a part of an international brotherhood needed to defend Christian Europe from being taken over by Muslims.[117] In the contemporary climate of an intensifying global anti-Muslim racism, white Christian aggrievement and rage discussed in this chapter is clearly not unique to Americans.

What do these massacres have in common with the enraged Christian parents insisting, sometimes with threats of violence, that Islam be purged from the school curriculum? Or, for that matter, what do they have in common with the policy insistence on the part of the U.S. Department of Education that Islam be covered less and always in the context of its brutal histories and that there must be no criticism of Israel? Clark, studying the Christian evangelicals and their leaders on tour in Jerusalem who spoke of "nuking Iran, blasting the temple of the Mount so that the Rapture might come more quickly," and who engage with Israeli generals about military strategy to further dispossess Palestinians, attributes such violent and militaristic sentiments to fear. Naming "fear of radical Islam, fear of Israel's extermination signaling a faith-destroying deviation from the divine plan, and fear of American's fall from grace with God into impotence and poverty," Clark's "fear-filled fundamentalist mindset" suggests a white Christian subject less afraid than vengeful and angry at those who stand in the way of their entitlements, although fear and anger may be two sides of the same coin—in this case the coin of aggrievement.

In her examination of the rise of antidemocratic politics in the West, Wendy Brown offers the Nietzschean concept of *ressentiment* and masculine dethronement to explain the quantity and intensity of aggression spilling from the right. Brown argues that "high levels of affect" animate populations mobilized by rancor and rage, "raw ressentiment without the turn toward discipline, creativity, and ultimately, intellectual mastery that Nietzsche tracks as slave morality in building Judeo-Christian civilization."[118] As she concludes: "This is ressentiment stuck in its trapped rancor, unable to 'become creative.' It has only revenge, no way out, no

82 "A New Phase of a Very Old War"

futurity."[119] If Brown's characterization of the far right describes the tenor of some of the responses to Islam and to Muslims, it does not fully capture the dimensions of the subjects who protest the presence of Islam in the curriculum. To be sure, the school conflicts discussed in this chapter are conflicts borne along a current of aggrievement and rage, emotions harnessed by Christian evangelical and Zionist organizations and mobilized to sustain a broad anti-Muslim politics. But as these networks of disparate anti-Muslim actors reveal, the emotions that power an anti-Muslim politics are a part of a white settler affect in which Muslims are seen as racial threats who undermine white settler entitlement in America and Israel. Ressentiment, rancor, rage—the reactions to humiliation and suffering that Brown describes are endemic to the white settler subject. When they appear to be heightened in right-wing populist movements, we forget at our peril that they are born not only of an intensified neoliberalism but of a structurally sustained white supremacy. White rage has a long and violent road to traverse before it runs its course.

Anti-Muslim affect, along with the wellsprings of aggrievement and rage it channels, does a great deal of hard work. White evangelical Christians find in Islam the perfect vehicle to carry racial aggrievement and rage. Bearing traces of the historical Turk, irreducibly foreign (Black American Muslims do not figure in the apocalyptic visions of the Christian right, a void filled instead by Arabic calligraphy and recitations of the Shahada), and now forever associated with terrorism and military tours in Afghanistan and Iraq, the figure of the Muslim stands in the way of the preservation of white, Christian life. If an abstract Muslim animates the homework assignments, and cartoon Muslims explain Islamic prayer to eight-year-olds, real live Muslims in the Middle East delay the eschatological scenario of the end of the world when Christ returns to Jerusalem. A generalized fear of the foreign and aggrievement over the declining influence of Christianity cannot power the expansion of anti-Muslim projects without an organized Christian right and Zionist base seeking to implement "God's foreign policy" in the Middle East. If anti-Muslim racism cannot bloom fully without the broader context of the rise of antidemocratic politics in the West that Brown charts, where rage replaces concrete grievances and vengeance becomes the only political goal, it is also nurtured by imperialism and by a liberal politics of inclusion in which the Muslim is granted conditional entry into the universal as multicultural difference, a place where Muslims cannot be recognized as targets of racism and or as oppressed. Although only one of several targets of white rage, the figure of the Muslim is perhaps singular in its capacity to reach into the affective Christian and colonial core of whiteness and to trigger specific fears of a lost white world. For this reason, anti-Muslim racism is not going away anytime soon.

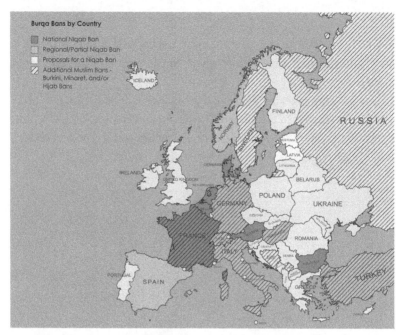

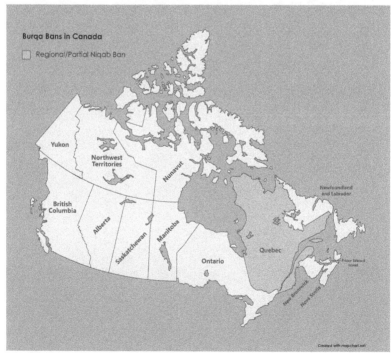

Figure 3. *(a)* Location of niqab/burqa/hijab bans by country in Europe. *(b)* Location of niqab/burqa/hijab bans by province in Canada. Created with mapchart.net.

CHAPTER 2

"I Can Never Tell If You're Responding to My Smile"
Desiring Muslim Women

We do not master by seeing; we are ourselves altered when we look.

—ANNE ANLIN CHENG, *SECOND SKIN: JOSEPHINE BAKER AND THE MODERN SURFACE*

Evidence or logic appear not to be measures used when managing issues involving women who cover their faces.

—NATASHA BAKHT, *IN YOUR FACE: LAW, JUSTICE, AND NIQAB-WEARING WOMEN IN CANADA*

In early 2017, an Australian television station sent a reporter clothed in a niqab (a garment that covers the body and face, leaving the eyes uncovered; often mislabeled as a burqa) to a mall. Within seconds of appearing at the mall, the reporter encountered a highly irate white man screaming abuses: "Did you come here on a boat?" and "Where's your f***ing face?" As he screamed at her, passersby looked on, saying nothing.[1] The confrontation is notable for the hierarchy of citizenship that is performed: an angry, threatening white man disciplines a woman he assumes to be a refugee. It is not hard to pin down the high emotion the man displays. The encounter is unmistakably gendered, boiling over with rage, and what Meyda Yeğenoğlu (following Fanon) has called "frustrated imperial ambition."[2] Suffused with longing and aggression in equal measure (yield to me, be grateful to me), scenes such as these, and the imperial sentiments they reveal, animate legal projects aimed at banning the wearing of Muslim women's head coverings from public life. Properly chastened, the covered Muslim woman must either yield to her

86 "I Can Never Tell If You're Responding to My Smile"

challenger or be legally banned from public space. As Fanon described for colonial Algeria, the rending of the Algerian woman's veil is an erotically charged act: "Straight off, with the maximum of violence, there is possession, rape, near-murder."[3] Unveiling provides the colonizer with power over the Algerian man and with "a practical, effective means of destroying Algerian culture," increasing the colonizer's aggressiveness.[4] Fanon does not consider the meaning of the act of rending the veil when it is performed by a woman, but we can speculate that the disciplining of a racialized woman by another woman provides a gendered form of racial power, allowing the woman who disciplines to come into her own personhood through circumscribing the choice of other women.[5] For the Muslim woman wearing the niqab, it seems possible that she prefers estrangement rather than risk the form of recognition the man in the mall is prepared to grant her. She refuses to meet him on his terms, and this rejection of his power invites sanction.[6]

Fraught with desire, the "ugly feelings" of the encounter in the mall are charged with political meaning.[7] The violence and intense emotion of the scene and its equivalent in the courtroom pushes me in the same direction of psychoanalysis as Fanon, albeit with an eye to the gendered dynamics he neglected. I hasten to say that I am not in a position to offer a fully fleshed out psychoanalytic account like Fanon's. In an effort to understand what is at stake for today's white, Western subjects in these social moments, I find myself having to think more about the role of colonial fantasy[8] and the nature of the subject whose coherence, as seen on the video of the shopping mall incident, cannot withstand the sight of a covered woman. The sexual nature of the responses to the Muslim woman wearing the niqab—the command to her to yield to the white masculine (and sometimes the feminine) gaze—prompts me to consider desire, whether understood as sexual or as a more diffused impulse for mastery. Bans in the West, I argue in this chapter, seek to reroute desire, damming up its flow and removing from sight the object of desire, declaring the covered Muslim woman a sight that cannot be borne.

Bans on Muslim women's clothing reveal "the sensuous and subliminal dimensions of politics," that is to say, the aesthetics of white power in law across the West.[9] When desire and repugnance form an anti-Muslim affect that travels through law and society, we know that we are in the presence of a subject who is apprehended as an Orientalized figure of the harem, a figure who is imagined to be coerced by Muslim men into wearing the niqab. Paradoxically, the niqab wearer is also considered a profound threat. She is assumed to be someone who deliberately rejects Western values and norms and who is likely to be the bearer of extremist ideologies. Presumed to be making herself sexually unavailable and thus refusing sexual freedom, the niqab wearer prompts a host of unruly feelings and emotions. She inspires desire and at the same time anger and frustration that she will not yield to those who would unveil her. A subject who is so overdetermined by notions of sexual and racial difference is not comprehended by universality.[10] That is, in all the phantasmic forms that she assumes, the niqab wearer stands in a negative relationship to law, a body that unsettles, threatens, and requires regulation. As the Introduction discussed, incoherence marks the spot where those in a negative relationship to law stand. If desire and repugnance signal her status, these emotions presage that the niqab wearer will not enjoy full personhood in the law. Her choice to cover will not be honored; a forced unveiling is the only legal outcome that secures the sovereignty of the man in the mall and, equally, the sovereignty of the nation, protecting all from an imagined threatening foreignness.

There is no question that Islamic specters of über-patriarchal and "terrorist" Muslim men and their differently aggressive veiled women haunt the political halls and courts of both Western and non-Western countries. The niqab wearer is the gendered phantom at the epicenter of anti-Muslim politics, a figure who is imagined to be both victim and threat. She has been banned from public life in the West from Canada to Europe. As Figure 3a depicts for Europe, where bans were first implemented in the West and where they proliferate, full or partial niqab bans prevail in Austria, Bulgaria, Denmark, France, Netherlands, Hungary, Germany, Italy, Spain, Switzerland, and Turkey.[11] Through such legal initiatives, Europe becomes one community that is racially structured. Niqabs and hijabs have also been banned in the Canadian province of Quebec (Figure 3b), where they serve as an ongoing battleground for French and English nationalism.[12] Easily connected to the bans passed in France, Quebec bans remain the only North American legal projects dedicated to Muslim women's head and face coverings. Fledgling efforts to introduce such bans in the United States have floundered on the shoals of the strong protection afforded to religious rights; notwithstanding this protection, a vigorous discrimination against Muslim women who wear head and face coverings persists and is legally sanctioned.[13] Niqabs have also been banned in non-Western countries from Algeria, Tunisia, Egypt, Syria, China, Cameroon, and Niger to India and Sri Lanka.[14] The sheer proliferation of legal projects targeting niqab wearers reveals the global reach of anti-Muslim racism. In seeking to exercise sovereignty over Muslim women, bans are a key part of maintaining a global color line in which white nations establish supremacy through the regulation of Muslim populations, and nonwhite nations position themselves within a global white supremacy that targets Muslims. Bans also serve the interests of majority-Muslim countries seeking to discipline their own populations by targeting conservative religion as inimical to national interests.

A virulent anti-Muslim racism is sweeping the globe, traveling through law and on virtual pathways such as YouTube, the place where I encountered the scene of the man in the mall. A circulating affect, the anger that is displayed toward Muslims is deposited in individual psyches, shaping future encounters. The anti-Muslim racism of public culture mostly circulates vertically, that is, from elites to ordinary people, gathering strength on its journey downward and inspiring acts of egregious violence. In Australia, where the scene in the mall was staged, Member of Parliament Pauline Hanson, a notable anti-Muslim ideologue, appeared in the legislature wearing a burqa in mockery of Muslims, an action that inspired condemnation but also garnered Hanson political attention and connection with voters who show social support for policies targeting Muslims.[15] Prone to similar tactics, President Trump's tweets sharing an incendiary video of Muslim Representative Ilhan Omar spawned a number of death threats against her.[16] More alarming, such acts have had lethal and international impact. Shortly after the "Muslim travel ban" was first instituted in the United States in 2016, a Canadian white nationalist, Alexandre Bissonnette, whose Facebook page showed him to be inspired by President Trump and to be linked to a number of white nationalist websites, walked into a mosque in Quebec City and shot six worshippers. Equally chilling, Fox News reported erroneously that the shooter was Moroccan, a man who was in fact one of the intended targets and who had called 911. The White House then quickly moved to exploit the Quebec City killings to support its travel ban, warning about "Islamic terrorists" even after the shooter was known to be a white nationalist.[17] A similarly inspired white nationalist who also maintained ties to other white supremacists on the internet killed fifty people at two mosques in Christchurch, New Zealand, in March 2019.[18] In both instances, apologists rushed to offer comments that the men were genuinely concerned about the threats facing the West from Muslims. Bissonnette has since been shown in the news during his police interrogation in a virginal white (and not orange) jumpsuit, softly explaining that he thought that his own family was under the threat of a possible attack from "terrorists."[19]

Shooters take bans to their logical conclusion. They show us that there is a connection between acts we label "extremist" (although white violence is rarely labeled extremist) and those that revolve around liberal inclusion: each act attempts to make true on the ground who is a part of the nation and who must be evicted from it. The Canadian province of Quebec, where Bissonnette went on his murderous rampage, provides an example of a legal environment dedicated to bans and from which shooters can emerge. Efforts to legally ban the wearing of the niqab began in 2010 when the government introduced Bill 94, which required "un visage découvert," a "naked face," when providing or receiving public services.[20] A decade later, the bill's present 2019 incarnation, Bill 21, anticipating challenges as to its unconstitutionality, required that the Quebec government override certain sections of the *Canadian Charter of Rights and Freedoms,* which it is able to do for a five-year period.[21] In April 2021 a Quebec Superior Court upheld Bill 21 by declaring that although the bill violated the rights of religious minorities in the province, the violations are permissible because of the Canadian constitution's notwithstanding clause, which permits Quebec to override certain sections of the constitution. Notably, the ruling declared that the ban on religious symbols for government employees could not be upheld for English-language schools in Quebec, since those schools are not covered in the notwithstanding clause.[22] Covered Muslim women continue to be in the line of fire as the Quebec Superior Court ruling is appealed to the Supreme Court of Canada and as French and English majorities in Canada continue to battle for supremacy over the bodies of Muslim women amid continuing violence directed at Muslims.[23]

The punitive effect of bans is breathtaking. They criminalize women, impose fines and prison terms, and exclude women from employment and from access to critical services. For example, Bill 21 makes it unlawful for niqab-wearing women to be public-service workers, including as teachers, police officers, prison guards, Crown prosecutors and judges, school principals and vice principals, peace officers and court agents (including clerks, sheriffs, and bailiffs), lawyers, and notaries working in the public service. One cannot board a bus, or take a child to a hospital emergency, or teach in a school while wearing the niqab. It is difficult to imagine that Muslims' basic rights will be honored in such an environment. Who will hire, for instance, anyone even remotely associated with Islam? Who will be civil toward such a person? Who will believe that such a person deserves not to be killed? The discourses of nationalism upon which bans rest prefigure the violence we see in the shooting rampages and employment restrictions alike. Bans make clear that the arguments they rest upon about secularism and gender equality function as technologies through which a racially stratified society is maintained. As Quebec scholars have argued about Bill 21, secularism is annexed to a type of nationalism that is deeply colonial at heart, inviting francophone Quebecers to understand their place in the nation as secured only by the violent eviction of Arabs, longtime phantasmic figures of French colonialism.[24]

In this climate of intensified racial violence against Muslims it is politically urgent to consider legal bans of all kinds and to examine their connection to the governance of racial populations, especially given that the global landscape is increasingly populated with such projects. Bans invite considerable violence against Muslims, but they also reveal a violence that is at the heart of liberalism itself, namely, the notion that those who refuse to enter the nation on the terms that are set out by normative citizens should be violently evicted, a feature that Étienne Balibar describes as the intensive universalism of contemporary nation-states.[25] Bans on wearing the niqab perform the eviction of those who must be excluded from the nation on the ground that their difference, deemed pathological, poses a threat. Bans have "a terrorizing effect."[26]

In a comprehensive review of bans on the wearing of the niqab in public spaces, Natasha Bakht (in this chapter's second epigraph) identifies what stands for me as their most revealing feature: they are marked by a striking illogic and lack of evidence.[27] When we are on the legal terrain of bans, nothing has to make sense. It is easy to find the illogic of bans. For example, when their proponents declare them necessary because niqab wearers are coerced, the evidence is overwhelming that Muslim women who cover make their own choices to do so.[28] Similarly, the argument that niqab wearers are aggressive proselytizers for a "radical Islam" has no foundation, but it invokes the fantasy of a "terrorist" religion. Legal arguments for bans are notoriously inconsistent. They reveal more about those invested in bans than they do about the women who wear the niqab. Marked by a profound antipathy and repugnance and a desire to control Muslim women, bans prompt us to consider the incoherence upon which they rest and to examine their productive function. Bans install imperial subjects whose racial superiority rests on disciplining Muslim women. It is pointless to search for their logic, but if we follow their emotional discourses, bans reveal how racial subjects are made and alert us to how a global white supremacy is consolidated through the figure of the Muslim.

In the first section of this chapter I make my case around desire, possession, and the limits of imperial ambition. I turn to legal cases banning the niqab, focusing on the phantasmatic scenes of their legal geographies. Together, these cases show that the primary legal logic on which bans rest—for instance, that an uncovered face is necessary for social interaction—is flimsy at best. These weak lines of argument are bolstered by the strong emotions that generate bans and are generated by them. Emotions reveal the racial fantasy that animates bans. If the law turns on racial fantasy, we can best understand bans by tracking the phantoms that inhabit law and the normative citizens they constitute. In the Western contexts I explore, white men filled with imperial rage and frustration, and white women seeking their own confirmation as modern European subjects, populate the legal and political texts dedicated to banning Muslim women's clothing. In the second section I turn to the spatial analytics of racial fantasy, exploring further the psychic underpinnings of bans, the ambivalence and desire that structure them, and the structure of racialized citizenship they maintain. I conclude that

92 "I Can Never Tell If You're Responding to My Smile"

bans are a key part of racial governance. Psychically, they are a protection against seeing what cannot be borne: the presence in our midst of those who challenge our hegemony and unsettle the desires on which it is based.

Phantasmatic Scenes in Legal Cases

I begin with scenes from a well-known Canadian case. *R. v. N.S.* is a sexual assault case, and I start with this case because it illustrates how much a ban is very much about a sight that cannot be borne, a sight that unsettles and challenges racial hierarchies. *R. v. N.S.* is all the more striking because of what the court refuses to see: the sexual assault of a child and young adult.[29] In *R. v. N.S.*, a sexual assault complainant wanted to wear her niqab when testifying. N.S. alleged that two of her male relatives had sexually assaulted her since childhood. She had tried on several occasions to do something about it, bringing it to the attention of a teacher, for example, but her father intervened and the matter was dropped. Now in her late twenties, N.S. had been wearing the niqab for about eight years when she brought her complaint to court. At the preliminary inquiry she wished to testify wearing her niqab, but the accused sought an order for her to remove it, alleging that the men's right to a fair trial was impaired if the court could not see N.S.'s face. It was argued that seeing her face was particularly crucial during cross-examination. The judge ruled in favor of the accused, noting that N.S. had previously removed her niqab for other public activities, such as getting her picture taken for her driver's license.[30] Equating this moment with the prospect of showing one's face for days on end while being cross-examined on the issue of rape, the decision installs the idea that N.S. is a fake whose religious beliefs change to suit her needs. The idea of the duplicitous Muslim renders this position reasonable.

N.S. appealed to the Supreme Court of Canada to permit her to wear the niqab in court. Several feminist groups, concerned with the implications for sexual assault survivors coming forward, intervened.[31] In the spirit of liberal inclusion, the majority opinion rejecting N.S.'s claim began by noting that Canada does not uncritically remove religion from the courtroom. Minority practices must be protected. Disapproving of the preliminary inquiry for its narrow approach to determining N.S.'s sincerity of belief, the court noted that sincerity does not mean that beliefs remain the same over time; religious beliefs may change according to circumstances. Nevertheless, the court agreed with the lower court and concluded that N.S. had to remove her niqab in order to testify. The case of N.S. in the Supreme Court of Canada turned, as it did at the lower levels, on the matter of demeanor evidence.

In her insightful analysis, appropriately titled *In Your Face: Piercing the Veil of Ignorance about Niqab-Wearing Women*, Natasha Bakht carefully unpacks the court's decision to require N.S. to remove her niqab on the basis that it interfered with the accused's right to a fair trial.[32] Bakht highlights the court's bias and the departure from a reasonable approach to the balancing of rights. First, in asking the question "Does permitting the niqab create a serious risk to trial fairness," the court was already privileging the men's right to a fair trial, and the focus is no longer on another question, namely, "How can the law accommodate N.S.?"[33] Notwithstanding the much-vaunted commitment to the principle of gender equality that proponents of bans often articulate, such concerns are clearly not paramount in the case of N.S. The court is unconcerned about the Muslim men who are accused of sexually assaulting N.S., a rare instance in the West where sympathy is extended to Muslim men. The figures I discussed in *Casting Out: The Eviction of Muslims from Western Law and Politics*—namely the dangerous Muslim man, the imperiled Muslim woman, and the civilized European[34]—may well have shifted in *R. v. N.S.*; when she contests patriarchy, the covered Muslim woman is no longer seen as imperiled but instead as aggressor and "in your face." Strangely, in this case Muslim men were no longer seen as dangerous or violent and may even have come close to being seen as victims of the aggressive niqab-wearing woman. From the outset N.S. was forced to justify the niqab, and the burden of proof was on her. Most important, and we will see this in other examples, the court simply accepted that seeing a face is of paramount importance when assessing a witness's credibility. Indeed, this position, offered as a quintessential feature of Western democracy, trumps any consideration of gender inequalities in a sexual assault trial.

As part of my argument about desire and the incoherence and strong emotion that signals it, I emphasize Bakht's argument that in the past

94 "I Can Never Tell If You're Responding to My Smile"

Canadian courts have been able to recognize the unreliability of demeanor evidence, but the court did not go down this road with N.S., in spite of the arguments proposed by the interveners that it do so.[35] The court did not consider, for example, social science evidence and simply repeated the common sense (as in the television show *Lie to Me*)[36] that we can easily tell when a person is lying by looking into his or her face. Bakht asks why the court "painted such an uncritical picture of demeanour, particularly in a case where full context was critical."[37] She speculates on whether the judges simply did not want to rock the boat when demeanor is such a pillar of the justice system (even though the minority opinion of Justice Rosalie Abella made it clear that demeanor is unreliable). It is noteworthy that the Supreme Court of Canada in *R. v. N.S.* showed itself to be remarkably inflexible and uncreative. Bakht notes that the court has been able to cope with other instances of confronting popularly held beliefs surrounding sexual assault, such as the belief that women who do not leave violent relationships are to be mistrusted.[38] (It is true, however, that the court did not come to this on its own. As Bakht points out, it took a great deal of lobbying.) Courts have often considered different forms of testimony, for example, where only female lawyers and the judge see the face. Finally, the court failed to consider N.S.'s own entitlement to a fair trial and the broader societal harm when sexual assault victims cannot testify. Ultimately, the decision avoided a clear rule, but it left a framework where, although trial judges can have discretion about the requirement to unveil, the bar is set high. The final result for N.S. was that when the case returned to the preliminary inquiry she was ordered to remove her niqab and the Crown subsequently dropped the charges against the men when N.S could not comply with the requirement to testify without her niqab.

As with other commentators puzzled by the Supreme Court of Canada's strange inattention to the context of the case (the long-term sexual assault of a child), Bakht focuses on Justice Louis LeBel, whose concurring opinion offers the best indicator of what cannot be borne. LeBel manifests what Bakht describes as "utter disapproval," but it is not disapproval of the act of sexual assault of a child. Instead, the judge disapproves of the complainant.[39] Since the niqab is considered to operate as a shield between N.S. and the public, we will not be able to tell if she is lying. The foreign woman who does not truly love us, who lies to us and rejects us, earns the judge's disapproval. Desire is thwarted, and the niqab wearer is rendered a censorious guest who disdains her host and disturbs a normally harmonious event. N.S. is considered to be in violation of the codes of civility.

Appointing himself the guardian of Canadian values, chief among them a secularism that must guard against excessive religiosity, Justice LeBel takes the trouble of noting that we are in a time of increased migration when the need to protect Canadian values from foreign intrusion is urgent.[40] The heuristic device is clearly announced: full and open communication requires seeing someone's face, and seeing someone's face is a fundamental value in an open and secular society—a society that must be protected from an onslaught of foreignness. LeBel declared that a trial is "an act of communication with the public at large" and that the public must be able "to *see* how the justice system works."[41] Maintaining what the philosopher Charles Mills described as "a principled anti-transparency on matters related to race" at the same time as a fidelity to the liberal principle of transparency, Justice LeBel is able to confirm law's objectivity at precisely the moment that it looks away from racial evidence.[42] The niqab wearer is deemed unfair to others because she does not allow them to participate in justice when she wears the niqab. Bakht is left to conclude that "the irrational insistence on seeing one's face defies logic": the niqab-wearing woman "sets the limit of the nation."[43] The niqab is the sight that cannot be borne if the nation is to exercise its sovereignty, expelling from political community those who threaten its borders.

Where does the exaltation of the face that we see in niqab cases come from? A similar proposed ban directed at niqab wearers reveals that the exaltation of the face supports the civilizational line that bans install and the white patriarchs whose desires drive them. The declaration in this other ban continues the insistence that seeing a face is necessary for interaction and similarly installs the Muslim woman as aggressively confronting others with her beliefs and posing a threat to a fragile nation. As with all bans, supporters do not have to offer rational arguments. Instead, emotional declarations invoking an imperiled, homogeneous white nation fills the void left by logic. Under the Conservative government of Stephen Harper, on December 12, 2011, the minister of citizenship,

96 "I Can Never Tell If You're Responding to My Smile"

immigration, and multiculturalism, Jason Kenney, introduced the ban on the wearing of the niqab while taking the oath of citizenship. Repeating the exaltation of the face-to-face encounter, Kenney made clear that this was not a technical or practical measure (and, indeed, as in other legal settings, there are numerous ways to adjust to a niqab-wearing woman in a citizenship court). For Kenney, as for Justice LeBel, it was a matter of protecting Canadian values through a symbolic gesture. Showing the face was an act of citizenship, an act that announced that one shared with others, freely and openly. The niqab is seen here as an *affront* to all those who participate in a liberal democracy, a community that Kenney names as "the Canadian family."[44]

Kenney revealed that the decision to ban the niqab had come about because he had received complaints that it was hard to tell if a niqab-wearing woman was actually reciting the oath, a facile argument that nevertheless carried the day.[45] If Canadians become offended because they cannot hear a citizenship oath performed (what of hearing-impaired oath takers?), Kenney makes clear that the real problem is threatening and confrontational difference. Sanctions become necessary in light of such challenges to national values. Asserting that "all new Canadians [must] participate in this ceremony in the same way" and that "we cannot tolerate two classes of citizens," Kenney's language of equality ironically establishes two classes of Canadians: those whose access to citizenship is unquestioned and those who must submit to additional testing.[46] His rhetoric organizes the pursuit of the niqab-wearing woman. When she is caught, the moment is marked by the cry "Yield to me or else." It matters little that the law organizes the chase on the strength of the logic that an oath that is spoken from behind the veil is not an oath. Nothing has to make sense.

The dogged insistence on homogeneity and protection from a threatening foreignness resolves the incoherence and conceals what is at stake. As many have pointed out, the full-face veil does not represent a pressing social problem, especially if one calculates the number of women involved. Rather, it is what the bans symbolize that counts. And in this regard, they symbolize the supremacy and desirability of European culture. There is much to gain politically from pursuing niqab wearers. As the Canadian scholar George Grinnell observed, the comments about the

"I Can Never Tell If You're Responding to My Smile" **97**

niqab and the citizenship oath were not "meant to solve a problem [but rather] to create and enflame one."[47] The emotions that underpin these moves, whether in the mall or in Parliament, are very strong ones—so strong that we must ask what the emotional terrain conceals and what the figure of the threatening Muslim woman installs: an imperiled and insulted white family and nation.

Muslim membership in the nation is always tenuous. Muslims must express restraint when making claims for inclusion or else risk expulsion, as Gada Mahrouse has argued about Muslim fears and anxieties in the wake of the mosque massacre of Muslim worshippers in Quebec.[48] Notwithstanding the harrowing experience of the mosque shootings, Quebec Muslims could not speak openly about anti-Muslim racism in the wake of a public response that resolutely avoided connecting the shootings to racial violence. Allegations of racism impugn the nation and undermine its claims to liberal neutrality and civility. Muslims who would speak of it cross a line, an infraction for which they are not forgiven and that earns them the label of ingrate if not terrorist. In a similar way, niqab wearers challenge the nation in their bid for inclusion, testing the limits of multicultural tolerance and leaving the nation open to the charge that it has been illiberal. Niqab wearers are often given the moniker "ingrate," but they are also likely to be considered aggressive and dangerous.

The racial hierarchy that the bid to exclude installs remains on record even when courts do not accept the arguments for bans, as was case when the niqab wearer of the citizenship ban won her case.[49] Repugnance and aggression toward niqab wearers form a circulating anti-Muslim affect, one that travels transnationally, in some of the examples above from France to French-speaking Canada. More clues about this affective landscape of threatening foreign women and the routes they travel are available from the French cases I now discuss. Although bans draw on a shared repository of European civilizational superiority, each nation takes care to dress the rationales for them in local fabric, styles that make bans acceptable to the public and to law and that obscure histories of colonialism and racism. In Quebec, as noted above, the ban on the niqab is typically defended on the basis that Quebec uniquely cherishes its secular identity, embedding the argument in the history of French/English relations in Canada and the bid to establish "an authentic Quebecois

98 "I Can Never Tell If You're Responding to My Smile"

identity."[50] Similarly in France, as Joan Scott argues, bans on Muslim women's clothing take the form of an insistence on the values and beliefs of the French republic, a mythical imaginary whose appeal rests on the demonization of Islam that it invokes.[51]

Reviewing the history of bans of Muslim women's clothing in France, Ratna Kapur observes the shift in the argument from the 2004 ban on the wearing of religious symbols and clothing such as the headscarf in schools to the 2010 ban on the wearing of the burqa (the term that is often used in Europe to include the niqab). While the ban on wearing of the headscarf or hijab rested on the notion of laicity (the separation of church and state), the ban on the wearing of the burqa and niqab emphasized the principle of "living together," a phrase meant to capture the idea that fully covered Muslim women refuse reciprocity and reject or are prevented from engaging in social interaction.[52] The concept of living together "demands compliance by Muslim women" and "operates exclusively in one direction—that is, in favour of majoritarianism."[53] There is no obligation on the part of the majority to respect the burqa wearer's own "existential, ethical and spiritual commitments."[54] Bans reveal a remarkable inflexibility where little attempt is made to accommodate Muslim religious practices. Muslim religiosity is simply declared offensive to national values.

While local inflections differ, what stays the same is the civilizational narrative that is declared through bans. Scholars participate in these imperial performances when they accept the rationales offered for bans as abstract declarations of principle unconnected to the colonial past and present. For example, noting that the debate in France is different for the hijab than for the niqab, Peter Baehr and Daniel Gordon insist that to better understand the origins of French bans we need to appreciate French democratic traditions. They assert that the push to ban the burqa in France is fundamentally a debate about democracy "independent of racial or gender prejudice."[55] Explaining why, comparatively, Americans have not favored legal bans on the hijab and niqab to the same degree as Europeans, these authors suggest patronizingly that social theorists (who can presumably explain the full meaning of French democracy) are more influential in the French context, both in popular culture and in legal projects, whereas in the United States the political process filters out social theory.[56] Racism against Muslims in France is thus seen as unconnected to legal responses to Muslim women wearing hijabs and niqabs. This scholarly interpretation preempts the question of what the invocation of such principles *does* in the present and indeed, what they did in the past. It is striking how even critical scholars who recognize the ways in which the modern secular European subject is made through the figure of the Muslim persist in the belief that Muslims have to be assisted into modernity, because they have failed to shed religion in ways that Europeans have long overcome.[57] As Mayanthi Fernando warns, the anxious invocation of secularism as the basis of French national identity is not simply due to the Republic's *contemporary* tensions with the formerly colonized, but is instead linked to long-standing contestations over the meaning of Frenchness.[58]

It is not political principles that dominate in the French cases but rather the phantom figures of the foreign woman who will not love us and the fragile nation whose culture cannot withstand the intrusion of foreign values. The well-known case of *S.A.S. v. France* shows the centrality of this phantom figure for jurists. In July 2014 the European Court of Human Rights (ECHR) dealt with the case of *S.A.S. v. France* and the issue of whether the state was allowed to criminalize the wearing of full-face veils in public spaces.[59] The court noted that France's position was that the wearing of the full-face veil was incompatible with French values and, specifically, with ideals of fraternity and civility. S.A.S. challenged the law, arguing that although she was willing to take off her veil for security reasons at airports and banks, she wanted to be able to wear it elsewhere for her own inner peace. The French government's response, as summarized by the ECHR, was the argument that concealing one's face in public places breaks the social tie and manifests a refusal of the principle of "living together," a phrase that recalls the Minister Kenney's declaration that wearing the niqab while reciting the oath of citizenship announced a refusal to join the Canadian family.

A majority of the judges of the ECHR agreed with France and ruled that the ban did not violate human rights. The court concluded that states have the right to insist on the values required in their society for equilibrium. In essence, if the French think the niqab contradicts its core values, it is at liberty to think so and to insist that all conform to its values.

100 "I Can Never Tell If You're Responding to My Smile"

Importantly, the two dissenting judges—two women—maintained that "living together" was too "far-fetched and vague" a goal and that respect for private life also encompassed the right not to communicate or to enter into contact with others.[60] As they suggested, human interaction is possible even if the full face is hidden and socialization works even "without necessarily looking into each other's eyes."[61] As the two dissenting judges clearly saw, vague and fanciful ideas structure the denial of niqab-wearing women's rights. It is hard to imagine that such a weak legal foundation would suffice in cases that do not involve Muslim women.

An excursion into French public discourse about bans further suggests that bans come to make sense to the public and to jurists and politicians alike through gendered discourses about Western superiority. What provides an underlying coherence to all the cases is that nations are constituted by their homogeneity, from which all foreignness must be excluded. Bordering the nation in this way requires an appeal to its unique and idealized national past and to abstract principles of democratic traditions, a drawing of a civilizational line between insiders and outsiders to the nation. A specific notion of gender is installed to carry the weight of racial superiority, the idea that it is the choosing, sexually available feminine subject who expresses modern femininity and citizenship.[62] For example, testimonies to the 2010 Gerin Commission, (a French parliamentary commission charged with investigating the imposition of a ban on the niqab) by academics, among them feminists, emphasize that bans are necessary in order to preserve a French notion of gender.[63] As Rey Chow argues of French feminisms, in this view, "feminization in its avant-garde form becomes racial power."[64]

In her very useful analysis of the testimonies given to the Gerin Commission, Kirsten Wesselhoeft shows the importance of the specific notion of gender that is invoked in the collective fantasy of unveiling.[65] Noting that the Gerin Commission heard from 210 individuals, including many academics and politicians from across France, and submitted a 658-page report, Wesselhoeft remarks on the paradoxes and contradictions that mark them. Strikingly emotional in tone, these testimonies offer unvarnished expressions of French superiority (as in the French art historian who argued that the culture of the West invests special value on the human face, as other cultures do not, and that this feature of Western

"I Can Never Tell If You're Responding to My Smile" 101

life must be protected at all costs from foreign intrusion).[66] Wesselhoeft shows that the report is animated by three paradoxes concerning the interpretation of the meaning of the veil. First, the paradox of femininity, where the full-face veil is read as the reduction of a woman to her femininity but also a negation of her ability to express her femininity or sexuality. Second, the full-face veil denies individuality, but the proposed law would deny women the right to express their femininity as they so choose. Third, the niqab wearer is imagined as aggressively and violently pursuing not being seen but is also seeking a passive public existence.[67] Each paradox is deserving of the detailed and insightful analysis that Wesselhoeft provides, but her argument about the single meaning that the Gerin Report attaches to gender demonstrates how a story about gender is simultaneously a story about the superiority of French culture, a plotline that rests on the covered Muslim woman as premodern and the sexually available French woman as modern.

Gender, French academics explained to the Gerin Commission, is about the right to a free sexuality, the right not to be a virgin on your wedding day, and the right not to answer to anyone, uniquely French values.[68] For some, it boils down to the protection of the desire to wear skirts. Elizabeth Badinter, a feminist philosopher, warned that if we allowed burqas in the schools, impressionable young girls might not be able to resist their families and communities who demand that they adopt the full-face veil.[69] Expressing "the ascendancy of the cosmopolitan woman as text—in the form of her open sexuality, her memory, her subjectivity," an ascendancy that, Chow notes, always requires the minimization if not the disappearance of the racial Other, Badinter declared that the wearing of skirts expresses a specific French femininity to which Muslim girls must have access.[70] A French politician, André Rossinot, similarly troubled, worried that women wearing the full-face veil are not free to seduce men and are presumably not free to be seduced either.[71] In sum, for these commentators, "a woman's liberty is best expressed, and her liberty best manifested, by exposing her form and face, not by concealing them."[72] For all these commentators on the meaning of gender, but for Badinter in particular, Western women do not encounter considerable violence from their own men, and are in a position to practice this normative femininity untroubled by harassment, rape, intimate partner violence, and so on.

102 "I Can Never Tell If You're Responding to My Smile"

It is tempting to dismiss such arguments, and easy to see their illogic and contradiction, but they make two things abundantly clear. First, a single notion of what gender means is the foundation of the civilizational divide between Muslims and the French: those who refuse to perform this version of femininity are simply premodern or antimodern and cannot be a part of the nation. A universal notion of gender thus relies upon the example of the oppressed third-world woman as necessary backdrop to convey the superiority of a Western notion of gender.[73] What we see in this move is the "rise of femininity as a form of racial power."[74] I would like to add to this argument a second point: the emphasis on seduction is telling. It announces desire and a considerable anxiety. As Fanon saw with the French in Algeria, the woman who sees without being seen frustrates the colonizer: "There is no reciprocity. She does not yield herself, does not give herself, does not offer herself."[75] Gendered colonial frustration marks the pages of the Gerin Report, a frustration expressed as resentment that the niqab wearer refuses to make herself available for social (and sexual) intercourse. Citizens are wounded by these aggressive acts and suffer. Abdennour Bidar (a philosopher and specialist in Islam, and like Badinter one of the most quoted academics for the Gerin Commission) made the argument to the commission that he, as an individual, suffers from violence when he cannot see the face of the Other. His suffering is none other than rejection.[76] The public must be protected from the affront of not being desired and from the suffering such rejection causes. Bans on the Muslim woman's niqab, a garment understood as psychic disruption and as giving offense, illustrate whose pleasure and desire the state is resolved to protect.

A Racial/Spatial Analytic: Sights We Cannot Bear

To further trace the psychic underpinnings of bans and to bring into view the subject whose coherence is secured through the eviction of covered Muslim women from public space, it is useful to employ a spatial analytic and to examine how racial categories are also spatial categories and where bans can be understood as a material defense against anxiety.[77] Bans expel from civic life Muslim women who are covered and are an example of the constitutive violence that is required to make a public.[78] They create a public that is made secure by the eviction of a threaten-

"I Can Never Tell If You're Responding to My Smile" **103**

ing foreignness. Banning the niqab protects the public from challenges to the meaning of gender as we know it. The niqab wearer is not sexually available and cannot be possessed. She seems to reject hegemonic gendered arrangements. Lauren Berlant suggests that the immigrant is defined as someone who desires America. Immigrant women, she adds, "especially are valued for having the courage to grasp freedom," a freedom defined as the free choice of love object.[79] Women of color—and, in this respect today, especially Muslim women—must confirm not only that freedom and democracy exist in the United States but also, significantly, that America and Americans are desirable.[80] In her refusal to be possessed and in her rejection of American life, the covered woman is an unbearable sight.

To think further about sights we find unbearable—sights that must be banned—I draw upon Susan Schweik's extraordinary book *The Ugly Laws* and rely on her analysis of the laws banning "unsightly beggars" to think through the spatiality and the scopic regimes of recent bans on the niqab and other veils.[81] Schweik explores laws colloquially known as the ugly laws. Ugly laws were city ordinances originating in Chicago that typically stated:

> Any person who is diseased, maimed, mutilated, or in any way deformed, so as to be an unsightly or disgusting object, or an improper person to be allowed in or on the streets, highways, thoroughfares, or public places in the city, shall not therein or thereon expose himself to public view, under penalty of a fine of $1 [about $20 today] for each offense.[82]

Schweik examines these ordinances "disciplining the 'unsightly beggar'" across the many cities that passed them, noting that a wave of ugly laws appeared at the height of the worst economic depression in the mid-1890s.[83]

What is at work in this codified impulse to protect the public from unsightly bodies? Schweik notes that there is deep ambivalence both in the moment of recognition of disability and in the moment of the ban, an ambivalence born in the case of the ugly laws in the space between "get out of my sight because you disturb me" and "there but for the grace of God go I."[84] Ugly laws were inspired by a fear of civic contagion, an outbreak of imperfect bodies. Such bodies raise anxieties about how they

104 "I Can Never Tell If You're Responding to My Smile"

have come to be. Have they come into existence through war? Through a bad economy where there are no jobs and people must beg? Should the state not look after such people? Such bodies haunt, and we want them to go away. They embarrass and worry us, forestalling our own insecure access to the space of the citizen. Recalling a friend with a visible disability who reported his own distress upon seeing an obviously disabled man on the street, Schweik suggests that we all write our own ugly laws to make disability go away, and then we have to write through them, by which I understand that we have to confront the urge to remove persons from public space who embarrass us, those who make us anxious, those who threaten us. If we were to do this with the niqab, we would have to ask why this practice so unsettles as well as who is unsettled by it.

Here I think of my own distress about the niqab. Like Schweik's friend, at least a part of my unease comes from my own insecure access to the space of the citizen. If any Muslimness in my biography must be erased as the premise of citizenship, then those who make public their own Muslimness will elicit unwelcome attention to all those assumed to be Muslim and/or foreign. As a woman, I also possess an insecure access to citizenship. Those who reveal the secret of the nation (that it is patriarchal) often have to pay for it. Women, including veiled women, must demonstrate that we like our subjection. We must make ourselves available, untroubled by unwelcome and often violent sexual attention or, conversely in the case of the niqab wearer, confirm our unavailability to all but our own male relatives. I wonder if the niqab-wearing woman thumbs her nose at patriarchy (I cannot be possessed) or publicly embraces it (I will be modest as is demanded of women). Either way, she introduces a conversation many of us would rather not have about our own relationship to patriarchy and to possession and sexual availability. It is hard not to wish that she would simply go away, a nuisance at best, a dangerous and unsettling provocation at worst.

In sum, the premise of the niqab wearer's exclusion is that through her foreignness and her expression of a version of gender inimical to Western norms, she disturbs the unity of the public sphere, a disturbance that is visible in her clothing. Both Western men and women must be protected from what the Canadian state (under the Conservative government of Stephen Harper) once termed "barbaric cultural practices."[85]

Again, visibility is key. As she moves through public space, the niqab wearer threatens and disturbs, and she introduces foreignness into what is imagined as an otherwise pure landscape. She haunts us because she represents the possibility that the nation is not fully governed by the male gaze and that it is not fully Christian. One wonders if it is the niqab wearer's autonomy (never acknowledged) that disturbs, her capacity, that is, to make a choice that challenges those who would insist on women's sexual availability. As Bakht comments, courts ignore the choices of niqab wearers and insist that they be protected from coercion even when the defendants demonstrate that they are clearly able to protect their own interests. In *Sahin v. Turkey* and *Dahlab v. Switzerland,* for instance, intelligent, well-educated women prepared to litigate domestically and internationally the violation of their rights were nevertheless seen as victims of passively accepted inequality.[86]

Faced with a sight we cannot bear, we project hostility onto the unsightly, performing our own aggression through the law. In ugly law cases, beggars are described as "people who thrust their deformities forward to the public gaze."[87] The unsightly can be silent, but they are nevertheless experienced as being too loud and "in your face." The niqab wearer is also experienced as powerful and powerfully disturbing. She inspires all kinds of aggressive acts, such as pulling her head covering off her head, but these acts also prevent her from accessing public services. We imagine that she is covering her body for antisocial ends, just as beggars were seen to be exposing their unsightly bodies for the purpose of begging, and we resent them both. Schweik notes that those experienced as unsightly were often imagined to be flaunting their difference.[88] For the crime of flaunting, ugly laws instituted harsh policing, systematized suspicion, the suppression of acts of solidarity with beggars, and structural and institutional repulsion.[89] Here it is useful to recall that French laws banning the headscarf rely on the logic that religion must not be flaunted in public space.[90] Flaunting one's difference, a sentiment behind laws that seek to regulate sexuality, is a powerful inversion of the violence the law performs. It is the law that flaunts an imagined bodily homogeneity and expels that which would undermine its own coherence. Such legally authorized aggression obscures how bodies come to be ugly and begging or homeless in the first place, just as bans on the niqab obscure how the nation comes to

106 "I Can Never Tell If You're Responding to My Smile"

constitute itself as only white, Christian, and defined by women's sexual availability. Two figures emerge in the colonial fantasy of Muslim women: a veiled woman, perhaps intent on tearing apart the fiction of homogeneity and perhaps not; and her slighted, vengeful lover, who mourns the intimacies he or she now actively repudiates. We see "frustrated imperial ambition" and sights we cannot bear in legal and social encounters, an oftentimes irrational insistence that the veiled woman yield to those who would possess her.

Let me spare a thought for emotions related to the frustrated desire that so clearly distinguishes these imperial and sexualized performances. Here I take seriously repugnance or disgust, emotions that establish social hierarchies. As William Miller has argued, disgust ranks people and is "the very substance of the civilizing process."[91] Far from being simply a natural impulse toward things or people we do not like or who are unlike ourselves, disgust is productive; it evicts from our consideration anyone who impairs the maintenance of self we need in order to establish belonging in the world. It is, as Miller suggests, "a nervous claim," enacting the very hierarchy we hope is true.[92] Douglas Husak reminds us that the readiness to demand a legal solution to the problem of disgust is a distinctive feature of modern society, an indicator of the collective anxieties of racial/colonial states.[93] Sianne Ngai observes that scholars pay more attention to the operation of desire than they do to disgust. Perhaps this is because "disgust is urgent and specific; desire can be ambivalent and vague."[94] "The disgusting seem to say 'You want me,' imposing itself on the subject to be mingled with and perhaps even enjoyed."[95] The niqab wearer is in our face, and we cannot forgive her for it.

What lies behind the cry to see the face—a cry that is alternatively plaintive and aggressive? Grinnell, utilizing a seventeenth-century example of an English aristocratic woman traveling through Turkey, notes that, in unveiling accounts, the English woman invited to the harem or the baths can display not only recognition (veiled women are like me) but a virulent repugnance.[96] His example, Lady Craven, displays feelings of disgust. She insists on humiliating her Turkish hosts whenever she gets the chance by aggressively maintaining an unveiled face. Admitted to the Turkish baths, she finds only fat and grotesque women there. Lifting the veil, Craven finds her own superiority in doubt and sets about confirming it through repugnance.[97] Drawn to Turkish culture, a desire that threatens her own sense of racial/cultural superiority, Craven transforms desire into distance. Grinnell writes that she was always ready to be disappointed and disgusted by the Turks, a positional superiority that is the end point of her journey into the harem. Despite her attraction to Turkish culture, a deep-seated, angry Orientalism persists and surfaces especially at those moments when she finds herself drawn to intimacy with Turkish women.[98] Disgust resolves the contradiction. Grinnell asks his readers to consider how the unasked-for experiences of shame that Lady Craven feels (she is desiring of kinship with the women yet knows she cannot give in to this desire) are the moments when we can consider how we are bound together. Remarking on the persistent hostility that the law directs toward the Muslim woman, a hostility that is obsessive, I can only speculate on the mechanics of desire and repulsion that drive bans.

As Ghassan Hage discusses in the Australian context, citizens defined as normative experience their own belonging as requiring them to be managers of public space. Hage considers people who pull the veils off the heads of Muslim women (among them other racialized people) as understanding themselves as preserving national space for its authentic citizens.[99] We might add that these are citizens driven to act upon feelings of disgust. As we have seen in the cases of legal bans on the niqab, such acts reach their apotheosis when the state itself performs its own unveiling through the courts and the legislature. When legal and political elites engage in unveiling, the ordinary citizen is emboldened to manage public space through the same violent maneuver, secure in the knowledge that his or her actions are sanctioned. The aggression behind such enactments of citizenship suggests that something very deeply psychically structured is at stake in these violent acts. Those who must know what lies behind the veil, who insist on the veiled woman's submission, and who must rend the veil betray an obsession with covered women. The niqab wearer is stalked.

In her analysis of the French debate and its misuse of Levinas, Chloe Patton offers a revealing example of colonial fantasy and its obsessive features. She explores a meeting on a French television program between a noted French politician and then secretary of the ruling right-wing party in France, Jean-François Copé, and Dalila, a twenty-two-year-old single mother who wears the niqab. Dalila was a challenging case for those who followed the state's logic that Muslim girls and women were pressured and duped into returning to the archaic tradition of their families. There was no father, brother, or man in Dalila's life to tell her she had to veil; her own mother was not a Muslim, and Dalila adopted the niqab at seventeen along with her twin sister after reading the Qur'an and a book on the Prophet's wives. Dalia is hard to pin down as coerced. Her position infuriates her pursuer and prompts him to become alternatively aggressive and wheedling. When he hears Dalila explain that she wore the niqab out of her own free will, Copé interjected: "But I can never tell if you're responding to my smile."[100] He later followed up with impassioned outbursts to Dalila, such as "stop lying to us."[101] Copé performs the French state's argument that the full-face veil destroys any fraternity, illustrating in the bargain the erotics of which Fanon spoke: smile; respond to me; don't lie to me. Patton explains these dynamics: "In Copé's face-to-face encounter with Dalila, the discomfort he experiences upon not being able to see her face leads him to withdraw from her."[102] He feels he cannot relate to her as an equal even though he is one of the most powerful men in French politics. Clearly, the colonizer is frustrated in his dream of possession. Like Lady Craven above, Copé does not assume any responsibility to discipline his own responses, to get past his discomfort, and to do some work in this encounter. The story that French law tells about Muslim women's clothing is indeed the story of frustrated imperial ambition. Desire and repugnance are the story's driving forces.

What does unveiling, when understood as an act of possession, provide to those who are compelled to engage in it? In her masterful book *Second Skin*, on the artistry and politics of the Black performer Josephine Baker, Anne Anlin Cheng remarks: "We do not master by seeing; we are ourselves altered when we look."[103] To look at the niqab wearer is to be altered, derailed from the path of racial and sexual mastery and confronted with the possibility that we do not know who she is or who we are. Faced with the prospect of alteration, we choreograph the encounter with Muslim women through bans on her apparel. Bans enable us to refuse to see, to block from our line of vision the sight that unsettles and that derails us from our plans of mastery. As dreams of possession, bans preempt any recognition of the Other's humanity and seek to ensure that we are not troubled by it.

"I Can Never Tell If You're Responding to My Smile" **109**

If it requires hard work not to see the imperial ambition behind bans in the West and the racial violence they inspire, supporters of bans warn of a competing harm that makes bans necessary: the covering of women's hair is a practice based on the idea that women possess a dangerous sexuality from which men must be protected, and in permitting a garment such as the niqab in the public sphere we ignore the fundamental gender inequality the niqab expresses. Confronted with this argument, a favorite in the law, feminists are meant to find themselves on the horns of a familiar dilemma: interrupt the imperial circuits that bans use, or encourage a deeply patriarchal project to control women. The terms of the debate themselves replicate a separation of patriarchal violence from imperial violence, inviting us to see the West as a place where there is a commitment to secularism and to women's equality and to see the Islamic world as a place of über-patriarchs. To go beyond these simplifications requires attention to the multiple ways in which patriarchal and imperial dreams operate through each other in space and time. There can be little doubt that bans are directly connected to keeping the Muslim foreigner out of political community. Equally, the control of women remains crucial for all projects of rule. We must also consider what is precluded in the formulation that wearing the niqab expresses a patriarchal logic. As Saba Mahmood observed, we do not consider the politics of piety in our assessment of patriarchal practices when we assume that covered women are dupes of oppressive men.[104] Women may choose to wear the niqab as an expression of piety regardless of its meaning elsewhere, and perhaps even because of it.[105] There is a pronounced unwillingness, Bakht observes, in accepting different forms of religiosity, a reluctance that is especially the case for Islam.[106]

Simplifications operate through the denial of history and context and through fidelity to legal and political abstractions. In the post-9/11 period, when Western states set out to deprive Muslim subjects of fundamental rights (for example, in antiterrorism legislation), they do so on the basis that Muslims are a particular kind of premodern subject noted for the oppression of women. The state has to protect its citizens from such premodern threats, and secularism of the Western variety is typically trumpeted as the best way to do so. As Talal Asad reminds us, the modern state secures its power as neutral arbiter by appointing itself as above warring religious factions, all the while guaranteeing the

110 "I Can Never Tell If You're Responding to My Smile"

social arrangements it wants.[107] Citizens owe their loyalty to the secular state, but the state reserves the right to manage populations and to determine which signs of religion's presence will be tolerated. When Muslims are deemed to have practices inimical to proper citizenship, their own grievances as subjects unequally treated, surveilled, and incarcerated have little traction. We should always ask, then, what an invocation of the secular secures in each context. If the idea of a monocultural, secular state holds dangers for women, stigmatizing and disciplining racialized communities, bans simply operationalize this eviction from the nation. They make clear who belongs in public space, and we would be naive to imagine that when a threatening foreignness is associated with the veiled woman, other racialized women and communities are safe from eviction.

Conclusion: A Rock-Bottom Minimum

In the last section of her book, titled "The End of the Ugly Laws," Schweik opens with an epigraph from Jacobus Tenbroek on the right to live in the world: "If the disabled have the right to live in the world, they must have the right to make their way into it.... A right on such terms to the use of the streets, walks, roads and highways is a rock-bottom minimum."[108] In this consideration of bans I have come to Tenbroek's "rock-bottom minimum." If we cannot offer that minimum, we are indeed in trouble as a society. Why is this minimum so hard to offer to Muslims? And what is the cost of not offering it?

To answer these questions for the bans on the unsightly, Schweik turns to Levinas. First, as Patton and Grinnell both do, she notes the face's ethical demand and Levinas's insistence on its unrepresentability (you cannot know it by seeing it).[109] Levinas writes of "nonindifference" and "the face as the extreme precariousness of the other."[110] The ugly laws were a "form of defense against being in proximity, being made awake to the face of the other."[111] Schweik recalls that those charged under the ugly laws felt themselves kicked in the face by those who were offended by their person. She discusses how much we would like to kick the unsightly beggar in the face and to not be troubled by the sight, to refuse to be made awake to the face of the Other. Veiled women often report the bodily disintegration or immobilization that they feel when required to unveil as equivalent to feeling kicked in the face.[112] Bans refuse "the possibility that an anomalous body might be seen in public and found pleasing," Schweik writes, and in this sense, the law "police[s] the sites of beauty as much as the situation of the ugly."[113]

The ban on niqabs and other veils similarly expresses the refusal to be in proximity, the refusal to be made awake to the Other's difference and to contemplate a diverse humanity and femininity. There is barely an attempt at defending such bans logically. Other than an endlessly repeated "the face must be seen," there is little substance, and still less appeal even to pragmatic considerations such as security. Instead, bans are rife with emotional discourses. One does not have to go very far to find highly charged phantasmatic scenes—from judges mindlessly insisting that the face must be seen, to politicians undone by not seeing a smile, to those who find our values reflected in open faces but not in making it possible for victims of sexual assault to testify.

In her discussion of Levinas, Patton begins with an image also commented on by Judith Butler, the popular image of the unveiled Afghan woman liberated from the burqa. As Butler comments, the unveiled face elides any real sense of the human. It is not a face that reveals anything about grief and the suffering of the war. In this instance, unveiling effaces rather than reveals a person's humanity. Patton follows Butler's lead to explore how Levinas sought "to advance an optics of ethical cohabitation between French citizens."[114] The Other teaches through her presence, and Levinas is concerned with how engagement can occur. As Patton notes, the key questions for him are: "How may I engage with the Other without reducing her to an extension of myself, an object of my gaze? How do I leave intact within her that which I experience as radically other?"[115]

Grinnell also reminds us that for Levinas the face requires respect, not sight. In the same vein, in *The Civil Contract of Photography*, Ariella Azoulay suggests that spectatorship must be anchored in civic duty. The reading of photographs of those who have suffered some form of injury requires civic skill and is not an exercise in aesthetic appreciation. Instead of empathy, pity, or compassion—or, I would add, in the case of niqab, repugnance and disgust—what is required is obligation. Spectators have a responsibility for what we see, reimagining the public sphere to form new communities in which what is repugnant can be borne. We crush the niqab wearer by stripping her, Wesselhoeft observes. Azoulay writes of the power Israeli soldiers have to make Palestinians strip, reminding us how the command to strip both requires and produces power over the bodies of Palestinians.[116] It is this power, and the desire that underpins it, that requires rethinking when we consider bans on the niqab.

I have been arguing that we must begin with the violence of bans and the embodied practices of citizenship they install. Niqab bans, hijab bans, burkini bans, minaret bans, bans on Muslim circumcision parties, calls for forcing fasting Muslims to be banned from work, and the requirement that the shaking of hands is required as a part of citizenship ceremonies (on the strength of the idea that some Muslim women refuse to shake hands)[117] all suggest that bans are an attempt to demarcate corporeally the boundaries of cultural and racial belonging. It is no surprise that phantasmic scenes mark this corporeal eviction of Muslims from political community. As Henk Van Houtum observes, we banish from sight what we desire and fear, building walls to ensure that we will not be in proximity to the Muslim.[118] Corporeal evictions from political community have been proliferating, inspiring along the way moral panics that serve to confirm the public sphere as a space from which all foreignness must be banned.

In the summer of 2019, Europe experienced an unprecedented heat wave. The French city of Grenoble shut down its two municipal swimming pools after several women, accompanied by activists, proceeded to swim wearing burkinis, swimming garments in which the hair and legs are covered. Announcing that the ensuing public furor made the pools dangerous, the shutdown was a salvo aimed at those who protested the convention that only conventional swimsuits and bikinis must be worn in swimming pools.[119] Conservative Muslim women's garments continue to serve as a battleground for citizenship. Bans in the West are a key plank in projects of racial governance and are unapologetically about keeping the foreigner out and preserving an imagined homogeneous (white) Europe. Bans on Muslim women's attire have always unfolded as a part of an anti-immigrant, anti-refugee agenda that includes such measures as the detention of children. This alone should give us pause. There is, as Ralph Grillo and Prakash Shah have shown, a "transnational intertexuality" among European nations banning veils and niqab, a shared repository that operates regardless of the specificities of each national context.[120] Such repositories are the technologies of a system of global racial governance.

Toni Morrison once urged a graduating class to imagine "what it would be like to live in a world where the solution of serious, learned people to practically every big problem was not to kill somebody."[121] In the same spirit, I propose that we imagine a world where bans are not the solution to every problem with Muslims. Although I acknowledge my own impoverished imagination in this regard, I feel sufficient apprehension about what bans do to urge that we heed Morrison's advice and stop turning to the law as a first and last resort. Bans do not push us to examine the basis of our own fragility and to ask why we cannot bear what we find repugnant. Instead, they unfold in the historical record as extraordinary and violent moments of longing and repugnance, moments born of dreams of possession.

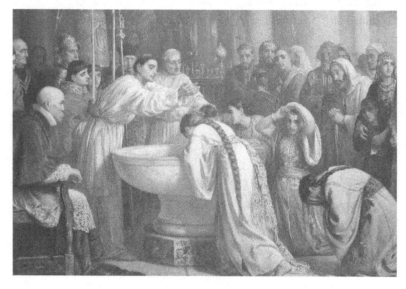

Figure 4. Edwin Long, *The Moorish Proselytes of Archbishop Ximenes, Granada, 1500* (1873). This painting depicts the forced conversion of Muslims during the Inquisition.

CHAPTER 3

"Terrorism in Their Genes"
Racial Science and the Muslim Terrorist

Poor prognosis is associated with being religiously devout. In other words, the more religious the person, the more poor the prognosis.

—MICHAEL WELNER, "TESTIMONY AT OMAR KHADR'S SENTENCING HEARING IN GUANTÁNAMO BAY, CUBA"

Have we become so assured of the inconsequence of millions of Arab and Moslem lives that we assume it is a routine or unimportant matter when they die either at our hands or at those of our favored Judeo-Christian allies? Do we really believe that Arabs and Moslems have terrorism in their genes?

—EDWARD W. SAID, "THE ESSENTIAL TERRORIST"

Race, religion, and blood came together five hundred years ago in Catholic Iberian Spain and profoundly shaped Spanish colonialism in the Americas. Two religions became races, and a legal bureaucracy worked hard to evict the targeted groups, Jews and Muslims, from law and political community at a time when each was imagined as a danger to the security and survival of the state. As the painting by Edwin Long (1829–91) in Figure 4 depicts, Archbishop Ximenes ordered the baptism of all Muslims as a part of the outlawing of Islam in the lands of the Spanish monarchy. As I discussed in *Casting Out: The Eviction of Muslims from Western Law and Politics* (and drawing on the work of Irene Silverblatt), we can look to the Spanish Inquisition to see an example of how such evictions from political community become socially and legally sanctioned through the concept of heritability.[1]

The question of heritability changes depending on each period's understanding of how culture, religion, and political sympathies are transmitted.

115

116 "Terrorism in Their Genes"

In Iberian Spain, for instance, it was feared that Moriscos, who had lived as Christians for generations, might revert to their earlier, Islamic cultures and develop sympathy for the Ottoman Empire. Moriscos had to be watched carefully for signs that Islam had reemerged. Lest their Christian sympathies falter, they were prohibited from speaking Arabic and from wearing clothing associated with Islamic dress, and were required to keep their doors open on Fridays in case they were inclined to observe Friday prayers.[2] As scholars remind us, historical events have an important role to play in the shape of anti-Muslim polemics and practices, and in Iberian Spain the threat of a Muslim enemy loomed large.[3] In our own time, the period we have come to call the "war on terror," the Islamic enemy is once again imagined to pose a political and cultural threat. Indulging in similar bans on Muslim clothing as in Iberian Spain, as chapter 2 showed, it is now common to consider how the apparently assimilated Muslim (the homegrown "terrorist") might carry the seeds of violence within his psyche. In the quest to determine if Muslims incarcerated on suspicion of having a connection to "terrorism" pose a threat, Western states today draw upon the ideas of racial science, watching for the signs of Islamic faith and cultures borne in the blood as zealously as their Iberian counterparts once did. Like the Moriscos imagined as unable to withstand the onslaught of Islam, the Westernized Muslim who is assumed to carry violence in his genes could never overcome his history.

The idea that Islam is a "terrorist" religion and Muslims are a people with a genetic capacity for violence does essential work in the trials and hearings of Muslim men and boys suspected of involvement in "terrorism." In the first section of this chapter I explore race-thinking and the idea of Muslims as carrying the seeds of violence in their blood as it operates in law. I do so through a close reading of the sentencing of Omar Khadr by a military commission at Guantánamo, and specifically of the testimony of the psychiatrist Michael Welner, which was the core of the state's case against Khadr.[4] Khadr, a Canadian, was held at Bagram and Guantánamo since he was fifteen, and accused of killing an American soldier, Christopher Speers, during a firefight in Afghanistan. In the chapter's second section I discuss the racial science we see in today's security hearing, which, while culturalist in tone, makes an affective appeal to biology. With its extravagant reference to "catastrophically damaged gene pools" and even its language of epigenetics, anti-Muslim racial science brings us full circle back to the nineteenth century but with the contemporary scientific twist of genetics.

Race-Thinking, Religiosity, and Future Dangerousness

Race-thinking, Hannah Arendt wrote, turns on the idea that culture and character are inheritable traits.[5] Europeans imagined that they possessed an innate capacity for rationality, while those whom they conquered and ruled over remained unable to move out of the state of nature. In *Casting Out,* I explored how race-thinking persists today in security hearings where Muslim men detained without charge and without full legal rights face a court that seeks to establish whether or not they will engage in "terrorism" against the state.[6] Race-thinking is evident in these hearings when Muslims, "Islamic extremists," and "terrorists" are all collapsed into one category and are imagined to share cultural and social characteristics (of tribalism, fanaticism, and a commitment to violence) that are innate. Importantly, in this imaginary, people of European origin also share innate social and cultural characteristics, but their gene pool produces civility, rationality, the capacity to live as autonomous individuals, and the capacity to exercise free choice. The racial Other who has yet to emerge out of the state of nature is necessary for the birth of rational man who knows of his triumph over nature, the triumph of mind over body, only through the existence of those beyond the boundary of humanity.

Race-thinking fuses culture and biology and is the basis of scientific racism. As David Goldberg reminds us, while a strictly biological racism in science gave way in the nineteenth century to "culturalist and class centered expressions of racist exclusion," ultimately, the end result was simply a more palatable form of racism.[7] The argument that Muslims have an inborn capacity for violence, and its obverse, that whites are inherently a rational and more civilized people, remains a long-standing plank in white supremacy and has become a staple in the study of genetics, where the propensity for violence becomes a genetic attribute of the racialized. One context in which scientific racism—or *racial science,* a term in widespread use—began to feature prominently with respect to Muslims is the dispossession of Palestinians and the birth of the state of Israel in 1948. The Palestinian, cast as "Islamic terrorist," came to be

118 "Terrorism in Their Genes"

known as a figure carrying violence in his genetic makeup. Edward Said identified this move in the proliferation of "terrorism discourses" in the 1980s, discourses that emerged in tandem with an intensified Israeli occupation and Palestinian resistance. Notably, "terrorism discourses" bore the hallmark that nothing has to make sense; facts, footnotes, or coherent argument were all beside the point. Instead, arguments rested on the powerful emotions aroused when the specter was invoked of the Muslim as genetically damaged. Reviewing a collection of articles edited by Benjamin Netanyahu, then Israeli ambassador to the UN and former prime minister of Israel (1996–99; 2009–21), Said shows that Netanyahu's argument that "violence emerges only out of communist totalitarianism and Islamic (and Arab) radicalism" erases the violence it takes to dispossess Palestinians and to bring into existence the state of Israel. If the enemy is, as Netanyahu put it then, "those with a disposition towards unbridled violence," then violence against them, such as the violence the Israeli army and its surrogates meted out in the 1982 invasion of Lebanon, and the massacres committed in the refugee camps of Sabra and Shatila, was not violence at all but defense against an enemy whose violence has no logic.[8] "The root cause of terrorism is terrorists," Netanyahu unabashedly proclaimed, illustrating in a nutshell the incoherence that is racial thinking.[9] Then as now, the idea of Islam as a "terrorist" religion required the ballast of racial science, knowledge offered by a coterie of scholars heralded as the accredited experts on the Islamic world and the new terrorism experts.

Like the refugee or the prisoner for whom time stands still[10] and who remains suspended in a spatial void,[11] the Muslim has no future when he is declared to carry the seeds of violence within him. The Muslim prisoner is removed from time itself, held indefinitely behind prison's walls, if not killed outright. We may not know precisely the origins of the term *Muselmann*, used by the inmates of Nazi concentration camp to describe a prisoner who was at the limit point of starvation and exhaustion and resigned to impending death, but this in-between condition connected to the figure of the Muslim describes one foot in and one out of the material world, a being outside time itself. It is a condition that the indefinitely detained terror suspect comes to inhabit on the basis that he possesses a cultural predisposition for violence and will never change. The argument

"Terrorism in Their Genes" **119**

for solitary confinement, indefinite detention, and assaults on the bodies and minds of prisoners all depend on the notion that the Muslim prisoner is a special kind of being against whom violence is authorized. The place of raciality in law where subpersons live is a place where nothing has to make sense.

To make an argument about a Muslim cultural predisposition for violence, Muslim savagery is read in the personality of the detainee and in his practices of religiosity. Psychologists and psychiatrists serving as expert witnesses guide the court in understanding Muslims and their cultural predisposition for violence. Such experts rely on ideas that circulate in the fields of evolutionary psychology and sociobiology, where scholars and anti-Muslim ideologues maintain that that there is a substantial genetic influence on Muslim expressions of religiosity. Genetic arguments, Dorothy Roberts reminds us, are used to rehabilitate a biological understanding of race. Pseudoscientific upon examination, the idea that Muslims possess a damaged gene pool draws on long-standing ideas in the history of racial science. As Roberts warns, we ignore pseudoscience at our peril, forgetting its role in establishing the idea that race is real and that populations may be usefully ranked on an evolutionary scale.[12]

When considering the role of racial science in the "war on terror," Omar Khadr's case is especially instructive. A thirty-three-year-old in 2019, Khadr became particularly important as a liminal figure, someone who was a child when incarcerated but who was nevertheless always treated as an adult in law. As I have shown elsewhere, passionate pleas that Khadr be considered a child soldier (and thus under the Optional Protocol for child soldiers) fell on deaf ears, despite the support of people like General Romeo Dallaire, Canada's most famous general (for his actions in trying to stop the Rwandan genocide).[13] The torture of a Canadian child at Bagram and Guantánamo prisons spectacularly failed to move both the Canadian population (polls suggested that 81 percent of Canadians did not want Khadr in Canada) and the Canadian government.[14] Neither of the West nor the East, neither child nor adult, Khadr was the limit point of justice, a body in which violence incubates and thus a body without a future. To mark the place where terror lives indefinitely, Khadr is someone who has to be shown to be the definitive Muslim "terrorist." In March 2008 a report was released indicating that the battlefield report that Khadr threw the grenade that killed Christopher Speers had been altered to cast blame on Khadr.[15] Weak on its own merits, the case against Khadr also required a conceptual arsenal of white-supremacist ideas about Muslims, chief among them the idea that Muslims carry the seeds of violence in their culture and religion and are deceptively normal until they strike. The notion of a worldwide Muslim conspiracy to wage jihad as the project of a cabal of violent jihadists in sleeper cells draws on long-standing racist ideas about Jews, an ironic historical connection given the contemporary appeal of such ideas about Muslims to Zionist groups. In examining closely what these ideas consist of and how they were deployed to condemn Khadr, we can learn a great deal about the contemporary structure of global anti-Muslim racism and its life in law. These ideas install the Muslim as someone who is fanatical, unable to think autonomously, angry, and dysfunctional. White-supremacist ideas have a wider appeal than is ordinarily imagined because they rest on the same liberal foundation of Western societies, namely, that people of European origin are rational individuals with an innate capacity to govern inferior races. In a hospitable legal environment, they blossom, upholding and upheld by a state of exception and other spaces in law where legal rights are suspended for those considered outside the boundaries of humanity and citizenship.[16]

A close look at how anti-Muslim racism operates in Khadr's case sheds light on the legal abandonment of Muslims, a practice that is institutionalized and actively promoted by well-resourced groups.[17] As occurred in the 1980s, these individuals and groups successfully circulate the position that the origins of terrorism lie in Muslim culture and in Islam, rather than in social and political contexts. Although, as Arun Kundnani suggests, conservatives stress that it is Islamic culture that is to blame and liberals emphasize that "the roots of terrorism are not in Islam itself but in a series of twentieth century ideologues who distorted the religion to produce a totalitarian ideologue—Islamism—on the models of communism or fascism," in practice the two views are reconciled on the matter of a fatal attraction between Muslims and terrorism.[18] The net result is that all Muslims are stigmatized. When radicalism comes to be seen as a cultural and psychological predisposition, we engage in race-thinking where culture and character become innate and inheritable traits.

"Terrorism in Their Genes" 121

In 2010, Khadr pled guilty as part of a deal to be returned to Canada. He was sentenced to forty years in prison for war crimes. The pretrial deal capped Khadr's sentence at eight years. The testimony of Welner, the state's expert witness on Khadr's capacity to commit violence, that Khadr was an unrepentant jihadist sealed his fate. Indeed, Canada gave as its official reason for delaying the transfer of Khadr to Canada until September 2012 that it had not seen the videotape of Welner's seven-hour interview and had formally requested an unredacted report in order to make the final decision about his repatriation.[19] Reviewing Welner's testimony in Khadr's sentencing hearing, one cannot help asking how illogical and contradictory ideas come to make sense in law, and how they continue to make sense when circulated widely in the media. How does a far-right, white-supremacist message come to achieve respectability? If one believes in Muslim irrationality, it is easy to follow and accept the many contradictions and inconsistencies in Welner's narrative. Racism gives coherency where otherwise there is none, allowing us to bypass illogic, contradiction, and duplicity in order to be rewarded with a world in which there are two levels of humanity and two levels of law.

Welner and the psychologist Nicolai Sennels, on whom Welner relies and who declared that Muslims have a catastrophically damaged gene pool, may be clearly visible as anti-Muslim, far-right propagandists, but in court at Guantánamo they become men of science who offer reasonable appraisals of Muslim degeneracy. Tracing how this transformation is performed in the military hearing and how the ideas in circulation there connect to general notions of racial science are the tasks I set myself in this section. The transformation of white-supremacist zealots into credible men of science is accomplished through the law's preservation of a space of law without law. That is, Khadr is evaluated in a court of law, but it is one in which he does not enjoy the right of facing his accusers. The legal environment at Guantánamo is such that processes such as cross-examination of expert witnesses are impeded by hidden forces. Khadr's lawyers claimed that prosecutors threatened to revoke Khadr's plea deal if they substantively challenged Welner's credentials.[20] While the "surrealism, absurdity, hypocrisy and capriciousness" of Guantánamo and its military commissions described by lawyers advocating for detainees[21]—features no less true today[22] than at the time of Khadr's sentencing—

122 "Terrorism in Their Genes"

are well known, it is the role of racial science that I wish to emphasize. Racial science invests these otherwise Kafkaesque proceedings with a surface coherency. Wrapped in a scientific cloak, racial "knowledge" is used to condemn Khadr, knowledge that requires men and women of science devoted to the idea that culture is inherited and that some populations are pathologically evil.

Terrorism was once understood as the work of rational actors. It is only since 9/11 that terrorism came to be definitively understood as the work of pathological evildoers, although as Zionist discourses show, the "terrorist" as evildoer has earlier incarnations. Evildoers lie outside the realm of moral consideration and exist in a negative relation to law. The legal proceedings of accused "terrorists" require experts in evil. While such experts operate "at the boundary between politics and science," as Lisa Stampnitzky argues, I suggest that it is racial science that gives them standing.[23] As experts, the white men who introduce to the court Muslim phantoms depend on our prior racial "knowledge" of the "terrorist" Muslim to make sense of the evidence.

As the expert witness for the prosecution, Welner was to conduct a risk assessment of Khadr in order to determine the likelihood of his re-offending, an evaluation, in his words, of "future dangerousness of a jihadi."[24] (Two mental health experts for the defense, Stephen Xenakis, a psychiatrist, and Kate Porterfield, a child psychologist, each concluded that Khadr did not exhibit "terrorist" tendencies.)[25] Importantly, Khadr is presumed at the outset to be a "jihadi."[26] Although Welner had no knowledge of "jihadis," he said that he was well versed in criminal recidivism and that he had developed a useful "depravity scale" that he hoped would assist courts in sentencing by providing a measure of the depravity of a crime. Welner refers to his scale as a means of measuring evil.[27] Locating himself firmly within the school of thought that considers evil as the explanation for terrorism, Welner then easily moved to considering what the signs of evil are in "jihadists" and how we might be able to predict who is and is not evil and who might be rehabilitated. As an expert for the prosecution, Welner assessed Khadr for "the risk for activities that would relate to violent or criminal expression of jihad"; for "the prospects for Omar Khadr's reintegration"; and for "whether there is a need for deradicalization with Omar Khadr or whether it can even be done with

Omar Khadr."[28] In the absence of actuarial data, Welner clarified that he had to go about learning about the population of "radical jihadists," beginning with the definition of "radical Islam" as distinguished from "traditional Islam."

It is important to pause here to follow the color line of the psychological radicalization model where Welner's assessment begins. Kundnani discusses the ideas behind a psychological radicalization model in his book *The Muslims Are Coming!* In the post-9/11 climate it was considered treasonous to consider the social and political roots of terrorism. Instead, terrorism was seen as originating in "the evil mind-set of the perpetrators."[29] While older forms of terrorism were understood to have political origins, "Islamic terrorism" was straightforwardly understood as originating in religious "fanaticism." Kundnani suggests that although this first step matured into a broader consideration of how terrorism develops, it was circumscribed by the demands of counterterrorism policy makers, whose interests lay in explaining terrorism as a product of how Islam was interpreted and not as a product of specific social and political circumstances.[30] Psychology and theology provided a comfortable ground on which such analyses can rest. With an emphasis on the individual psyche, it was not long before a mini-industry of scholars, intelligence analysts, and policy makers grew around the idea that Muslims move to "extremist" views because of an underlying cultural predisposition. Identifying the historian Walter Laqueur (ironically a scholar who has written persuasively of the social and political factors that produced the Holocaust)[31] as someone who provided a bridge between older "terrorism studies" and the new focus on the psyche, Kundnani shows how Laqueur, a Washington insider with connections as Israel's representative to the CIA-funded Congress for Cultural Freedom, developed the idea that al-Qaeda emerged because of Muslim religious commandment to jihad.[32] For Laqueur, Muslim communities in Europe failed to integrate and wanted to preserve a separate religious identity. In this environment, the second generation, sexually repressed and aggressive, and angry at non-Muslims, turned easily to "terrorism." As Kundnani notes, such explanations set the stage for a radicalization focus on religious beliefs, anti-Western attitudes, and youth alienation where "terrorism" is seen as a kind of virus that some people can catch. Law enforcement has

124 "Terrorism in Their Genes"

to prevent exposure but also to look for indicators of the patterns and beliefs that indicate "terrorist" risk.[33]

As I detailed in *Casting Out* regarding Canadian security cases in the first half of the decade, intelligence services seeking to detain Muslim men whom they believed had the potential to engage in "terrorist" activity needed only to make the case in court that the defendants had a profile that made them of use to al-Qaeda. Courts were by and large persuaded that those who held Muslim religious beliefs, who had certain histories (for example, those who went to Afghanistan during the 1980s), and who appeared "normal" were simply waiting for the ideal time when their true natures would be revealed.[34] Omar Khadr presented Welner with an ideal opportunity to illustrate the psychological and theological foundations of the process known as "Muslim radicalization." Since Welner was expected to assess whether or not Khadr could be "deradicalized," a process understood as involving an alternative interpretation of Islam, his assessment had to explore whether Khadr exhibited the signs that scholars such as Laqueur identified. Laqueur invited policy makers to examine the presence of anger and aggression and disaffection, as well as the extent and direction of religious commitment. The incoherence that is a feature of racial explanations gave Welner free rein to articulate his theories, and the military hearing at Guantánamo, as a space of law without law, restricted opportunities for challenging his views.

Omar Khadr was considered a violent "jihadist" because he threw a grenade that killed an American soldier. Khadr denies killing Speers, but he had to admit to it as part of the plea bargain for a lesser sentence and for the chance to return to Canada. The fact that he was fifteen, and that the circumstances of the firefight in which Speers was killed are in doubt have no bearing on the outcome. Khadr, Welner reminded the court, was a convicted war criminal. In Welner's words, "Well, he's murdered. He has been a part of Al Qaeda, and we're still at war."[35] Moreover, "the war is not ending soon." Under these circumstances, the "prognosis" for rehabilitation was grim. Welner considered whether Khadr was in a financial position to facilitate violent attacks and whether he was a leading figure who had the capacity to commit "terrorist" acts.[36] Since Khadr had no financial resources, Welner focused on his potential as a leader of jihad. It is here that the question of Muslim religiosity becomes central.

"Terrorism in Their Genes" 125

A leader of "jihad," for Welner, is someone who leads prayers and who inspires others through his increasing religiosity. Religious devotion in this formulation becomes a feature of "radical" behavior. To assess a "radical jihadist," something Welner had not previously done, Welner turned to Nicolai Sennels, maintaining that Sennels was one of very few people in the world who had studied young Muslims in a correctional setting and who had treated them therapeutically. It is Sennels's articulation of the psychological "radicalization" paradigm elaborated earlier by Laqueur that becomes the foundation of Welner's analysis.

Sennels's views are frequently profiled on a large number of anti-Muslim and white-supremacist blogs, something that was not brought out in court.[37] A young psychologist whose first job was working in a Danish youth prison, Sennels (who was fired for his anti-Muslim views) wrote a book titled *Among Criminal Muslims: A Psychologist's Experience from the Copenhagen Municipality*. In this book he presented his findings about the psychological characteristics of Muslim youth in prison. In his three years at the youth facility, Sennels claimed, he conducted individual and group therapy with 150 Muslim and 100 Danish clients (the terms Muslim and Danish are incommensurate for Sennels). He concluded that anyone reared in a Muslim environment was likely to develop antisocial patterns, because Muslim culture "supports the development of certain psychological characteristics."[38] Chief among these characteristics is Muslim proclivity for aggression and anger, particularly when criticized or made fun of, as in the Danish cartoon controversy. Muslims are also unable to take responsibility and to act autonomously. In Sennels's phrase, their "locus of control" is outer-determined rather than inner-determined. That is, Muslims are unable to decide how to live their own lives and are guided instead by "a fearsome God, a powerful father, influential imams, [and] ancient but strong cultural traditions."[39] Given these characteristics, they are unable to integrate into Western society, and Sennels has spent considerable time promoting his views that Muslim immigration to Europe should be halted. He believes that Muslims will always refuse to integrate, will push for the Islamization of Europe, and will provoke a "continent wide civil war."[40] For Welner, Sennels's work is especially pertinent because he compared Muslims to non-Muslims. Welner admired what he regarded as Sennels's humility. Sennels, he told

126 "Terrorism in Their Genes"

the military court, was not afraid to admit that he had failed in his therapeutic work in curing young Muslims of their religious propensity for violence. From Sennels, Welner concluded that remorse and Westernization were the two factors that led to "a positive prognosis."[41] Westernization, in this view, is the opposite of religiosity, and the religiously devout Muslim has the poorest prognosis of all of reintegrating into society.

The First Sign: Memorizing the Qur'an

For Welner, memorizing the Qur'an revealed that Khadr became more religious while in prison. He also saw this achievement as Khadr's rejection of secular studies. Cross-examined, Welner did not recall that Khadr had also explained to him that he had memorized the Qur'an because he didn't have much else to do and also because, even though he wanted to study medicine one day, he found it hard to slog through the high school science and math curriculum unaided. Asked about leading prayers, Khadr noted that since he was able to memorize the Qur'an while many others hadn't, he was able to lead the prayers.[42] Khadr represented his own religiosity as consisting of "living as strict as he can" and figuring out the meanings of the Qur'an by himself.[43] Admitting on cross-examination that "radical" and devout need not be the same thing, Welner insisted nonetheless that "The problem is radicalized jihadists who happen to be devout, because the more devout they are, the more it increases the risk of a poor prognosis."[44] In this logic, "radical jihadists," who are by definition devout because they believe in a holy war to establish Sharia, bear a special burden of showing that their religiosity is declining rather than increasing.

Religiosity has a major role to play in revealing the contours of the "terrorist" psyche. Drawing closely on Sennels, Welner concluded that Khadr's apparently increasing religiosity was a sign that he was fanatical, submissive to the will of others, and without remorse. Welner explained to the court what he derived from Sennels:

> [Sennels's] best sense is that part of the observance and adherence to Islam is submission, submission to the Qur'an, submission to what the Imam says, submission to paternal and superior influences and while that may cultivate obedience and it may enhance structure and order in a certain context. At the same time what

"Terrorism in Their Genes" **127**

he finds, as a clinician, a drawback of that is that it makes it much more difficult for somebody to be introspective. The locust [*sic*] of control that someone has on their life is always someone else. It's always someone else's fault. It's someone else who has control. And in someone who is more introspective and more self-reliant, the person takes responsibility, takes ownership, takes a look at the predicament they are in and says "What can I learn from this? How can I go forward? How can I better myself? How can I develop? How can I grow?" That, from his experience, is the best explanation for the relationship between how devout a person is and how that devoutness actually increases a risk of poor prognosis.[45]

Although the argument is declared to be about violent "jihadists," for both Sennels and Welner, the broader problem lies with Islam and with Muslim culture. Muslims "have a God that decides their life's course," Sennels has written, and clerics who tell them what to think and do.[46] Muslims, as unthinking fanatics who look to others for direction, only become more devout in prison and more devoted to the cause of jihad. Khadr is at particular risk of succumbing to what Welner never fails to represent as a disease with a poor prognosis. He lost his father and is particularly sensitive to "pseudo parents," "people who might be older and who might take him under their wing," and people who are ideologically hardened and mature, as are the detainees of Camp 4. (Camp 4 is one of the camps at Guantánamo where prisoners who are considered compliant live in communal dormitories.)[47] Notably, here Khadr is considered a child whereas throughout, he has been tried and sentenced for the crimes of an adult.

The Second Sign: The "Rock Star" Who Leads Prayers

Welner reported to the court that Khadr was considered by fellow detainees as a "rock star," with the capacity to inspire and lead them. He gleaned this information not from interviewing Khadr's fellow prisoners but from Khadr's interrogators and guards. Indifferent to the contradiction of a portrait of a "rock star" leader who is also submissive and seeking "pseudo parents," Welner's argument about the detainees of Camp 4 as ideologically hardened "jihadists" who both follow Khadr and influence him runs aground quickly, as even the prosecution seemed to have

128 "Terrorism in Their Genes"

recognized. Reminding Welner that Camp 4 detainees are supposed to be the most compliant of detainees (they are given the freedom to associate with each other), the prosecuting attorney, Captain Chris Eason asked Welner if their compliance might also mean that they were "deradicalized."[48] Welner is able to navigate these contradictions through appeal to a long-standing racist idea of the sleeper cell with its population of patient, calculating, and duplicitous "Orientals" (as the term was first used during World War II) waiting to strike at an unsuspecting West:

> Radicalized Islam works at its own timetable just because it is a—it is a movement that dreams and at some times actually implements apocalyptic violence doesn't mean that it doesn't have the patience to wait for opportunity. And many people who are housed in Camp 4 have extremely destructive pasts and legacies but they are just smart enough to know to follow the rules, and keep themselves quiet and compliant, and they will have an uneventful incarceration. And so this is the example that is provided for Omar Khadr and it's an example that he follows and so he is well behaved in the custodial environment as are they, but it does not at all speak to their mission; it does not at all speak to their ideology. What it does speak to is that Mr. Khadr, when he chooses, has perfectly good impulse control and in a certain kind of risk of dangerousness assessment that would be relevant. That's not the kind of risk of dangerousness assessment that I am asked to do here. I did not do a psychopathy checklist [PCLR]. I did not assess whether he is a psychopath or not. He may be, he may not be, but were I to have done that assessment, impulsivity, which is one of the measures of the PCLR, his time in Camp 4 reflects on him as someone who is not impulsive.[49]

Patient and calculating, and with "good impulse control," Khadr's good behavior and apparent rationality is only a cover until he can strike, an argument I have previously tracked in Canadian security cases where detainees are condemned for being too normal. A "rock star," someone who has memorized the Qur'an, a murderer, the revered son of the famous Ahmed Khadr, and someone who has even spent time with bin Laden, Khadr is also fluent in English, multilingual, charming, good at

"Terrorism in Their Genes" **129**

sports, and someone who has attracted NGO support. As Welner itemizes these qualities, he adds a few incidents that under cross-examination are revealed to be fabrications. For example, apparently wanting to check Khadr's interactions with non-Muslims, Welner tells the court that Khadr had a confrontation with an African American female guard, calling her a slut and a whore.[50] (He does not consider what might have provoked such an incident.) While Khadr acknowledged that he sometimes cursed at the guards out of frustration, it was also clear that he was not yet in Camp 4 when the incident with the guard took place. When they are revealed, such fabrications do not appear to damage Welner's credibility, a feature of legal processes that achieve their coherence from racist ideas.

Having entered the domain of religion, the violent "jihadist" can never emerge, a position that depends upon racial thinking, the idea that culture is innate and inheritable. "Deradicalization," Welner explains, means changing one's interpretation of the Qur'an, and there is little chance that this can happen in Omar's case because he has a family that is deeply "radicalized."[51] Using a biological metaphor of "a fungating tumor" that requires a skilled surgeon, Welner declares that the level of skill required to do the operation simply doesn't exist.[52] In fact, there is nothing that could interrupt Khadr's journey of "radicalism."

The Third Sign: Failure to Acculturate

The argument that violent "jihadists" have the capacity to seem otherwise carries the risk that we will not know one when we see one. Khadr generates anxiety, an anxiety comparable to long-standing white-supremacist anxieties about Jews who are regarded as deceptively white and normal but are behind-the-scenes manipulators.[53] Khadr is of the West but is not Western. How would we know whether a charming, apparently Westernized boy from Toronto is a seasoned, adult killer, steeped in Muslim and non-Western culture, and with the potential to lead a jihad? Khadr is the limit test for "jihadism" precisely because he does not appear to be the fully formed Middle Eastern Muslim "terrorist" and because he spent his childhood in both the West and the East. The anxiety is mitigated through an old sociobiological idea: Khadr carries his potential for dangerousness in his history. As inheritance, Khadr's culture and religion can only condemn him to his fate. He may look and sound like he is of

130 "Terrorism in Their Genes"

the West, but an Eastern cultural inheritance runs through his veins. He carries within him a predisposition for violence.

Welner is at pains to establish that while Khadr is from the West, he is not Westernized.[54] Rather, he is the quintessential duplicitous "Oriental" whose duplicity is never more apparent than when he appears most Western. It is not surprising, then, that any evidence that he is behaving as an ordinary Western teenager and then a young man of twenty-five becomes evidence that he is secretly a violent "jihadist." The question of Khadr's acculturation is complicated by the fact of his personality. As Welner acknowledged, Khadr was charming and comfortable with everybody and was therefore "very different from a number of the other al Qaeda folks that he would run into who are more limited in their cultural experience."[55] He seems normal. He reads Harry Potter novels, for example, which helped him (in his own words) to "just get away, to not think about things." For Welner, Khadr's indulging in "escapist literature" only indicated a desire to avoid facing reality and to dissociate from his environment.[56] Khadr was very angry about being in custody, Welner reported, and "does not involve himself in the kinds of things that would acculturate him to this Western environment." Welner is not pressed to say what such things might be at Guantánamo, or whether Khadr, imprisoned at fifteen and tortured, might in fact have reason to be angry, and reason to want to get away from it all, if only via a fantasy novel.

When, under cross-examination, Welner is asked to explain why Khadr also read books by Mandela and Obama, he refuses to reply on the grounds that he would need to see the exact place in the transcript of his interview with Khadr in order to comment. A rather transparent obstructionist tactic, Welner is never fully called to account for his selective use of the interview data. The same tactic serves him well when he is cross-examined about his conclusion that Khadr wishes to return to Canada, not because it is his native country, but because he wishes to replace civil law with Sharia law. As Khadr's defense counsel pointed out, Khadr communicated to Welner that he believed the opposite of what Welner alleges: in Khadr's words, "I can be a Muslim. You can be a Christian. It doesn't have to do with anything."[57] Welner again refuses to comment when Khadr's words are quoted, until he can see the transcript.

Since the defense cannot locate the exact page number for this quote, the matter is dropped after Welner offers an inchoate and rambling explanation for his belief that Khadr secretly wanted to establish Sharia law:

> Again, just as an example of the sort of cherry picking with one of the questions that had just come up only a couple of minutes ago about Mr. Khadr and—in which a question came up of whether he could be around Christians, the significance of that was I didn't even ask him that. But he was so coiled, and he was so calculated, and he was so ready for that question to come in that he took me to a different area. I merely wanted to ask him, "What's it like for you when you need to practice around people who don't share the same beliefs?" Not whether you're willing to live with anyone. I mean, look, there are Christians in Tehran. There are gays in Tehran. While the leader there wants to destroy the world, and it doesn't mean that you can't practice Christianity.
>
> You know just because somebody espouses a theocracy, it doesn't mean that they're not aware or may even be friendly to people practicing something else, as long as they are submissive. You know, that's—and that's the way a theocracy would work. Now that's not a reflection on Mr. Khadr. He's devout in his belief. I just wanted to get a feel for him. That's all I was after.[58]

The vagueness of racist thought is a reminder about the racial fantasies at work and the incoherence that accompanies them. The "all over the place-ness" quality of racism that Ghassan Hage identifies is fully in evidence in Welner's meandering explanations of Khadr's psyche.[59] Questions are rhetorical, and logic is beside the point. Khadr wants to establish Sharia law in Canada but hides his true intentions with an apparent broad-mindedness. His Westernized tastes are merely evidence of his deception. Legal procedures permit the incoherence to stand, as the attempts by the defense to point out Welner's selectivity and the contradictions of his claims come to naught because the appropriate pages of Welner's interview with Khadr were not marked and tagged in advance. The defense asks questions that remain rhetorical. The logical circularity of Welner's argument goes unchallenged. No one pursues how Welner knows that Khadr killed in order to martyr himself or how he knows that Khadr is

132 "Terrorism in Their Genes"

"al Qaeda royalty." There is no need for serious consideration of these matters, and they can be dealt with in sound bites gleefully consumed by the media and replayed for several years.[60]

Nowhere does the legal process seem more complicit in providing a platform for white-supremacist beliefs than when Welner is challenged about his reliance on the work of Nicolai Sennels. Welner acknowledges that although he relies on Sennels, he really does not know a great deal about the man or his work. His knowledge of Sennels was mainly based on a telephone conversation with him. Cross-examination of Welner begins with the inability of the defense to say Sennels's name correctly. Defense counsel Major Matthew Schwartz establishes that Welner has not interviewed other "jihadists" and had no prior experience with evaluating the future dangerousness of a "jihadi."[61] Sennels, it seems, is Welner's only source of information. Asked about the peer review process and the details of Sennels's research (which Sennels himself has made clear in interviews was not a research project), Welner reiterates that he was impressed with Sennels because he acknowledged that he had failed to "deradicalize jihadists" (because they are beyond help). Sennels's research methodology, he elaborates, was simply that he worked with Muslim patients and treated them therapeutically. Research has no place in the military hearing when it involves Muslims.

The defense presented Welner with three short articles and an open letter to British prime minister David Cameron, all written by Sennels or featuring interviews with him (and widely circulated on the internet on a number of Islamophobic blogs and websites). The court is not told where these articles appear, and the vague discussion about peer review and its meaning only hints that Sennels does not do academic research. Welner is unable to confirm that he has read any of Sennels's work. He responds that he recognizes only some parts. He is surprised when he learns from the defense that Sennels is only thirty-three years old. He has never seen interviews with Sennels about his book, nor has he seen the open letter Sennels wrote to Cameron in which he urges the prime minister to deny Turkey entrance into the European Union because Muslims are unable to integrate into European society. Welner recognizes some parts of Sennels's article on the psychological differences between Westerners and Muslims, but when asked about Sennels's opinions about "Muslim inbreeding," in an article in which Sennels refers to the "catastrophically damaged gene pool" of Muslims, Welner repeats that he does not find these ideas relevant and so did not read them. Given time to peruse the documents over lunch, he is asked whether the articles have changed his opinion of Sennels. Confident to the end, Welner replied that the articles are "just a political comment from a political opinion," adding, "I believe I heard Chancellor Angela Merkel say something of the sort probably within the last 2 weeks."[62] The cross-examination ends with Welner maintaining that he agrees with a significant amount of the content of Sennels's work.[63]

Welner's views remained the key testimony about Khadr's "risk of dangerousness." As *Toronto Star* reporter Michelle Shephard reported, when forensic psychiatrist Marc Sageman rebutted Welner's professional expertise in the field of "terrorism," the military judge presiding over Khadr's case "allegedly quipped to the defense that 'Dr. Welner would have been as likely to be accurate if he had used a Ouija board.'"[64] No one, it seemed, expected an expert on evil to make sense. In the strange ending to Khadr's sentencing hearing, an avowed white supremacist, Nicolai Sennels, is held up as an expert, and his anti-Muslim rhetoric remains on record as scholarly research. Welner's credibility is not damaged by his lack of familiarity with Sennels, an ignorance that puts in doubt his own scholarly expertise and record, and his refusal to condemn Sennels for his racist views. Instead, Welner feels free to state that after reading the materials on Sennels provided by the defense, that "Dr. Sennels' work is actually more impressive than I ever gave him credit for."[65] If we are tempted at this point to believe that Khadr's sentencing hearing was meant to be a farce, that impression is solidified when Welner closes his testimony with an opinion that dispenses with the arguments around religiosity made earlier and stresses instead that it is Khadr's history and his family and his supposed capacity "to inspire and to be incendiary" that indicate his future dangerousness.[66] History, family, and an inherent deviousness make the case for future dangerousness. Blood, it seems, trumps all.

It is instructive to end this exploration of white-supremacist views in Omar Khadr's sentencing hearing with a psychiatrist who worked with Khadr's defense team and who was not called to testify. Retired U.S. Army brigadier general Stephen N. Xenakis, a child and adolescent psychiatrist who assessed Khadr and found that he shows no proclivity for committing "terrorist" acts, wrote to the *Washington Post* expressing his outrage at Welner's testimony.

> As I listened to the prosecution's expert testimony depicting Khadr's state of mind, I was reminded of psychiatry and the politicization of mental health under the Soviet regime. Those were the years when political dissidents were accused of insanity simply because they had the audacity to challenge the Soviet system. The medical profession, especially psychiatry, was a political instrument of control and repression.[67]

What I can add to this is that racial thinking—the belief that Muslims carry the seeds of fanaticism and irrationality in their culture—helps to smooth the way to this repression. Psychiatry is best able to work as a political instrument of repression when it is harnessed to ideas about humanity and subhumanity.

Gene pool and heritability claims are never claims divorced from racial hierarchy. Though they may sound like pseudoscientific gibberish, they contribute to the sentencing hearing's legitimacy and make possible the accomplishment of its objective: Khadr received a forty-year sentence, reduced to eight years in a plea deal. Their effects go far beyond Khadr, however. Productive of white European subjectivity as a superior state of being, blood narratives bring race into existence far beyond Guantánamo. Like a tidal wave, stories about "catastrophically damaged gene pools" travel through the media, wiping out any good sense in its path. We come to believe in the truth it establishes, or worse, that we have no need of any truth but the truth of race. Resisting the urge to quarantine the narratives in which Welner trafficked at Khadr's sentencing hearing merely as pseudoscientific or illustrative of the absurdities of Guantánamo's military commissions, I examine below the provenance of these ideas and the work that blood narratives about Muslims do as they travel through contemporary society.

"Stained Blood" and Other Stories

Established to determine if Jews, Muslims, and others deemed heretics posed a threat to national security, the Spanish Inquisition pursued its goals by attempting to determine who held beliefs or engaged in life practices that threatened the state. The Inquisition did not concern itself with

"Terrorism in Their Genes" **135**

crime but with what we might today call pre-crime (a focus on crimes not yet committed in order to identify criminals before they have committed an offense, as in the film *Minority Report*),[68] the identification of those with *limpieza de sangre* (stained blood) who could not erase the stains of a heretical religious past and who possessed latent qualities of disloyalty. In these respects, the Inquisition bears a close resemblance to the contemporary security hearing. Accused Muslim prisoners who lead prayers, or indeed who pray at all, those whose histories include a too close familial relation to people and places now deemed "terrorist," and those who are imagined to be hiding their disloyalty behind a cloak of normalcy, are marked as possessing a latent capacity to be violent. In her exploration of stained blood as it operated in colonial Mexico, María Elena Martínez concludes that religion, lineage, and blood organized the Spanish colonial world.[69] Martínez emphasizes that racial discourses were remarkably flexible, invoking nature, biology, and culture interchangeably. Heretical tendencies were considered to have been learned from parents, and "blood was a metaphor for indoctrination within the family rather than for biological reproductive purposes."[70]

As in Catholic Spain and colonial Mexico, religion, lineage, and blood provide the bedrock upon which rests the claims of those who maintain that Muslims have "terrorism" in their genes. And, as in those contexts, blood functions as a metaphor for heritability. Ideas of heritability proliferate among right-wing and white-supremacist ideologues[71] and are invested with an academic and feminist patina—glosses we find in the journals devoted to evolutionary psychology and to "terrorism studies." Some of the earliest articulations of blood discourses occur in the work of scholars who sought to explain "suicide terrorism" committed by "Islamic terrorists." For many of these scholars, the context most commonly discussed is Israel/Palestine. For example, tabloid realism[72]—controversial and extravagant claims and phrases—is the defining feature of the work of Satoshi Kanazawa, an American-born British evolutionary psychologist based at the London School of Economics. Kanazawa, known for his incendiary opinions and florid writing style, is often a subject of protest. (The students of Northwestern University, for example, protested his guest lectureship there, pointing to his articles "Are All Women Prostitutes?" and "What's Wrong with Muslims?"; the students were able to secure a promise from the administration that guest lecturers would be

136 "Terrorism in Their Genes"

better vetted in the future.)[73] In his article "The Evolutionary Psychological Imagination: Why You Can't Get a Date on a Saturday Night and Why Most Suicide Bombers Are Muslims," published in the *Journal of Social, Evolutionary, and Cultural Psychology* in 2007, Kanazawa claims that Muslim men are conducting suicide bombings because they want to have sex with seventy-two virgins in heaven. He offers his own contribution to evolutionary psychology, named the Savanna Principle, an argument repeatedly circulated in *Psychology Today* and other journals[74] that "the human brain has difficulty comprehending and dealing with entities and situations that did not exist in the ancestral environment."[75] Circulating the idea of the significance of ancestral environment, Kanazawa's claims rehabilitate biological racial differences, differences that emerge out of geography and an unchanging culture and religion.

As they apply to Muslims, arguments about biological racial differences often take this turn through the ancestral and the cultural. The biological as metaphor easily twists into a story about heritability. Nancy Hartevelt Kobrin, a psychoanalyst and self-described "counterterrorism specialist" who works with military, law enforcement, and mental health professionals, is the author of four books that discuss the Muslim psyche.[76] Kobrin has also enthusiastically introduced the work of Nicolai Sennels, an indicator of the tightly formed networks of "terrorism" experts.[77] Departing from a strictly genetic explanation in that she argues that nobody is born a "terrorist," Kobrin maintains that "Islamic suicide bombers" and the "jihadis'" "lack of empathy" can all be explained by their early childhood.[78] Beginning with the extraordinary claim that "Islamic suicide terrorism" is a new variant of domestic violence, Kobrin explains that Muslim children experience their mothers being physically and mentally abused by their fathers. Such children are not "loved and hugged appropriately," and the baby boy, who wants nothing more than to bond with his mother, is destined to be thwarted. Frustration builds, turning boys into men who are full of rage and sexual frustration, feelings that come to be expressed in "terrorism." Littered with sensationalist claims (for example, that Muslim/Arab families routinely masturbate their sons' penises to enlarge them), Kobrin's book *The Banality of Suicide Terrorism* offers a detailed psychological portrait of the dysfunctional Muslim/Arab family. An introduction by feminist psychologist Phyllis Chesler (Chesler is well known for her presence in organizations in Islamophobia net-

"Terrorism in Their Genes"   137

works and for her books which discuss that Islamic "fundamentalism" threatens women and that critics of Israel are anti-Semitic)[79] succinctly sums up Kobrin's key points as contributions intended "for those who love America and Israel." She writes that Kobrin has enabled us to see that "barbarism is normalized within the Arab and Muslim family" and that "Islamic suicide terrorism may also be psychologically understood as 'displaced rage against one's childhood mother.'"[80] In this view, Arab/Muslim mothers, targets of abuse themselves, pass on the violence directed against them.[81]

Kobrin has circulated her ideas for more than a decade, maintaining the same links between psychology, culture, and passed-down qualities that amount to a latent capacity for violence. Her articles and books on "jihadi terrorism," for instance, build on the idea that Muslim children grow up with feelings of revenge directed at the world, and at Jews in particular. Referencing neuroscientists who claim that brain imaging reveals that even six-month-old babies can already possess problems with aggression, and expanding on her theory that "jihadis" lack empathy, Kobrin cites works that discuss the link between "Islamic terrorism" and autism, domestic violence, and children reared in "shame honor cultures."[82] Emphasizing the devalued females of "honor cultures" and the "tribal thinking" inspired by the Prophet Muhammad, a heritage that produces cognitively impaired children and men, Kobrin alerts those in the "terrorism" field to pay attention to "dismantling ticking human bombs before they detonate."[83]

Others sound the same warning notes about the destructive core of Muslim culture. In *The Path to Paradise: The Inner World of Suicide Bombers and Their Dispatchers*, Anat Berko makes claims identical to Kobrin's, using the same concepts and words. Claiming to have accessed the inner world of suicide bombers through prison interviews with those who dispatched suicide bombers or those whose bombs did not go off, Berko describes a dysfunctional Palestinian family "that has lost much of its patriarchal power and is suffering from a process of disintegration."[84] Arab children, under the thumb of their parents, "direct their feelings of jealousy, inferiority, and deprivation at Israel and the West in general."[85] Anxious to please their mothers specifically, whose daily abuse they witness, boys grow into men who have trouble realizing their masculinity. Farhad Khosrokhavar pursues the same psychological line, arguing that

138 "Terrorism in Their Genes"

Muslim men act out of an injured masculinity because they have been vanquished by the West and can only hope to "humiliate the humiliator."[86] Since in this view Muslims do not dread death and in fact wish it for the sake of Islam, men who are emasculated in this way turn to a politics of death. Together, such books and articles form a small corpus of works that circulate on websites devoted to anti-Muslim projects.[87] They have had an impact on policy and find resonance with increasingly popular ideas from the fields of genetics and epigenetics.

It is tempting to dismiss evolutionary psychologists as a fringe group and to consider their work to be in limited circulation and confined to a particular genre that features ideas about dysfunctional races and cultures. It is important, however, to remember the enduring link between racial science and politics, and to note the vigor with which such ideas are circulated by elites. Tom Griffin, David Miller, and Tom Mills, writing about the think tanks of the neoconservative movement and their impact on Islamophobia, offer the instructive example of the importance of the ideas of Daniel Patrick Moynihan, a policy analyst in the Johnson administration whose writing about the dysfunctional "Negro family" (a dysfunction he attributed to the higher numbers of single-parent families led by women) had considerable circulation and influence. As they remind us, the idea of dysfunctional Black families enabled the state to dismiss Black claims for justice.[88] As several scholars have shown, evolutionary psychology ideas inform policy initiatives around the issue of "deradicalization" and the prevention of "terrorism," initiatives underpinned by the same arguments that meld biology, culture, and religion and that identify the "Islamically inspired terrorist" as a product of his cultural and religious environment.[89] Reviewing scholarship on "radicalization" and political discourse, Jonathan Githens-Mazer concludes that government reports unfailingly reduce the phenomenon of "radicalization" to Muslims and to their "breeding grounds." Scholars offering a more complex account of the causes of violence still focus their efforts exclusively on Muslims.[90]

Those who write about the pathological Islamic family and the cultural and religious roots of "radicalization" are of interest to, and are often funded by, Zionist political interests, as Said and other scholars noted. For example, as Sarah Marusek traces, there is considerable

Zionist funding of Islamophobic texts and their circulation in policy circles and on websites.[91] Kobrin's work is regularly featured on the website of the Clarion Project, a nonprofit organization that describes itself as educating the public about the dangers of "radical Islam."[92] The recipient of multiple grants, and enjoying the patronage of notable anti-Muslim ideologues, Clarion produces films that emphasize patriarchal and "extremist Islam."[93] It maintains a website on which users can learn of "extremist" groups in their area. The list includes individuals and organizations whose connections to "extremist" movements can be as remote as pointing out that Hamas funds hospitals in Gaza. It would not be too far-fetched to conclude that such sites incite persecution. For example, Congresswomen Ilhan Omar, who has received death threats for her criticisms of Israel, is regularly featured as an anti-Semitic sympathizer of "terrorists." Academics who voice the same criticisms are also labeled "extremist" and become persecuted for their views.[94] Clarion takes care to include as regular contributors "moderate Muslims" who are able to denounce "terrorism" in the name of their own religious beliefs. As Nathan Lean reminds us, the "Islamophobia industry" comprises "a ferocious squad of propagandists" as well as "a more measured group of policy-oriented warriors who inject prejudiced view of Muslims and Islam into legislative and governmental arenas."[95] If each group supports the other, as Lean suggests, it is also the case that anti-Muslim ideologues and scholars draw support from a wider social context in which ideas about genetics and race have strong popular support and are widely promoted by elites.

Conclusion: Biology as Destiny

In *Superior: The Return of Race Science*, journalist Angela Saini opens with a claim: "No place or people has a claim on superiority."[96] The counterargument is that we are born different with innate qualities and capacities that explain the progress of the groups to which ancestry has confined us. Saini's critics typically begin with Charles Darwin. As Bo Winegard and Noah Carl, reviewers who are critical of Saini's book, offer:

> The truth, as we see it, is that human populations differ in important and fascinating ways, and they do so for straightforward evolutionary reasons: such populations have been living in different

140 "Terrorism in Their Genes"

environments from one another, under different regimes of selection, for thousands of years. Saini wants us to ignore the basic tenets of Darwinism. Moreover, she wants us to equate any claim that genes might contribute to psychological differences between populations with racism.[97]

The psychological differences between populations, articulated by Welner, Sennels, Kobrin, and others and endorsed by these reviewers, is at the very heart of the claims of racial science in our time. The genetic basis to psychological differences in *populations* has powerful political utility. Genetic arguments concerning the existence of race hail us into an imaginary where the white European subject as a superior subject has far outpaced all others. As Angela Saini observes, at the time when race labels such as "black" or "white" emerged, the "power hierarchy had white people of European descent sitting at the top" and inevitably understood as the "natural winners" of the genetics game.[98]

The crux of the matter, as Dorothy Roberts has written, is the "devastating political consequences"[99] of a world so persistently imagined as racially structured. In her book *Fatal Invention,* Roberts puts it starkly: "The state's power to control life and death relies on classifying people by race."[100] When the state of California collects DNA samples from everyone who is arrested, becoming the third-largest DNA bank in the world, and when DNA is used to identify populations imagined as predisposed to crime, it is only a short step to determining that it is acceptable to police and punish such populations. A dehumanizing brutality against such targeted populations becomes necessary.[101]

From Abu Ghraib to torture in U.S. prisons to the caging of children at borders, damaged gene pools mandate such violence. We become inured to the violence through a casual belief, instilled by racial science and circulated widely, that some populations are simply more genetically advanced than others. It becomes possible to accept that a gene exists that shows a predisposition to join gangs, as one study purportedly showed.[102] Studies show that people who believe Black people are uniquely descended from apes also condone police brutality against them.[103] Roberts's impassioned argument about the consequences of the ideology of biological race is amply demonstrated in the case of Muslims. If we can believe that the higher fertility rates of less-intelligent groups

"Terrorism in Their Genes" 141

produce social disparities, an argument made in the book *The Bell Curve,* we are certainly easily primed to accept that Muslims carry genes that predispose them to violence.[104]

Those who appeal to genetics to argue that racial differences are real emphasize that the truth of racial difference is intuitive to most people. We can see it. What this ignores, of course, is the meaning we ascribe to what we see. Both genetic and epigenetic arguments have anchored claims that race is real. In her study of the biopolitics of emotion, Kyla Schuler shows that from the nineteenth century on, the key idea installing racial hierarchy was not biological race but the notion that humans are impressible and always changing in response to environment. The question became who was most capable of evolutionary change and who remained unable to move out of a state of nature.[105]

Epigenetics begins with the premise that genes and environment interact, changing the chemical composition of genes and altering which genes get expressed and which do not. The right kind of educational environment can alter, for instance, how mental illness develops. However, as the *New York Review of Books* contributors Israel Rosenfield and Edward Ziff have suggested in their review of recent books on epigenetics, the field "has also made clear that the stress caused by war, prejudice and other forms of childhood adversity may have consequences both for the persons affected and for their future—unborn—children, not only for social and economic reasons but also for biological ones."[106] The Muslim male subject loses in two ways in this epigenetic field. First, he may be considered to have a damaged gene pool owing to long-standing cultural practices. Second, his already biologically impaired makeup deteriorates rapidly in the environment of the Muslim family, whether it is that of war or everyday cultural and religious life. As critical disability studies scholar Tanya Titchkosky comments, the growing belief in epigenetics that the first two thousand days in a child's life matter most enables researchers and, I would add, ideologues, to home in on mothers and caregivers and on familial environment: "The focus becomes what do adults and their environments make of a child's pre-given genetic material," Titchkosky writes.[107] As we have seen with Kobrin and Chesler, the Muslim child has no hope in this respect; he is unable to rely on his abused mother, and what may have begun as a minor genetic predisposition soon devolves

142 "Terrorism in Their Genes"

into an inherent capacity for "terrorism" through his mother's and his family's failure to nurture him.

Inhabiting both law and popular culture, the figure of the Muslim in racial science contributes a great deal to the argument for global white supremacy. A newly targeted group as well as an old one, Muslims are easily cast in the story of ancestral gene pools gone amok. As with other groups so marked, racial science does not have to make sense. Instead, networks of powerful interest install the figures of civilized Europeans and their opposite, "Islamic terrorists." The historian Linda Gordon notes that mid-nineteenth-century ideologues who promoted ideas of racial science were elite men whose status enabled them to pass off bogus claims as science.[108] The same is true for today as well-funded networks circulate the idea of Muslims as possessing a damaged gene pool. As Roberts makes clear, racial science makes it possible to accept a never-ending brutality against racialized groups, whether in wartime or peace-time, as it has in the past for eugenic projects. As outlandish as the claims argued at Guantánamo or in the pages of *Evolutionary Psychology* are, they perform an eviction of Muslims from political community. In their compatibility with prevailing popular ideas about genetics, they contrib-ute to global race making in ways that are far from small.

In her discussion of the promise of Sylvia Wynter's work for social justice, Katherine McKittrick argues passionately that "scientific racism cannot have the last word."[109] The biometric model of humanity (racial-anatomical difference) and "Darwinian 'survival of the fittest' narratives seep into our intellectual struggles and consequently render particular academics and their projects more likely to *naturally* (read: economically) survive the world than those of their nonconforming counterparts."[110] Racial science is not easily countered by showing that groups have outper-formed what we might expect from their genetic or epigenetic forecasts. Wynter emphasizes that we end up simply arguing how humans move up and down the evolutionary scale, entrenching in the process Man (a bio-economic being) as fully human and all others as defective and endlessly catching up. In McKittrick's words, we fail to radically unsettle "Man-as-white-heterosexual-breadwinner-and-measuring-stick-of-human-normalcy, or Man-as-human," unless we challenge "*where* humanness takes place."[111] Placing her faith instead in the artist who "solders together self, flesh, physiology, and the word-bios-mythoi, cognition-neurology-creativity, phylogeny-ontogeny-sociogeny,"[112] McKittrick reminds us that we cannot look for humanness in a science intent on demarcating levels of humanity. The same is true for law premised on installing the boundaries of the universal and establishing those who must be violently excluded from it.

CHAPTER 4

"We Didn't Kill 'em, We Didn't Cut Their Heads Off"

Torture and the Making of American Innocence

Memory says, "I did that." Pride replies, "I could not have done that."
Eventually, memory yields.

—FRIEDRICH NIETZSCHE

How can one examine the experience of phenomenal violence without giving in to explanatory categories that mitigate it, fetishize it, or turn it into pornography?

—ANUPAMA RAO AND STEVEN PIERCE,
"DISCIPLINE AND THE OTHER BODY: HUMANITARIANISM,
VIOLENCE, AND THE COLONIAL EXCEPTION"

If, as chapter 3 shows, brutality and torture become authorized and acceptable when we are able to imagine Muslims as requiring violence, how do torturers and their communities live with torture? Memory must insulate the psyche and protect us from the possibility that we have inflicted harm and wanton violence upon another. To believe that we are innocent of torture, we must work hard to establish that barbarians require force. As the torturers at Abu Ghraib prison reveal, establishing innocence is a collective project that requires the assistance of lawmakers and cultural producers alike. Few can walk the path alone—a reminder that we are all implicated in racial violence.

In this chapter I discuss cultural memory of the torture of prisoners at Abu Ghraib prison by American coalition forces during the occupation of Iraq in 2003–4. If the nation remembers that American soldiers tortured Iraqi prisoners, memory yields to pride, as Nietzsche famously

145

146 "We Didn't Kill 'em, We Didn't Cut Their Heads Off"

said. The cultural memory of torture at Abu Ghraib is thus not one of torture at all but rather a memory of a traumatic moment in the nation's history when Americans, and not Iraqis, encountered a horror they had not known before. Remembering neither the victims of torture nor the Iraqi community upon whom extraordinary violence has been visited, American soldiers who engaged in torture and the American nation itself recall only that all were duped by unscrupulous leaders and pressed into service to discipline and keep in line an Islamic enemy. Innocence, the Caribbean Canadian poet Dionne Brand observes, referring to white people who refuse to acknowledge their implication in transatlantic slavery and its afterlives, is "politically, economically and psychically lucrative."[1] Memory transforms a tremendous violence into a lucrative innocence. It enables the soldiers and the imperial nation of which they are a part to leave the violence behind, ready to start life anew once the occupation ended. The cleansing that memory provides leaves Iraqis excised from the story of the occupation, neither victims who suffered nor moral subjects. Memory may thus be regarded as one more item in the constellation of U.S. power in a region where "the horrific effects of U.S. power cannot be overstated."[2]

How does memory yield to pride, transforming torture into the trauma endured by the torturer? In popular culture, and in the film discussed in this chapter, *Standard Operating Procedure,* American soldiers at Abu Ghraib are not remembered as torturers; indeed, the word *torturer* is rarely uttered in connection with Abu Ghraib. Instead, the nation remembers its soldiers duped into "prisoner abuse" by their duplicitous leaders. The innocence of the torturers stands in marked contrast to the duplicity and capacity for "evil" that is associated with the tortured, as was believed of Omar Khadr, the Canadian teenager tortured by U.S. forces at Bagram and Guantánamo and discussed in the preceding chapter. It goes without saying that the innocence of the torturers in popular culture is also the innocence of the nation, a story of American exceptionalism that is achieved through the tortured bodies of an Islamic enemy.

Cultural practices are a form of historical remembrance. Offering the term "historical remembrance" to describe the way that cultural practices interpret the past, drawing on both memory and history, Jay Winter observes that historical remembrance unites people.[3] There is something

"We Didn't Kill 'em, We Didn't Cut Their Heads Off" **147**

of the familial about it. The film *Standard Operating Procedure* is not just a history nor just a memory, but instead a stage where people who share a familial bond face their shared past together. Emphasizing that remembrance is performative and that "it is materialized in the gestures and statements of the actors, those whose actions constitute remembrance," Winter offers us a way to think about how a film that purports to tell critical truths about an occupation becomes instead a part of war making and empire, an active and embodied forging of national community and empire long after the occupiers have gone home.[4]

Remembering begins immediately, even before the torturer leaves the site of torture. If spectacular forms of violent discipline are reserved for those beyond the pale of rationality, torture at Abu Ghraib is memorialized in the same way as colonial violence: as "grim necessity in dealing with a reified other."[5] The thousands of photographs of torture at Abu Ghraib materialized an ideological enemy that required torture and translated the prisoners' suffering into American triumph. The alchemy was only possible because the Islamic enemy as imperial enemy par excellence was already well known. Approached as a culturally different kind of enemy who required culturally specific torture, it was a short distance from cultural difference to racial difference and to levels of humanity with which Americans were already deeply familiar. As Angela Davis insightfully observes of torture at Abu Ghraib, "to explain the tortures within this pseudo-cultural framework is to define the people who are being tortured as already inferior."[6]

In the prisons of the "war on terror," including Abu Ghraib, Guantánamo, Bagram, and a host of secret sites, torture was from the beginning narrated as grim necessity and as aberrational, a contradiction reconciled through the idea that the Islamic enemy always requires violence. Remembered as practices of "abuse" taking place in exceptional spaces against an exceptionally violent enemy in an exceptional time, torture's connection to empire and to the routine practices of American prisons is repressed and rendered ghostly. The special circumstances of the "war on terror" and an enemy especially deserving of torture transform torture into nothing more than an enhanced interrogation technique. From bakers to generals, all those confined at Abu Ghraib were scripted as carrying the seeds of violence in their own bodies, a situation that required

148 "We Didn't Kill 'em, We Didn't Cut Their Heads Off"

violence from their jailors. The prisoners' lesser personhood provides coherence to the legal story that is told about the acceptability of torture and its transformation into practices that are simultaneously regarded as aberrational and as standard operating procedure.

The cultural memory discussed in this chapter, the story of duplicitous leaders and likable torturers, is mainly circulated among critics of torture, those who believe that the torture of prisoners at Abu Ghraib was not the work of a few bad apples, as the Bush administration claimed, but was instead legally authorized interrogation techniques that were endorsed by the state and a part of governmental practice in U.S. prisons. Decrying the Bush administration's policies, critics emphasize the legal excesses of the "war on terror," thereby reifying the "war on terror" as an exceptional war. The story of exceptionality installs an innocent America and obscures the war making of an empire. The connection between torture and empire disappears, and we do not see how torture is the story of imperial/racial power written on the bodies of the tortured and on the social body. Tortured prisoners slip from view amid the policy debates about the legalities of torture, their transformation into abstract objects made possible not only by an abiding belief in U.S. hegemony and the rightness of American presence in Iraq but also by the failure of the region's Arab inhabitants to come into view as human beings. Even critics of torture policies could not see them, and they are rarely mentioned as persons with real lives and families. When the profound suffering of the tortured prisoner is eclipsed, "it reveals the extent to which the reverberations of morality can support the very racism that enabled the torture in the first place."[7]

The argument I make in this chapter is as follows: cultural memory of torture at Abu Ghraib constructs a story of likable torturers and duplicitous leaders that is told in *Standard Operating Procedure*. The story sidesteps the wrongness of torture committed against a racialized Other, replacing it with the story of American innocence and a people betrayed by their leaders. Exceptionalist constructions of the United States, Gwen D'Arcangelis points out, reverses the story of American aggression by installing an America at the mercy of Iraq, al-Qaeda, and other Arab/ Muslim groups and nations.[8] The story of national fragility traffics in discourses of feminized vulnerability where the nation is itself feminized

"We Didn't Kill 'em, We Didn't Cut Their Heads Off"   **149**

and where all soldiers, but white women in particular, feature as emblems of the nation's vulnerability. As I discuss below, vulnerable white female soldiers were especially necessary to the story of Abu Ghraib as a story of American innocence, given that the women were themselves torturers. The story of vulnerable soldiers confronted by an especially barbaric enemy in a barbaric place creates a moral community that approves of torture and is ultimately complicit in the project of empire. Cast only as people in the wrong place at the wrong time, American soldiers who tortured their prisoners are never portrayed as a part of a brutal occupation. Involving as it does a complete erasure of the geopolitical role of the United States in global domination and requiring a menacing Islamic enemy who could only be controlled through torture, the story of duplicitous leaders and innocent soldiers is a quintessential and lucrative story of empire.

In the first section that follows, I consider the racial line that runs through torture, starting with the idea that torture is a narrative of power written on the body of the tortured and on the social body, a line intended to establish the victory of civility over savagery. I emphasize the imperialist and Orientalist fantasy that runs through torture, the notion that a culturally different enemy requires torture. I make the argument that race, the hierarchy invoked by one of the female soldiers who tortured prisoners at Abu Ghraib, Lynndie England, in the title of this chapter, is crucial to the persistence of torture *and* to cultural memory of it. Although I make passing reference to them, I devote little space to those narratives that openly endorse what went on at Abu Ghraib. I do not discuss Hollywood films that continue to render torture as necessary in the "war on terror," such as *Zero Dark Thirty* and *The Hurt Locker.*[9] Instead, I examine *Standard Operating Procedure* by the noted filmmaker Errol Morris, a documentary that is critical of what happened at Abu Ghraib and that takes an anti-torture stance.[10]

It is the greatest of ironies that those who are critical of torture contribute to the story of American innocence and that their contributions install white goodness and Islamic barbarity and affirm that white vulnerability legitimates imperial violence. In the second section, I examine anti-torture narratives and their installation of likable torturers. Focusing on *Standard Operating Procedure,* I show that what critics of Abu

Ghraib have emphasized is the innocence of soldiers who participated in torture. The emphasis in these anti-torture narratives is on the feelings of the torturers, who in the main feel sorry for themselves. In this redemptive narrative, the lives of those who were tortured do not come in for consideration, and the narrative of torture as a triumph of civility over savagery remains in place. A moral community is created that at worst approves of torture and at best is not disturbed by the suffering of those who have been tortured. The redemption that both torture and its memorialization offer is long lasting, enabling Americans to continue to know themselves as humanitarians who suffered a national tragedy from a merciless Islamic enemy.

In 2009 President Barack Obama declared that "America does not torture" and that "a new era of engagement has begun."[11] By then, Abu Ghraib had been rebuilt, ironically, in the image of a model American prison. Obama's words are often considered to have ushered America officially into a "post-torture" age, but it should not be forgotten that President George W. Bush had also declared in 2007 that America does not torture.[12] Despite his ringing declarations, under President Obama there was little accountability for torture, and Guantánamo remains open for business. Torture continues apace, at Guantánamo and at black sites where "terror" suspects are sent for interrogation. The force feeding of detainees, a practice many maintain is torture, remains authorized although carefully kept away from the public eye.[13] Secret prisons remain secret, and less-secret ones are renamed.[14] Throughout, Americans as a people remain innocent of torture and empire, their innocence reaffirmed each time the fabric is rent and they are confronted anew with evidence of torture at American prisons abroad. In December 2019, graphic illustrations of his torture drawn by Guantánamo detainee Abu Zubaydah and released in a report written by his lawyer attracted little national attention or critical introspection. Americans appeared to have moved on. Paradoxically, the illustrations of Abu Zubaydah may have operated to cement into American consciousness that torture, if it happened at all, is something an empire has to do, and can do with impunity when confronted with terrorist masterminds of the Arab/Muslim variety. As with the photos of the torture at Abu Ghraib, the illustrations are both a reminder and a reenactment of the force of imperial power: look how we

"We Didn't Kill 'em, We Didn't Cut Their Heads Off" **151**

can stuff a full-grown man into a small box for hours, making him "scream unconsciously" from the muscle pains he endures.[15] In October 2021 the U.S. Supreme Court began hearing arguments concerning whether Abu Zubaydah can subpoena testimony from the CIA contractors who supervised his torture, a national moment in which torture may be simultaneously acknowledged (in the form of widespread coverage of the torture in the public narratives of both Abu Zubaydah and the CIA contractors who tortured him) and denied (if the Supreme Court declines to hear both their testimonies).[16]

Torture and a Culturally Different Enemy

What are the explanatory categories that mitigate violence, fetishize it, or turn it into pornography, questions Anupama Rao and Steven Pierce ask in the epigraph above? If it is abundantly clear that torture is an American tradition upheld by all segments of the political spectrum, it is also true that the nation has always debated its legitimacy.[17] Race is the explanatory category that is always key to these debates, resolving the debate in favor of torture. Race assumes a centrality in explanations that deny torture and those that justify it. As W. Fitzhugh Brondage concludes in his historical review of torture, "Perhaps the most enduring characteristic of the American tradition [of torture] is the compulsion to restore national innocence so that Americans can once again take comfort that torture is something done by other people elsewhere."[18] "We didn't kill 'em, we didn't cut their heads off," Lynndie England, one of the soldiers charged with "prisoner abuse" at Abu Ghraib, tells us, defending her involvement in torture at Abu Ghraib and expressing a quintessential American innocence defined against those who cut heads off, as ISIS has done. Democracy, the authors of an anthology on torture remind us, simply "transfers torture to those we consider to be others, those we have deemed less than human, in spaces that we consider distant."[19] The racialized story of Muslim-as-savage fuels both the official and the popular story of Abu Ghraib so that today, if Abu Ghraib is remembered at all, it is remembered as a time when leaders were corrupt, the people were innocent, and the Islamic enemy behaved as barbarically as it always has.

A racial story line enables the West, and not just Americans, to forget decades of imperial violence in the region. These events of empire do not often feature in accounts of torture at Abu Ghraib, either pro or con. The imperial line that connects Iraq to the United States is well known yet often in shadow when torture is discussed: overt support for the Baathist regime of Saddam Hussein in the Iran-Iraq War of the 1980s, the U.S.-led but UN-backed support of the bombing campaign of 1991, the first Gulf War, the decade of sanctions in which nearly five thousand Iraqi children died each month at the height of the sanctions, the deposing of Saddam Hussein, and the invasion in 2003. There is little to suggest that Americans understood the occupation of Iraq as connected either to these recent events or to their own imperial histories of the theft of Indigenous lands and the pursuit of global dominance. Instead, most understood the invasion of Iraq as a necessary confrontation with an Islamic enemy who had bombed the World Trade Center and the Pentagon. That there was no evidence of weapons of mass destruction or acknowledgment that the Baathist regime of Saddam Hussein, a former ally, was the most secular of regimes in the Middle East was irrelevant to the story of the need to confront a barbaric Islamic enemy.

The Muslim who populates torture narratives is an enemy rendered as cultural and racial Other, a figure imagined as inclined to homosexuality yet sexually puritanical, and one who required specific sexualized practices of interrogations. It is likely that soldiers were always conscious of a civilizational line between themselves and their prisoners, prisoners they forced to eat pork, wrapped women's panties around their heads, sodomized, and filmed naked and in positions of masturbation. If, as I have argued elsewhere, the sex and the photos revealed more about the jailors than it did about the prisoners, their participation in sexualized racial violence confirmed that the encounter in Iraq was a fully colonial one.[20] Colonial fantasies animated the sexualized violence that provided such an embodied sense of racial mastery. The soldiers could understand themselves as racially superior through the sexualized degradation of their Iraqi prisoners, establishing their superiority and crossing a forbidden racial, gender, and sexual line at the same time. Even soldiers of color could enjoy the race pleasure[21] that sexualized violence secures, the violence providing assurance that one is on the correct side of the civilizational divide. As with lynching, the violence transforms whiteness into "something visible and terribly tangible," something the photos

"We Didn't Kill 'em, We Didn't Cut Their Heads Off"   **153**

recorded for posterity.[22] Sexualized torture is an effective way to make whiteness on the ground; it yields a deep *embodied* sense of participation in American empire.

Empire, where a superior civilization defends its values from barbarians through annihilating them, is evident in torture talk, *whether pro or con,* whenever the idea is invoked that an all-powerful America confronts an especially savage, culturally different enemy from which it must defend itself. In 1987, Michael Taussig pinpointed the racial divide that lies at the heart of this contest that is imagined as one of savagery over civility. Writing on colonialism's culture of terror, Taussig ventured that neither the political economy of rubber nor that of labor accounts for the brutalities against the Putamayo Indians of Peru during the rubber boom. Terror—that is to say, violence that is widespread and systematic—he reminded us, is the mediator of colonial hegemony par excellence, an "inscription of a mythology on the Indian body, an engraving of civilization locked in a struggle with wildness whose model was taken from the colonists' fantasies about Indian cannibalism."[23] Despite a persistent belief that torture is instrumental—designed, that is, to extract lifesaving information from an enemy who would not otherwise divulge it—torture is intrinsically about the staking of identity claims on the bodies of the colonized. Because torture is first and foremost a "memorializing" or imprinting of power on the bodies of the colonized,[24] it has an intimate connection to terror, as Taussig emphasizes. Marnia Lazreg explains, for example, that for the colonial Algerian context, torture defined "a genuine battle between two embodied realities: in this case, colonial France with its unbounded power and mythologies, and colonized Algeria, with its claim to a full share of humanity. Conversely, the fact of doing torture allows the torturer to voice (albeit freely) *his* identity claims."[25] Torture links the body to the state—individual bodies as well as the military itself. In Algeria, torture "reached deep into the military body which it tied to the political system in a way that supplemented the esprit de corps that normally characterizes the army. Torture was the source of social integration that melded the political and the military, and consumed the structural transformation of the state into a militaristic institution."[26] If the state enjoys its identity through torture, individuals who participate in torture do the same: "Imperial identity is achieved through torture."[27]

154 "We Didn't Kill 'em, We Didn't Cut Their Heads Off"

In contemporary narratives about torture, the struggle with wildness and the fantasy on which it is based (the imperial identity alluded to by Lazreg) is visible in the idea that a culturally different enemy requires torture. Even critics of torture find it difficult to abandon ideas of civilizational difference, ideas that enable them to acquiesce to torture. For example, at an academic workshop, a former military interrogator, an anthropologist, a psychologist, and a philosopher each discussed the justification for "new methods of interrogation." We are dealing with a culturally different enemy, several of these academics and military personnel advised. The Arab enemy is more "ideologically driven and more religious."[28] Unlike during the Cold War, the "war on terror" and the occupations of Iraq and Afghanistan have produced conditions where military interrogators need cultural help. Without it, "the 18-year-old interrogator will fail and will be driven to more violent means to obtain information," warned the interrogator. A well-known anthropologist suggested that with a clandestine enemy, standard ways of operating are no longer useful. (The enemy is usually seen as clandestine, as Joshua Dratel points out, but when Communists were viewed as clandestine there was no argument that torture was the only option for confronting the communist threat.)[29] The anthropologist's suggestion was only a hair's breadth away from the logic of torture itself. As Stephen Holmes explains, the logic behind torture is simple: "To respond to the savages who want to kill us, we must cast off our Christian-liberal meekness and embrace a 'healthy savagery' of our own. We must confront ruthlessness with ruthlessness. We must pull out all the stops. After victory we will have plenty of time for civility, guilt feelings, and the rule of law."[30] Savagery or wildness, as Taussig reminds us, is the stuff of colonial fantasy.

The idea of a culturally different enemy and a healthy savagery of our own first circulated upon the release of the photos of Abu Ghraib. The theory that went the furthest to provide an explanation for the practices shown in the photos was the idea that sexualized torture was simply a culturally specific interrogation method. Fitting in nicely with the "clash of civilizations" thesis[31] that had come to dominate Western explanations for conflict between West and non-West, and the Islamic world in particular, pyramids of naked men forced to simulate having sex with each other was everywhere to be understood as nothing more than a

"We Didn't Kill 'em, We Didn't Cut Their Heads Off" **155**

contemporary form of interrogation. Few in the media questioned the Orientalist underpinnings of this claim. (Unlike us, they are sexually repressed, homophobic, and misogynist and are likely to crack in sexualized situations, particularly those involving women dominating men or those involving sex between men.) No one asked whether such methods would in fact humiliate men of all cultures, both because they are violent and because they target what it means to be a man in patriarchy.

The "clash of civilizations" approach to torture reinforced the idea of their barbarism at the same time that it enabled the West to remain on moral high ground. Through the idea of cultural difference, sexualized torture became something more generic—torture for the purpose of obtaining information, something that was not even torture at all. Sexualized torture, then, was simply "to attack the prisoners' identity and values."[32] Believing that the fault had to be traced back to the top, Mark Danner declared the photos "comprehensible" given the cultural characteristics of Arabs *and* the CIA's manual on interrogations. The photos are "staged operas of fabricated shame intended to 'intensify' the prisoners' guilt feelings, increase his anxiety and his urge to cooperate," Danner wrote, quoting parts of the CIA's interrogation policy.[33] Photographs are a "shame multiplier," according to the Red Cross, since they could be distributed to the prisoners' families and used to further humiliate detainees.[34] Through the idea of culturally specific interrogation techniques, Americans were installed as modern people who did not subscribe to puritanical notions of sex or to patriarchal notions of women's role in it. The Iraqis, of course, remained forever confined to the premodern in the narratives of critics and supporters of torture alike, a place where torture is necessary.

The idea of a culturally different, more savage enemy persists in several contemporary journalistic accounts that approve of torture. For instance, Heather MacDonald, a journalist and frequent guest on Fox News, writes: "The Islamist enemy is unlike any the military has encountered in the past."[35] The difference, it turns out, is a cultural one. "Islamists" don't give up information, don't play by the rules of the Geneva Convention, and are mainly interested in homosexual sex. MacDonald illustrates in this comment the incoherence of racist positions. If the Iraqis were especially humiliated by the idea of men having sex with men, why would they

156 "We Didn't Kill 'em, We Didn't Cut Their Heads Off"

also be characterized as mainly interested in homosexual sex? Confronted with such an uncivilized enemy, Americans had no other choice but to turn to various "stress techniques," some of which may have gone too far (she dislikes the use of dogs and is a little concerned about waterboarding). The prisoners who were moved from Camp X-Ray to Camp Delta at Guantánamo were really only upset because they could no longer have homosexual sex. Acknowledging some practices of torture and echoing the sentiment expressed by Lynndie England, MacDonald concludes: "We don't gas people like the Nazis did." One sees only a slightly more restrained culturalist argument from lawyers and policy analysts, many of whom use the culture argument to downgrade what happened at Abu Ghraib from torture to interrogation. For example, Andrew McCarthy describes the "mortification" of Iraqi prisoners at Abu Ghraib and argues that with a new clandestine and ruthless enemy, America had to legally authorize "a bending of the rules." Dismissing any connection between lawlessness (as in the refusal to grant POW status to detainees) and torture, McCarthy simply agrees with Alan Dershowitz that we should have a system of torture warrants where we apply for permission to torture especially high value and presumably especially savage detainees.[36]

In view of the mediation of "terror" through narration, it is not surprising that news coverage of Abu Ghraib in North America, both then and now, does not typically use the word *torture*. As Timothy Jones and Penelope Sheets found, only 19 percent of the American press articles on Abu Ghraib referred to torture, in comparison to 81.8 percent of European press (Canada and Australia referred to torture 41 percent of the time).[37] Americans and American soldiers are massively opposed to torture but not to abuse or mortification. Polls indicate that many Americans are in favor of sleep deprivation and other techniques.[38] As I show in the next section, narratives about a few bad leaders effectively limit the extent to which Americans can see themselves as implicated in torture, and by extension in empire.

Anti-torture Narratives and Likable Torturers

Many scholars now unambiguously condemn torture and show "the mundane banality with which cruelty and torture became official policy of the United States Department of Defense."[39] If it is clear that the treatment

"We Didn't Kill 'em, We Didn't Cut Their Heads Off"   **157**

of prisoners at Abu Ghraib was not an anomaly, practices of torture being already deeply embedded in the institution of the prison, it is also the case that the dominant impulse among critics of torture is to maintain that the abuses at the prison were due to the exceptional circumstances in Iraq. Nearly two decades after the events at Abu Ghraib, we can add a second dominant impulse: to maintain that the abuses were the work of an aberrant U.S. administration. Analysts share the conclusion that under President George W. Bush, as David Cole put it, "an amoral, blinkered pragmatism ruled the day."[40] How do contemporary narratives about the *wrongness* of torture at Abu Ghraib mediate "terror"?

A collection of articles on the torture debate in America begins with the observation that Americans have been remarkably "apathetic" about the question of torture in the "War on Terror." The editor speculates that Americans are not uncaring but simply confused about the issue.[41] The spate of films about torture and other excesses in the "war on terror," however, suggest otherwise. Americans *have* engaged in a public discussion of the meaning of Abu Ghraib, Guantánamo, and other sites of torture, and they have mostly done so as critics. Documentaries such as *Standard Operating Procedure* (the focus of this section) and *Ghosts of Abu Ghraib*, as well as books such as Jane Mayer's *The Dark Side* and Hollywood movies such as *Rendition,* have become a genre of sorts, works united by a common criticism of the torture policies of the Bush administration. If the majority of critics of American torture policies of the past decade (most do not spare the time to discuss pre-9/11 American torture) focus on the corruption, immorality, and illegality that characterized the Bush administration, very few consider torture itself: what is torture, who is tortured, and what made it so easy for the regime, ordinary soldiers, and ordinary people both to torture and to accept torture as official policy. Although we have all become familiar with the list of torture practices and with the legal legitimization of torture,[42] it is as though these acts were not in fact committed by people we can name. Instead, the discussion has largely been an abstract one about policies and immoral leadership. On the rare occasion that the questions "Why was it so easy for American soldiers to be amoral?" and "What enabled torture?" are asked, they are answered by the theory that once you create a torture culture, ordinary people find it easy to torture (Stanley Milgram's Yale

158 "We Didn't Kill 'em, We Didn't Cut Their Heads Off"

experiments are often cited). Importantly, psychological explanations turn our gaze away from history and context, and there is little chance to explore what kind of Americans the soldiers imagined themselves to be. "Rumsfeld made them do it" (a reference to Donald Rumsfeld, defense secretary under President George W. Bush) seems to suffice as explanation. Such explanations do not explore torture as an identity-making practice. In fact, they studiously avoid *embodying* torture at all; torture remains a particular policy or law. We seldom hear the voices of the tortured of Abu Ghraib, Guantánamo, and elsewhere, although the information from interviews with detainees compiled by the International Committee of the Red Cross is one exception.[43]

It is said that Americans must now live with the story of torture. As Danner wrote after reading the Red Cross interviews, the decision to torture "sits before us, a toxic fact, polluting our political and moral life."[44] To confront this toxic fact requires confronting what torture *is:* a systematic dehumanization of the Other. In both popular culture and officially, America has yet to acknowledge and confront the fact that its soldiers were able to torture with abandon. The soldiers involved in torture at Abu Ghraib appear neither to regret it nor to face social censure for it. The remarkable disavowal of the fact that prisoners were *persons* who were tortured and the compulsion to exonerate the rank and file ensure that Americans do not confront the toxic fact of empire. Here I will argue that this is about the persistence of racial terror in narratives even as America announces itself to be against torture. Specifically, I suggest that the soldiers at Abu Ghraib have often aroused compassion and understanding. As a culture, North Americans appear to sympathize with many of them, perhaps believing the Milgram experiment to be a good explanation for their behavior. I note here that less good feeling has been spared for the Winter Soldiers[45] who protest the war and the terrible things they were required to do in Iraq and Afghanistan. Through the redemption of the soldiers involved in torture and an almost exclusive focus on the legal and political authorization of torture, Americans have successfully stopped torture from penetrating their consciousness. Along with scholars exploring the productive function of apologies, truth and reconciliation commissions, and other national moments where state violence is confronted, I suggest that an important question to ask about

"We Didn't Kill 'em, We Didn't Cut Their Heads Off" **159**

these ostensibly critical narratives of torture is quite simply "How do the stories make us feel?"[46] Put another way, "What kind of a moral community is created by contemporary critics of torture?"

There is something deeply productive about the argument that *only* the leaders are to blame for torture. American innocence is secured through this focus in much the same way that Canadians peacekeepers were able to affirm their innocence in abuses of Somalis they had come to protect.[47] Both the nation and its soldiers become mere dupes of a corrupt leadership. The work of empire can go on apace when we rest on the assumption that all the bad guys have gone home. What was done to Iraqis disappears into a story of American innocence, a strange time in American history when "our children," as the filmmaker Error Morris called the soldiers, were coerced into "animal house on the night shift" at Abu Ghraib, a phrase he borrowed from former defense secretary James Schlesinger.[48] Morris is reluctant to name what went on at Abu Ghraib as torture, and the soldiers whose faces appear in the famous pictures are never labeled torturers. At worst, the soldiers who were charged with abuses at Abu Ghraib are referred to in the media as the "seven bad apples," and their activities are described as "unseemly."

I rely on the documentary film made by Morris titled *Standard Operating Procedure* and the book he coauthored with Philip Gourevitch based on extensive interviews with the soldiers to illustrate my argument about the nature of "post-torture" recollections of Abu Ghraib.[49] Sabrina Harman, Megan Ambuhl, Lynndie England, Jeremy Sivits, and Javal Davis—five of the seven soldiers charged for their role in torture at Abu Ghraib—have told their stories in two documentaries and a book; two others, Charles Graner and Ivan Frederick, remain incarcerated and inaccessible to the media.[50] Critics have been remarkably unanimous in their responses to *Standard Operating Procedure,* finding the occasional fault (particularly with Morris's decision to reenact scenes of torture) but agreeing for the most part with the story line that the real culprits are the leaders. Although I rely on the documentary and the book *Standard Operating Procedure,* and critics' responses to them, it is possible to turn to other documentaries and films, such as the documentary *Ghosts of Abu Ghraib* by filmmaker Rory Kennedy, which shows fidelity to the argument that the most important conclusion we can come to about Abu

160 "We Didn't Kill 'em, We Didn't Cut Their Heads Off"

Ghraib is that torture was official policy and that soldiers did what they were ordered to. Like Morris, Kennedy feels sympathy for her documentary subjects, believing them to be the likable, hapless victims of a corrupt administration. As Kennedy told Amy Goodman in an interview:

> And what I found was that they were, in fact, very likeable, and that I could see their humanity in looking at their eyes and was able to connect with them. And it was very hard to reconcile that experience with the reality of what I was seeing in the photographs and images.[51]

For Kennedy, as for so many, it is possible to reconcile the photos with the niceness of the soldiers by focusing on the responsibility of the chain of command and on the idea (citing Milgram once again) that ordinary people will easily commit acts of torture if someone in authority tells them to do so. What enables this exoneration of ordinary torturers? While there are several reasons, I propose that a crucial part of this response originates in the belief that Arabs/Muslims are culturally different and less than human. As such, they are prisoners who require torture. An anti-Muslim affect circulates throughout discussions of torture, providing memory with its opportunity to cede to pride. "Memory is life, borne by living societies founded in its name," Pierre Nora reminds us.[52] If memory is a bond tying us to the eternal present, as Nora suggests, then it "only accommodates those facts that suit it."[53]

Post-torture Memory: "I Don't Know What I Could Have Done Different"

By way of moral contrast, let us first consider some altogether different narratives about Iraq than are found in the discussions of Abu Ghraib. In March 2008, hundreds of veterans of Iraq and Afghanistan gathered in Maryland to give their eyewitness accounts of the occupations of both countries. The veterans modeled their testimony after the Winter Soldier hearings organized by Vietnam Veterans Against the War in 1971. As Amy Goodman reported, "the war veterans spoke of free-fire zones, the shootings and beatings of innocent civilians, racism at the highest levels of the military, and the torturing of prisoners."[54] Most major news outlets did not cover the Winter Soldier event. Goodman broadcast the hearings, in

"We Didn't Kill 'em, We Didn't Cut Their Heads Off" **161**

which soldiers tearfully described in detail (often illustrating with pictures of themselves) the acts of violence they perpetrated upon Iraqi and Afghan people. In one such account, Jon Michael Turner stripped his medals and ribbons from his chest and ended his testimony as follows:

> I just want to say that I am sorry for the hate and destruction I have inflicted on innocent people, and I'm sorry for the hate and destruction that others have inflicted on innocent people. . . . I am sorry for the things I did. I am no longer the monster that I once was.[55]

Carl Rippberger, commenting on a slide of himself in Iraq, said:

> I am extremely shameful of it. I'm showing it in hopes that none of you people that have never been involved ever let this happen to you. Don't ever let your government do this to you. It's me. I'm holding a dead body, smiling. Everyone in our platoon took two bodies, put them on the back ramp, drove them through a village for show, and dumped them off at the edge the village.[56]

As these excerpts reveal, the Winter Soldiers acknowledge personal responsibility for their actions in Iraq and Afghanistan, even as they believe that they were a part of a systematic campaign of violence orchestrated from the top. Their stories confirm that a pattern of terror begins with individual soldiers who are asked to do, and who do, unspeakable things. Some find the courage to say no on the spot; most do not. But in the case of these soldiers, all now believe that what they were asked to do, and what they did, was wrong. Their testimony is intended to rectify these wrongs by taking personal responsibility and by speaking out against practices of torture and terror, and against war and occupation. This response is not one that has occurred to the majority of the soldiers at Abu Ghraib, and it is not one that Morris or Gourevitch ever consider possible. "I'm sorry" has not been uttered by any of the torturers, nor have any of those who condemn torture uttered these words. The politics of apologies are well-known productive acts. As Richard Weisman discusses (drawing on others), expressions of remorse have to include an unconditional acknowledgment of responsibility, sincere self-condemnation, and, crucially, an awareness that the victim has suffered.[57] Without these components, we are not being invited into a moral community in which

162 "We Didn't Kill 'em, We Didn't Cut Their Heads Off"

torture is wrong. If no one thinks that the acts of torture at Abu Ghraib were really wrong, then are Muslims/Arabs full members of the human and political community?

In *Standard Operating Procedure*, Morris intersperses vivid reenactments of torture, the Abu Ghraib photographs, and interviews with the soldiers, the latter often shot close-up so that their faces fill the entire screen. The viewer has a sense of being face-to-face with torture and torturers. The tortured do not speak; their bodies are meant only to contrast to the calm and reasonable voices of the soldiers who give us their accounts of what they did in Abu Ghraib prison. There remains a voyeuristic gaze throughout as we are invited to consume pyramids of naked prisoners alongside close-up shots of the female soldiers in particular that emphasize their femininity and youth. As Lazreg writes, today for the French, as the former colonial power in Algeria, the "cumulative effect of this speaking and writing about the war [of independence in Algeria] has resulted in a trivialization of the significance of torture as glossy pictures turn war into *an orgiastic intellectual entertainment.*"[58] Similarly, documentaries such as *Standard Operating Procedure* offer avid descriptions and images of torture and cinematic close-ups of torturers.

The documentary begins by informing us that American soldiers as a group were so deeply depressed when they got to Abu Ghraib that they felt "already dead." In the book, Gourevitch and Morris ensure that their readers understand that Abu Ghraib was an intolerable place that was constantly under mortar fire (although in 2003 no American soldier was killed from this). The 372nd Military Police Company, a reserve unit based in Cresaptown, Maryland, finds out that instead of going home they will be posted to guard duty at Abu Ghraib, something for which they are not trained. As we observe them in this environment—untrained, alienated, stressed, frustrated, and overcome by the climate—we are coached to understand that normal, wholesome American soldiers, all with their own dreams, soon fall apart in the hell that was Abu Ghraib. The film and the book both begin with this equivalent to Marlow's journey into the heart of Africa, Joseph Conrad's European character in the novel *Heart of Darkness* who travels by river into the dangerous jungle, encountering along the way savageries that reveal the darkness that lies within man and not within the imperial project.

As I have shown elsewhere in the case of the violence of Western

"We Didn't Kill 'em, We Didn't Cut Their Heads Off" **163**

peacekeepers toward the populations they supposedly came to help, the savagery of the racial Other and the savagery of the place of the racial Other become the reasons why violence is authorized against them.[59] As Hugh Ridley memorably put it, recalling the themes of colonial novels and the mind-set of the masculine subjects who inhabit these fictional colonials worlds, "In Africa, who can be a saint?"[60] The civilized man "loses" it in Africa on account of the dust and heat, as Canada concluded in its inquiry of the violence of Canadian peacekeepers toward Somalis. In Africa, the soldier feels compelled to engage in violence *anticipating* the savagery of the racial Other and the hardships of the land. It is this narrative line, a combination of "Rumsfeld made me do it" and "In Iraq who could be a saint?," that runs through the accounts of the Abu Ghraib soldiers, accounts very much fostered by Morris and carefully, and even lovingly, crafted in the film and book.

What stands out the most about the narratives the Abu Ghraib soldiers offer to the cameras is the almost complete absence of moral conflict. The soldiers do not believe that they *personally* did anything wrong. Instead, we see subjects who are intent on presenting themselves as victims. Presumably asked by Morris (who does not appear) how they feel now, the soldiers display no shame, little interest in the impact of their actions, and an intense self-absorption. Asked what she could have done differently, Sabrina Harman appears puzzled and replies, "I don't know what I could have done different," and as an afterthought adds, "I wouldn't have joined the military. It's just not worth it." In the interview quoted in the book, she expands on what she means:

> You always feel guilty thinking you could have changed something—or, I guess, dereliction of duty for not reporting something that went on, even though people did know. I guess you could have went to somebody else. So I accept the dereliction of duty charge. Personally I accept that one. It would be nice just to put everything behind me. It sucks, but it's a learning experience, I guess. It helps you grow, getting screwed over. I don't know.[61]

The spark of remorse that leads Harman to accept the dereliction of duty charge for not reporting the abuse is quickly put out by the predominant feeling of "getting screwed over." Similarly, although he felt sorry for a prisoner who died in a bombing just as he was being released,

164 "We Didn't Kill 'em, We Didn't Cut Their Heads Off"

Javal Davis remains most rueful about the loss of his dreams. Davis offers the camera his final thought: "A big chunk of my life is gone. I can never get it back." Jeremy Sivits is sorry that he couldn't make his family proud. Megan Ambuhl (who later married Charles Graner) simply concludes: "Life's not fair, that's for sure," and if we are in any doubt about whose life is not fair, it is quickly put to rest when, reflecting on her own life, she declares, "I've always known that." Lynndie England announces that she wouldn't change a thing, because she got a son out of her relationship with Graner. For her, regret is centered around Charles Graner himself. Believing herself to have been taken advantage of by Graner, England says that Abu Ghraib has left her with one predominant feeling: "Learn from your mistakes. I learned from mine. It's like I don't need a man to survive. Forget 'em. . . . It's just being young and naïve."[62] If self-pity runs like a stream through these narratives, and a gendered story enables some of the women to cast themselves as special victims, the soldiers are clearly not sorry for what they did to Iraqis. Their recollections reveal that little about the situation troubled them in the first place, other than their own personal discomfort, the discomfort of being in a savage place at a savage time. They work hard to make a moral distinction between humiliation and torture, believing nonetheless in their absolute right to engage in both.

The journey into the heart of darkness, where torture is transformed into humiliation, is a gendered one. As D'Arcangelis observes, drawing on the work of Gil Hochberg on women in the Israeli army, nationalist narratives frequently deploy tropes of femininity to conceal state violence.[63] Both the book and the film begin with the story of Sabrina Harman as the epitome of feminine innocence defiled. Harman's soft, girlish voice reads from her letters to her wife, Kelly.[64] Faithful to the story line of someone who descends into hell, Harman writes of the first time that she saw a prisoner with underwear on his head, stripped naked, and handcuffed to the rails with arms extended over the head in the "Palestinian position," made famous by the Israelis for the extreme discomfort in which it places the prisoner. Like most soldiers, Harman understood that the prisoner, a taxi driver, was most likely innocent, something that did not stop her from engaging in humiliation and torture. She recalls for Kelly that at first she found the prisoner's situation funny and initially laughed

"We Didn't Kill 'em, We Didn't Cut Their Heads Off" 165

when someone "poked his dick." Editorializing quickly, Harman writes: "Then it hit me that this was molestation." Molestation, but not torture. Claiming that she knew that much that went on was wrong, she nonetheless participated and took pictures, apparently believing that the pictures would later serve as proof of the ill-treatment of prisoners. At no time does it occur to Harman to try to stop the practices or even to complain about them. If she gives a thumbs-up or gleefully smiles for the camera, Harman suggests that this is simply what she always did in front of a camera.

Morris and Gourevitch sympathetically portray the young girl who dreamed of becoming a forensic photographer. In Harman's letters, the story of taking pictures for the purpose of documenting abuse is undermined by her recounting of the casual details of life at Abu Ghraib, where "we stripped prisoners and laughed at them; we degraded them but we didn't hit them." These casually inserted details of her direct participation in torture, practices that she clearly does not consider to be torture, take second place next to the accounts Harman gives of her kindness. She writes of the young boy who was covered in ants and whom she tried to help, and the general whose eyebrows were shaved and whom she tried to console for this humiliation. On camera she comments on the famous photograph of the prisoner who was made to believe that the electrodes attached to him were live wires and that he would be electrocuted if he fell off the box: "It would have been meaner if the electrodes were hooked up." Gilligan, as this prisoner was nicknamed, was never physically touched, Harman insists, puzzled by those who saw the photograph and thought that it was torture.

The contrived and contradictory nature of Harman's recollections give Gourevitch and Morris pause, and they notice that she is working hard to construct herself as innocent: "By the end of her outpourings she repositioned herself as an outsider at Abu Ghraib, an observer and recorder, shaking her head, and in this way she came clean with her wife. In this way she preserved her sense of innocence."[65] Noting that Harman "imagined herself as producing an exposé" but that "she did not pretend to be a whistle-blower-in-waiting," they can make no further sense of her performance and instead accept her explanations. When she acknowledges that the grin and the thumbs-up she offered to the camera in most

166 "We Didn't Kill 'em, We Didn't Cut Their Heads Off"

of the photos "look bad" and suggests that this was simply how she always poses for photos, there is little in the book or the film to imagine that this might not be true. Harman's narrative is indeed full of contradictions. Documenting abuse yet giving an unself-conscious account of her own involvement in various torture events, it is nonetheless clear that "she was as forgiving of her buddies as of herself."[66]

There is a strange structure to the soldiers' narratives of "the first time I saw abuse." It is the naked detainees wearing women's panties that shock, but not the repeated violence. Initially sure that what they were seeing was wrong, they soon participate in acts of abuse and describe their participation in various contradictory ways: the leaders made me do it; others did far worse; I just followed orders; the prisoners were ordinary innocent people; the prisoners were people who had happily blown us up; the prisoners had information that would save lives; the prisoners didn't have information; and so on. No soldier takes responsibility for acts of humiliation and torture. If it is ever acknowledged that most of the people in Abu Ghraib were simply ordinary people, this does not give anyone pause to acknowledge that what they did was wrong.

Davis knew from his first encounter with naked prisoners wearing women's pink panties over their heads that "something's not right here." Describing his initial attempt to complain, he notes that the chain of command simply abandoned the rank and file, confirming that however they felt, they had to do the bidding of Military Intelligence. He grew numb but participated nevertheless, by his own and others' accounts, often with enthusiasm. He acknowledges that they would simply go and sweep up every single male "from kids to the local baker" and then set about humiliating them. He soon determined what would work best, playing rap music and country music loudly and without cease in order to destabilize the prisoners. In his view, what he participated in was not torture but humiliation. "We don't have photos of torture," he states, even though he believes that torture happened all the time. The real torturers, he implies, got off. Megan Ambuhl also insists that the photographs don't show torture, and goes further by maintaining that they in fact make things look worse than they were. "We softened them up," she casually explains. "We would burn them with a cigarette. We'd just do what they [Military Intelligence] wanted us to do. It didn't seem weird; it was saving lives." Other soldiers calmly describe their own role in water torture: "We turned on the showers and wet the detainee until it was hard to breathe through the hoods."

Alternately excusing themselves on the grounds that they were simply following orders and insisting that what happened was not torture or was in the interest of saving American lives, the soldiers speak casually of the horrors they were involved in, lamenting that the incidents for which they have been condemned were far more innocent than others they knew about. They tell of prisoners whom they were "humiliating" who were already dead, of being asked to help out and doing so in order to be "nice." Harman is able to draw diagrams in her letters home of how dogs are used on prisoners. Others announce their belief that most prisoners were ordinary people who were innocent, yet they could recall soaking sandbags in hot sauce to be placed over a prisoner's head because "these guys have info." They were able to participate in the brutal beatings of prisoners and maintain at the same time that the most that ever happened was "a really, really bad case of humiliation." As "helpers," Anthony Diaz and Jeffrey Frost (who were not charged with prisoner abuse) describe the order to tie a prisoner in a higher-stress position. They find out after some time that the prisoner they were allegedly softening up was already dead. "It kinda felt bad. I know I am not part of this but," offers Diaz in the film, illustrating the acknowledgment of violence and disavowal of his participation of it in one breadth. If what felt bad was when the prisoner died, it did not feel bad to spend days tying prisoners up into intolerable stress positions, stripping them naked, and turning on the showers for water torture. The mundane work of torture elicits little moral conflict. It is work that is never named as torture.

The soldiers are not only forgiving of themselves and of each other for engaging in torture; they are also absorbed in the tragedy of what happened to *them*. Lynndie England, described as a girl who once looked like a boy and who enlisted at seventeen in order to be able to attend college and to lift herself out of a life working at a chicken-processing plant, is dismissive of the public who saw her holding the leash on a prisoner and called it abuse. "It was no big deal," she observes, explaining that Charles Graner asked her to hold the leash for the photo. Maintaining throughout that she only did was what she was told to do, England presents herself

168 "We Didn't Kill 'em, We Didn't Cut Their Heads Off"

as a woman victimized by a man. "I'm in the brig because of a man," she states flatly to the camera, explaining that women in the army either had to prove their equality to men or be controlled by them. A man's place, the army also turned out to be a place where "people wanted to mess with the prisoners." Offering no comment on this state of affairs, England remains unrepentant as she describes her involvement in the scenes of sexual torture: "We didn't kill 'em, we didn't cut their heads off." Unconsciously comparing herself to the barbaric enemy who kills and cuts off heads, England secures for herself a higher place on the civilizational scale.

If the soldiers seem unmoved by their acts of torture, those who bring us their story share this indifference to what was done to Iraqi bodies. Although Gourevitch and Morris write passionately that "the stain is ours," the stain is only torture as policy and the crimes of the upper levels.[67] Of the soldiers they conclude: "Even as they sank into a routine of depravity, they showed by their picture taking that they did not accept it as normal. They never fully got with the program. Is it not to their credit that they were profoundly demoralized by their service in the netherworld?"[68]

> Inexperienced, untrained, under attack, and under orders to do wrong, the low-ranking reservist MPs who implemented the nefarious policy of the "War on Terror" on the MI block of Abu Ghraib knew that what they were doing was immoral, and they knew that if it wasn't illegal, it ought to be. They knew that they had the right, and that it was their duty, to disobey an unlawful order to report it to their immediate superior; and if that failed—or if that superior was the source of the order—to keep reporting it on up the chain of command until they found satisfaction.[69]

If they had the right to refuse to commit acts of torture, and this was surely their duty, why didn't they do so, and what do we think about them not having done so? These questions are answered in the film: they didn't do so because it was hard to do, and we should forgive them.

The film and the book are both assembled so that the complicity of the lower ranks is a light one. Tim Dugan, a civilian interrogator, explains to us at the start that the rank-and-file soldiers were a "bunch of unpro-

"We Didn't Kill 'em, We Didn't Cut Their Heads Off"   169

fessional schmucks that didn't know their damn jobs, all thrown together, mixed up with a big-ass stick." By the end of the film he no longer holds this view, and we can guess that he now believes that torture was policy. Brent Pack, lead forensic examiner of the computer crime unit of the U.S. Army, who analyzed the thousands of photographs, lends the full weight of his science to the diagnosis: the pictures depict several events of what was often "standard operating procedure." He classifies the acts of torture and humiliation, clarifying that physical injury amounts to a criminal act, sexual humiliation is dereliction of duty, but most other practices are simply standard operating procedure. Agreeing with the other experts who are interviewed that the soldiers were mostly people in the wrong place at the wrong time, Pack feels sorriest for England. Lynndie was "just in love." If the photos tell us anything, he implies, it is the story of a woman in love. Neither Lynndie England nor Sabrina Harman, who writes so lovingly to her wife, is presented as a torturer. Although we have little on the two men serving the longest sentences (Charles Graner and Ivan Frederick), their stories, too, are ultimately presented as the stories of victims. Their country betrayed them, we are led to believe.

Perhaps the end point of the equivocation about the soldiers is best revealed in the many interviews Morris has given (some with Gourevitch) in which he explains what most concerned him about Abu Ghraib. Professing himself to be most interested in the role of the photos, Morris wonders about what they reveal and what they conceal. Often turning to Sabrina Harman as an example, he notes that it is tempting to conclude from the thumbs-up and the smiles in the photo of herself with the dead, tortured Iraqi prisoner that she participated in his death or at least approved of it. The smile is an uneasy one, Morris suggests, and Harman's crime is nothing compared to the soldiers who actually murdered the prisoner. In this moment we are invited to forget that while Harman did not murder prisoners, she did participate directly in moments of torture. Challenging his audience to answer the question "Did Sabrina Harman commit a crime?," it is clear that for Morris the answer is no. Although she may not be "lilywhite" or "uncompromised," we are invited to consider that she is not the culprit.[70] In the end, although he wished to interrogate complicity at the bottom rather than the top, and imagined himself making a film that did more than focus on the chain of command, we arrive in

170 "We Didn't Kill 'em, We Didn't Cut Their Heads Off"

the same place. At no point does it really occupy Morris's attention that American soldiers such as Sabrina Harman *tortured* Iraqis. The unchallenged assumption throughout, shared by Morris, Gourevitch, and their subjects, is that there is a valid reason to treat Iraqis as they were treated in Abu Ghraib prison, even if things did go a little wrong.

"Frightened, Disoriented Men and Women"

With some of its plot devices rather obvious, it is surprising that reviewers find so little to critique in the work of Morris and Gourevitch. In a review of the book and the film published in the *New York Review of Books,*[71] Ian Baruma begins, as so many reviewers do, by reminding us of Susan Sontag's argument that the torture photographs "were typical expressions of a brutalized popular American culture," but adds approvingly that Morris's documentary "complicates matters." The complication is that the pictures don't tell the whole story and may "even conceal more than they reveal." What they conceal is torture as policy and the practice of using untrained soldiers, among them those with a "bad boy" reputation such as Charles Graner. Of the other soldiers who participated, Baruma has only kind things to say. Harman, in particular, draws his sympathy, as Morris intended. She is the person about whom her colleagues say that she wouldn't hurt a fly. We are reminded of her dream to become a forensic photographer. For Baruma, Harman is simply telling the truth when she says that she took pictures in order to document abuses. She committed no crime, he insists, since the real crime lies in those who tortured a prisoner to death. England was simply in love and did whatever her man told her to do. The photos, Baruma concludes, were "fun and games" compared to the darker secret they hide. The most condemnation Baruma offers is that everyone probably got a little "erotic frisson" from their participation in these acts. He recalls that Sontag may have been right about the pornographic nature of the encounter, but lying at the heart of pornography and the Abu Ghraib encounter is the capacity to objectify and dehumanize, something that contemporary Abu Ghraib commentators such as Baruma seem not to notice. Not surprisingly, any comparison between the soldiers of Abu Ghraib and the Nazis is rejected outright, although it is interesting that reviewers such as Baruma feel compelled to deny the similarity.

"We Didn't Kill 'em, We Didn't Cut Their Heads Off" **171**

Baruma's response is a typical one. The Canadian reviewer Peter Goddard[72] also agrees that England was merely goofing around for her boyfriend when she took part in the photo of "Gus," the name given to the prisoner on a leash: "The picture isn't about Gus being dominated by England. It's about England being dominated by Graner." Apparently buying England's gender defense—that she wasn't humiliating prisoners but just trying to please Graner—Goddard is able to sidestep the fact that a prisoner was still in the end being humiliated by jailors who had considerable power over him. Graner's interest in documenting the terrible conditions of his job, Harman's wish to use photos to deflect her own humiliation at being a spectator at a demeaning ritual—all these are accepted at face value. Goddard concludes: "The theatricality of the Abu Ghraib photos only adds to the shock of what was really happening there. It's as if Graner and the rest of the picture-takers understood implicitly that they were in that awful place to play a role in this war fantasy. So, they did just that, with great big smiles on their faces."[73]

One is struck by the extent to which reviewers are forgiving of the soldiers. They emphasize their "uncertainty and confusion" as well as their "posing and posturing." As Michael Roth (president of Wesleyan University) writes, "through the soldiers we are able to grasp the 'slapdash ineptitude' and the incoherence of the war itself."[74] In his review, Michael Chaiken takes Morris to task for "the heavy-handed reliance on re-creations to shock the audience into recognizing the magnitude of the horrors being recounted."[75] Chaiken's argument is that the re-creations "divert attention from that for which there is no substitute: the faces of those frightened, disoriented men and women tearfully coming to terms with historical forces of which they too are hapless victims." Bemoaning that we suffer a failure of empathy and imagination when we are overly exposed to images of horror (as Sontag argued), there is little doubt whom our empathy is supposed to be for—the soldiers, not their Iraqi victims.

As many reviewers agree, Morris is asking us to think about the relationship between the photos and truth. As Cynthia Fuchs put it, "the movie is more deliberately and (for lack of a better term) more poetically invested in how the crimes were defined by the images."[76] Fuchs notices England's "oddly detached" stance as she explains that the problem was

172 "We Didn't Kill 'em, We Didn't Cut Their Heads Off"

that she was a woman in a man's world, and she reminds us that England's "seeming lack of a perspective becomes a perspective." Again, however, the lack of perspective that is so remarkable is simply evidence of the degree to which these practices were policy. The pictures assembled into a timeline by Pack don't tell us about the "stunning policy-making that determined that sequence." For Fuchs as for all the other reviewers, the real story lies elsewhere. It does not lie with the strange detachment that England and others reveal to this day except insofar as the detachment confirms that they too were merely hapless victims of a corrupt leadership. The reviewer for the World Socialist website, Joanne Laurier, is the only one to suggest that Morris seems to display "an unwillingness to see how far things have gone," that is, to acknowledge that America "terrorized and intimidated an entire population."[77] But how terror and intimidation is performed by individuals who continue to be feel blameless and who are apparently without remorse is not something any reviewers have pursued. Instead, they have sought redemption for the soldiers who tortured and, by extension, for all Americans.

Conclusion: "I Want You to Feel That Iraqi Life Is Precious"

Torture has what we might regard as a built-in connection to race. Quite simply, torture is permissible against those whom we have evicted from personhood and humanity, even as torture itself guarantees this outcome. Torture's connection to two levels of humanity can thus be located in law. Whether "enemy combatants" or inhabitants of a refugee camp, the legal distinction that marks who enjoys the rule of law and who does not often thinly disguises that the camp's inmates are *already* regarded as a lower form of humanity. Lazreq comments regarding Algeria that the French classified Algerians as "French Muslims" and as "protected subjects," the latter an especially ironic moniker given that those in this category were marked as outside the law's protection. Similarly, the Bush administration produced Arabs/Muslims in a state of exception when the rule of law could be suspended in their case. That torture at Abu Ghraib could be defended through reliance on the principles of American law, however, indicates that no special measures were necessary to authorize torture. Prisoners are already a category of people easily evicted from the universal through ideas about persons who bear a negative relationship to law, a status that race makes defensible. The Islamic enemy, racialized as a category of persons against whom force is necessary, was easily accommodated in the legal space for subpersons.

Drawing on Elaine Scarry's argument that torture is work mediated by the labor of "civilization," Lazreg notes that "torture finds justification in the alleged barbarity of the enemy."[78] In Algeria the French would often set up torture centers in old wine storehouses. Prisoners would often die from the sulphuric gases from the remnants of fermented alcohol, but there would be the added bonus of "simply allowing alcohol, the object of a Muslim taboo, to work its invisible magic on the Muslim body."[79] We should not, therefore, be surprised that torture talk and culture talk merge so often. Cultural difference, the enemy's innate barbarism, is an important element in the eviction of the tortured from the rule of law, and thus from humanity. The bikini panties wrapped so diligently around the heads of the prisoners tortured at Abu Ghraib was a lesson intended for the torturer more so than the tortured, reaffirming the former's cultural superiority and the latter as a lower form of humanity.

Post-torture discussions create community as much as torture itself does, continuing racial terror through cultural memory. In memory, torture is not torture at all but interrogation methods gone awry, or soldiers carried away at a frat party. Culture talk, or in its absence simply an outright dehumanization of Iraqis, undoubtedly helps Americans to become reconciled to having tortured. President Obama's statement that Americans don't torture and President Bush's justification for torture may in the end come to mean the same thing when we consider not only that officials have not been prosecuted for their role in torture but that those of the lower ranks who *have* been charged remain for the most part unrepentant and socially embraced. Their refusal to take responsibility and the public's forgiving of their acts reminds those of us who share color, religion, region, or simply personhood with the tortured that our lives are similarly valued. The white femininity of some of the torturers, so celebrated by filmmakers and reviewers alike, strikes terror in the hearts of anyone who watched and waited for an acknowledgment of the violence done to Iraqis.

For their part, Iraqis have certainly understood the meaning of American actions. On May 4, 2008, an intriguing story appeared in the

174 "We Didn't Kill 'em, We Didn't Cut Their Heads Off"

Los Angeles Times: "Blackwater Shooting Highlights a U.S., Iraq Culture Clash." In September 2007, Blackwater workers killed seventeen Iraqis, including the son of an Iraqi man, Abdul Razzaq, in what the Iraqis called a massacre and what Blackwater called a "situation" that arose because their workers feared for their lives. U.S. officials were investigating the shooting, but in the meantime they attempted to provide monetary compensation to Mr. Razzaq, who refused it. The reporters offer their analysis of this strange impasse:

> Far from bringing justice and closure, the investigations underline the frictions between Americans and Iraqis that have plagued the five-year U.S. presence. The shooting and its aftermath show the deep disconnect between the American legal process and the traditional culture of Iraq, between the courtroom and the tribal *diwan*. U.S. officials painstakingly examine evidence and laws while attempting to satisfy victims' claims through cash compensation. But traditional Arab society values honor and decorum above all. If a man kills or badly injures someone in an accident, both families convene a tribal summit. The perpetrator admits responsibility, commiserates with the victim, pays medical expenses and other compensation, all over glasses of tea in a tribal tent. "Our system is so different from theirs," said David Mack, a former U.S. diplomat who has served in American embassies in Iraq, Jordan, Lebanon, Libya, Tunisia and the United Arab Emirates. "An honor settlement has to be both financial and it has to have the right symbolism. We would never accept their way of doing things, and they don't accept ours."[80]

"I want you to feel that Iraqi life is precious," explained Haitham Rubaie, a physician who lost his wife, a physician, and his son, a medical student, and who rebuffed efforts at compensation (offered in the form of a donation to an orphanage). "No amount of money," he added "will sweep this under the rug."[81] It seems certain that the United States really will not accept this way of doing things, this quaint cultural way of acknowledging that Iraqi life is precious and that fathers whose wives and children have been blown to bits require a meaningful apology. The American system is indeed different from the one Rubaie and other Iraqis know. In 2021, as

"We Didn't Kill 'em, We Didn't Cut Their Heads Off" **175**

President Trump left office, he pardoned several soldiers guilty of torture and murder in Afghanistan and Iraq.[82] The making of American innocence goes on apace and largely through the story that the Islamic enemy requires the level of violence unleashed against them.

Critics of what happened at Abu Ghraib contribute to the making of national innocence by losing sight of the fact that Iraqi life is precious. It is never easy to navigate between being critical of torture and reifying it. Indeed, I seriously doubt that I have been successful here. At the end of the day, the sentence "Iraqi life is precious" stays with me as a reminder of how difficult it is to reclaim the humanity of the tortured once it has been taken away. We can begin to do this by making reparations and by starting with the investments we have in installing subjects who are innocent, ourselves included. We shield ourselves from the reality of torture in any number of ways, by insisting that it works or by declaring that it is the only way one can respond to a culturally different enemy. In other forms of protection from the truth of torture, Abu Ghraib is remembered as a unique example of the worst excesses of the "war on terror," an exceptional moment in an otherwise unblemished history. We continue to imagine that torture is inimical to liberal democracy, Jinee Lokaneeta writes, an assumption that helps us to deny how routine torture is, both in war and in everyday policing.[83] If we are to look torture in the face and avoid these narrative shields, refusing to make ourselves innocent is the first place to start.

When the Iraqi American poet Dunya Mikhail writes a poem issuing an urgent call to Lynndie England to return home immediately to have her baby (fathered by Charles Graner), she urges her not to worry about the future. There are prisons everywhere, she reassures her, and Lynndie will be certain to find work. To help her, the poet will send an email to God explaining that "the barbarians were the solution." In a final instruction, the poet warns Lynndie not to forget to hide the terrible pictures in case her child should one day find them: "You don't want your child to cry out: the prisoners are naked . . ."[84] Like Lynndie England, we are the ones entrusted with the memories and the photographs. We must take care what we do with them lest our own children cry out when they find them.

Conclusion
Arriving as Muslim

> How did we get here, to this place of hijab bans and outlawed mina-
> rets, secret renditions of enemy combatants, Abu Ghraib, and GTMO?
>
> —SOPHIA ROSE ARJANA, *MUSLIMS IN THE WESTERN IMAGINATION*

Despite a belief propagated by some that anti-Muslim racism is an imaginary racism, and that Muslims are a religious group and not a racialized
one, race is clearly central to how Muslims are apprehended and treated
in many parts of the world.[1] Racism changes character with the wind and
according to geopolitics. One day I realized that the racial epithet "damn
Hindu," hurled at me when I was an undergraduate by teenaged white
boys on the streets of Vancouver (boys still stuck in a nineteenth-century
world of early Sikh immigrants unsettling white people of Canada), had
changed. Hate mail now arrives with demands that I go back to the harem
and enjoy being one of the many wives of Osama bin Laden or be grateful that the West has saved me from the excesses of Islam. From "Paki,"
a favorite slur of the 1970s directed at anyone Brown, to "damn Hindu"
and to unrepeatable epithets uttered to women who wear the niqab and
the hijab, racial slurs reflect historical contingency. Whether it occurs
through acts of individual racism or institutionalized racism through surveillance, incarceration, or curricula, anti-Muslim racism changes character according to geopolitics and is largely driven by an affective relationship to a mythical "Islamland," a place Lila Abu-Lughod names as
the fantasy space constructed by anti-Muslim ideologues such as Ayaan
Hirsi Ali.[2] Decades of imperial wars and occupations, including the un-
ending "war on terror," have ensured the racial and imperial fantasy's en-
durance and its destructive effects far beyond the world of casual racial
epithets uttered on the streets of North America.

178 Conclusion

This book has been an exploration of this fantasy space "Islamland" in law and politics. The journey has entailed charting anti-Muslim racism as it travels through legal and cultural sites in the West, consolidating whiteness as it goes and contributing to a global white supremacy. Now at the journey's end, I begin by reviewing the features and landmarks of the place to which I have arrived as Muslim and consider the question that Sophia Rose Arjana asks about how we, those of us imagined as the inhabitants of "Islamland," got here. In the second section I venture outside the confines of this study to consider how anti-Muslim racism unfolds in the global South and the East, driving genocidal campaigns against Muslims. I consider what the making of Islam and Muslims as global threats portends for departure from "Islamland." In the closing section I suggest that the global dimensions of anti-Muslim racism, the consolidation of a global white supremacy, and the increasingly genocidal quality of anti-Muslim campaigns make an international antiracist and anticolonial politics urgent. I hope that this book contributes to such a politics.

Arriving as Muslim

This book traces the emergence of aggrieved white subjects through ordinary as well as legally sanctioned anti-Muslim feelings and emotions. It explores legal challenges that are driven by the bad feeling a white Christian woman has when she sees that her child has an art assignment on Arabic calligraphy, the unrestrained aggression displayed by a white man or woman who meets a woman wearing a niqab in a shopping mall or a school, and the sanctimony and patriarchal aggression that judges display when attempting to protect their nations from imagined Muslim foreigners. Such quotidian emotional scenes are remarkable for the ordinary and official places where many of them take place: homes, malls, streets, schools, and courts among them. They are also highly consequential: they produce routinized violence as well as racist legal precedent.

Emotions run high. Veils must be ripped off the heads of covered Muslim women in the name of feminism. White men insist on being able to see the smiles of Muslim women, and white women passionately protect Muslim women's right to wear short skirts. A "Muslim travel ban" attempts to keep Muslims out of the United States and politicians raise

Conclusion   **179**

the specter of ISIS and honor killers at the border as a justification for it. Paroxysms abound. The mere mention of Islam in a homework assignment unhinges parents; the impulse quickly comes to a white Christian father that he should go to the school with a gun to protest the assignment. It is possible to live with the torture of Omar Khadr, first detained as a fifteen-year-old Muslim Canadian, and to use the crudest versions of racial science—that Muslims carry a gene for violence—to condemn him to forty years in prison. In contrast to the response to Muslim teenagers, their torturers earn the nation's sympathy. The soldiers at Abu Ghraib prison who readily engaged in sexualized torture during the occupation of Iraq in 2003 are forgiven; they have yet to acknowledge the value of their prisoners' lives. Americans look on with indifference. Some are willing to condemn the leaders and architects of torture, but only as aberrations and stains on an otherwise pristine national landscape. It is sobering how quickly racial feeling can be harnessed to war making and the pursuit of imperial power, reminding us that such projects are dedicated to keeping property and power in white hands and require the making of a global whiteness. In other words, that affect results in very material effects. The ease with which the Western world has accepted extrajudicial killings of Muslim enemies and the dropping of bombs on village compounds, schools, and hospitals by drones reveals the extent to which the continuous death of populations deemed to stand in the way of accumulation is the structuring principle of Western life.

If Muslims are caught in a necropolitics that brings death and destruction, they are also part of the everyday calculus of living and dying that is a part of liberal modernity. Because they are framed as incompletely modern, their eviction from law and politics often occurs under the guise of a liberal politics. Muslims experience a differential inclusion when they are tolerated as a faith community on the condition that racial grievances are left at the door. Nations are prepared to save Muslim women from their oppressive cultures, announcing that women's rights are human rights even as a terrible violence is directed at Muslim populations. It is entirely possible to practice a multicultural inclusion while remaining defined by the imperatives of an empire premised on the disposability of targeted populations. As Richard Slotkin shows, the scripts of cultural mythology about a multicultural, egalitarian nation are easily

180 Conclusion

rewritten to adapt to the needs of political projects of a white "gun-fighter" nation and empire.[3] The Muslim's many phantasmic forms—as "terrorist," as global enemy, and as slyly aggressive covered women of the harem—lurk in the background, readily activated when required in the interests of empire and the racial state.

The conjured objects of white anti-Muslim feelings, Muslims matter to these schemes of global whiteness and imperial power. Whether deemed religious foes who stand in the way of the end times, a Christian religious scenario that accommodates the dispossession of Palestinians and the pursuit of American hegemony in the Middle East, or imagined as threatening to white Europeans anxious to ensure that colonial spoils are not available to the formerly colonized and to those fleeing imperial wars and occupations, Muslims are in the line of fire. In Europe and North America, organizations and legislatures pursue anti-Muslim legal projects with concentrated fury, and disparate networks mobilize to circulate an anti-Muslim affect globally. The point is to circulate anti-Muslim feelings and to proclaim who are rightful citizens of the nation and who stand outside of it. Anti-Muslim legal strategists seem to know that nothing has to make sense in law when the subject is Muslim; reasoned argument is readily abandoned in favor of passion. For those committed to anti-Muslim racism, facts don't matter. The courtroom, operating uncannily like the minaret from where Muslims are called to prayer, becomes instead a place where faithful white Christians gather and are reminded of their common identity. The goal of anti-Muslim actors is race making, and whether it is done in the name of Christianity or secularism, each legal battle begins by declaring that white European civilization and modern life itself is under siege from Muslims.

When nothing has to make sense and racial feeling and emotion do the work of securing white interests in law, concepts such as ideology and class antagonisms have less analytical purchase than they might have. They do not seem able to bear the weight of the fears, anxieties, and desires that anti-Muslim racism entails as it travels through law and society. A racial project of accumulation through late capitalism in the West certainly does (Fanon had it right); the ways in which we have become accustomed to hierarchies of the human that lie at the base of this project still stops the heart. It is difficult to absorb European indiffer-

Conclusion 181

ence to the deaths of so many refugees crossing the Mediterranean and into Europe. For instance, the Italian coast guard waited more than five hours before rendering assistance to a migrant-carrying boat, resulting in the death of 268 people.[4] Such indifference cannot be explained as mere anti-immigrant feeling fueled by declining economic prospects for the white working and middle class. The same is true of the American turn to a more aggressive white nationalism; economic aggrievement tells only half the story. As the historian Walter Johnson reminds us, the economic anxiety felt by white Americans is "ineluctably racial," and white male vulnerability never fails to express itself in the language of racial entitlement.[5] Something important about imperial projects of rule and the relentless dehumanizing and disposal of surplus humanity they require demands an analysis of race making, and specifically what it means to live in a world where, as Ghassan Hage writes, quoting Genesis, the operating logic is that "every living thing shall fear you and shall be meat for you."[6] Charting torture in secret and known prisons, indifference to bombs dropped on the children of Gaza and Yemen or to those unleashed by drones on Muslim populations in the name of "taking out" noted "terrorists," the questions persist: How did we get here? How do we change course?

I hear the question Sophia Rose Arjana asks as one full of anguish: How did we get to this place?[7] Exploring the history of Muslims as monsters in the Western imagination, Arjana observes that today's Muslims provoke "old anxieties" and are constructions that for thirteen hundred years have been simultaneously fantasies about Jewish and African bodies. "The homicidal terroristic Muslim man" featured in tales of Muhammad in the European medieval period survives in stories of Black Saracens and monster Turks during the Ottoman period and in New World accounts of Indigenous people as Moors. Medieval Muslims are well-traveled monsters who were once depicted with black, blue, or purple skin, large lips, and curly hair. "Hybrid monsters" in which the categories of Saracen, Jew, and Black African melded, they serve as racialized constructions that establish white Christianity as normative white humanity.[8] Today, monster Muslims who help Christians to imagine themselves as a superior racial community populate an imaginary filled with sexualized images of monsters with giant penises violating white womanhood

182 Conclusion

and looking forward to sex in heaven. As chapter 3 discusses, the pages of the journal *Evolutionary Psychology* offer the same gendered and sexualized imagery relatively unchanged for use by prosecutors of Muslims accused of having the potential to commit "terrorist" acts and for policy experts on Muslim "radicalization." Hindu nationalists borrow the same ideas about the Muslim man as rapist, the sex in these fantasies concealing desire and bearing the full weight of racial hostility.

The world has been unwilling to do without its Muslim monsters and rapists, white fantasies that have traveled transnationally for several centuries. Shared expressions of anti-Muslim feeling flowed between Anglo-Americans and Britons in British-ruled India. Eighteenth-century Americans absorbed English views of Muslims, even though they possessed little direct knowledge of them. A shared Europeanness and Christianity easily made up for the distance between continents. Then as now, colonialism built the racial infrastructure required to carry anti-Muslim affect. As Junaid Rana shows, the technologies and structures of detention, rendition, and torture depend upon a particular racialization of Islam and Muslims as disposable and marked for death.[9] Christian evangelical sources, as chapter 1 discusses, circulated anti-Muslim sentiments between continents, discourses littered with impassioned war cries of "Islam or Christ."[10] The status of Muslims today in Europe and America is foregrounded by these long-standing ideas about Islam and Christianity locked in mortal combat. Christianity announces whiteness in many parts of the world, and phantom Muslims are never far behind.

The figure of the Muslim that haunts Western consciousness as a reminder of the Crusades, as the Antichrist, or as Hollywood's Dracula is a figure who stands in the way of white Western superpower and who is imagined as already having breached the gates of Europe and America. Hage offers the metaphor of wolf to describe how Muslims are experienced in the West today, feared Others who cannot be integrated into the modern and who are ungovernable waste, surplus populations who must be disposed of.[11] If we have traveled from the casting out of Muslims from law and society to aggressively disposing of them, it is because Muslims stand in the way of accumulation, "abandoned subjects" relegated to the role of "superfluous humanity," as Achille Mbembe suggests of populations whom "capital hardly needs anymore to function."[12] The whiteness that is secured through bans on Muslim women's hijabs and niqabs enables Canadians and Europeans to understand themselves geopolitically as a family of nations of a superior civilization, but it also enables such nations to close their gates to refugees and to engage in a politics anchored in keeping out the "barbarians." A circulating colonial affect of the Muslim as premodern and patriarchal accompanies border policies that contribute to the deaths of thousands trying to make their way into Europe. American Christian evangelical local projects to ban Islam in the curriculum have a similar material impact when they facilitate the continued dispossession of Palestinians. Wars in the Middle East accomplish the same deterritorialization as chaos is sowed and whole swaths of populations are forced to be on the move as refugees in wars often understood as "Muslim wars."

If North America and Europe are centered in the analytical frame of this book, it is nevertheless clear that the international whiteness that is made through the figure of the Muslim underwrites imperial projects the world over. Muslim parts of the world come to be seen as legitimate sites for plunder and rule through wars and occupations, projects that utilize the anti-Muslim discourses of the West grafted onto local anti-Muslim narratives to enact the destruction of Muslim communities. Anti-Muslim racism contributes to the unwavering support the United States gives to Israel, most recently endorsing plans for the Israeli unilateral annexation of the West Bank. American support for the Saudi-backed bombing of Yemen secures privileged access to oil markets and brings unimaginable violence to that country, a violence now increasingly referred to as an impending genocide. Genocidal campaigns against Muslims are proliferating.

Genocidal Scenes

The figure of the Muslim that I follow in this book contributes to the making of the transnational community of white people in an increasingly globalized world in which violence against Muslims is proliferating. What has become clear, however, as I discussed in the Introduction, is that there are the cracks in the color line, as Sedef Arat-Koç put it, referring to Eastern European nations deemed insufficiently white who seek to access the benefits of whiteness through distancing themselves from Muslims.[13] Non-European nations widen the cracks further when they

184 Conclusion

locate themselves on the terrain of international and imperial whiteness through an intensified and genocidal eviction of Muslims from political community. India and China are two examples of this development, each country designating Muslim minorities with whom they have long been in conflict as global "Islamic terrorists" and individuals and groups to be added to the "Consolidated List" of global "terrorists" and communities targeted for disposal.[14] As Ben Emmerson, the former UN special rapporteur on counterterrorism and former judge of the United Nations International Criminal Tribunals for Rwanda and the former Yugoslavia, observed, the Chinese Communist Party uses "counter-terrorism as a fig-leaf for cultural genocide."[15] *Genocide* is a word that has also been applied to the treatment of the Rohingya by Myanmar[16] and the bombing of Yemen supported by Saudi Arabia.[17] If these genocidal scenes seem a world away even from torture at Guantánamo and Abu Ghraib, genetic arguments in sentencing hearings, and bans on the veil and on Arabic calligraphy, they can be easily connected to these events in the West though their emphasis on humanity/subhumanity and the racial infrastructures necessary to accomplish the disposal of populations. Reliant on the same technologies and infrastructures—of surveillance and social media, for example—and legal narratives about the pathological psychology of Muslims, these events link us all in a global circuit of anti-Muslim racism and of war on disposable populations.

Perhaps nothing portends the disposability of Muslim populations as much as does the intensified campaigns to create Muslim as a race. There is a growing tendency to focus on Muslim genetics by states anxious to regulate and surveil Muslim populations; anti-Muslim states find it increasingly important to invent a Muslim race. China offers one of the most notorious examples of race making as key to its genocidal campaign against its Muslim Uyghur minority. As a part of a massive DNA project to create the image of a person's face, China has collected blood samples from the Muslim Uyghur population, a million of whom are currently interned in what many have described as concentration and forced labor camps.[18] Assisting the state to identify who is Uyghur and who is not, phenotype genetic research is openly declared to be for the purpose of surveillance and control. Sharing the goal of surveillance and control of Muslims, American firms who were a part of the Chinese project only

Conclusion **185**

suspended their involvement when it came to light in the media that the samples were likely obtained without Uyghur consent.

Genetic research has long been yoked to political concerns, as chapter 3 discussed. In a 2007 research study that collected blood samples from Shia and Sunni Muslims, Indian researchers hoped to establish whether present-day Muslims were mainly descended from "invaders" or from Indians imagined as being forced to convert to Islam.[19] The researchers concluded that although it seemed that Shias were more recent on the Indian landscape than Sunnis, most Indian Muslims were genetically Indian and descended from Muslim males who came to India, married local females, and settled down. The study concluded that Muslim genes were closer to those of upper-caste Brahmins and Rajputs, which in turn showed that Indians were not forced to convert to Islam, since forced conversion is typically associated with lower castes. It is hard to see how blood samples can reveal so much about ancestry and the heritability of beliefs. The politics visible in the research suggest a troubling logic that divides Indians into authentic and inauthentic citizens, a division secured by reference to genetics. One can only imagine the conclusions drawn by more racially hostile genetic researchers today in an India where the state has pursued the legal disenfranchisement of Muslims through a National Register of Citizens that has evicted two million mostly Muslim Assamese Indians from citizenship on the premise that they are not of Indian ancestry. At the same time as Muslims are evicted from citizenship, a policing of the gene pool as it is imagined is occurring with legal efforts to stop interfaith marriages.[20]

An emphasis on race as real and consequential is ominous. The division of humanity into races has always smuggled in hierarchy, arrangements that can quickly turn to concentration camps and genocides. For this reason, it is imperative that we analyze a global order in which the Muslim is declared to be a universal enemy through the prism of racism. It is of vital importance to understand how the racialization of Muslims occurs and the role it plays in projects of rule and capitalist accumulation. This book has pursued this goal through an examination of how white subjects and white nations in the West consolidate their whiteness in law and politics through the figure of the Muslim. It argues that the Muslim as "terrorist" is a figure of global importance, maintaining white

186 Conclusion

supremacy and contributing to the structure of a world divided between the deserving and the disposable according to a racial logic whereby people of European origin are the former and all others are confined in various ways to regimes of disposability. Reviewing the book's conclusions, two questions arise: How does the racialization of Muslims and the hierarchies of the human it installs operate outside of Europe and North America, and what does an international whiteness and a global imperial structure presage for an oppositional politics that seeks to undo racially structured projects of accumulation and their deadly arrangements? Although this book has not explored anti-Muslim racism in the global South, the destruction of Muslim life that is unfolding in such places as India and China confirms that the violence directed at Muslims in these regions relies on a form of race making similar to that in the global North and is critical to vesting property and profits in the hands of elites who imagine themselves as racially superior and who are a part of an international elite capitalist community.

Arundhati Roy writes of the Indian context that we "can only hope that someday soon, the streets in India will throng with people who realize that unless they make their move, the end is close."[21] The end that Roy fears for India is the wholesale dispossession and eviction of Muslims from national community in the name of Hindu supremacy, a neoliberal project that vests power in the hands of elites and dispossesses Muslim, Indigenous, and poor communities across India.[22] The targeting and dispossession of Muslims is accomplished by highly organized mob killings, the brutal military occupation of Jammu and Kashmir (provinces summarily stripped of their special status under the Indian constitution), and the legal disenfranchisement of Muslim Assamese Indians from citizenship. The evicted are held under lockdown, herded into concentration camps, and subjected to torture. Observing that Hindu nationalist organizations and the ruling party (the Bharatiya Janata Party) together command an infrastructure that is able to accomplish racial violence directed at Muslims at a level and speed previously unimaginable, Roy considers the militias of men and women trained to execute violent pogroms, the media infrastructure that circulates anti-Muslim feeling, and the political and legal elites that authorize the violence and concludes that even if India does not "get to the Zyklon B stage" (a reference to the gassing of Jews during the Nazi regime), "there's plenty of money to be made."[23] Noting the close connections between Prime Minister Modi and former president Trump, she reminds us that anti-Muslim projects are shared between nations of the North and the South.

The near genocidal violence reported by scholars in the Indian context reveals the racial lines that run through the Indian Hindu-supremacist project. The Muslim as phantom rapist, "terrorist," and religious enemy gives birth to a modern superior race obliged to guard the gates of the nation from atavistic Muslim marauders. Requiring a dominant group who comes to believe in its (gendered) racial entitlement through religion, the Hindu-supremacist project assembles men who see themselves as soldiers and warrior monks, and women who are able to participate directly in the violence on the same premise of defending the nation from Muslims who defile the nation as they are imagined doing to Hindu women.[24]

Feminist scholars, troubled by events of the 1990s in which Hindu women "led mobs and dragged Muslim women and children into the streets, applauded their gang rapes and joined men in stoning Muslim women and setting them on fire," have sought to explain how it comes to be that women, scripted as subordinate in Hindu nationalist mythology, nevertheless gain a measure of agency and freedom (sometimes expressed in protofeminist terms) through their participation in violence against Muslims.[25] As the Indian historian Tanika Sarkar observes, the eternally lustful Muslim male with evil designs on Hindu women is not only a powerful vector in anti-Muslim violence more generally, but a myth that enables Hindu nationalist women to focus on anti-Muslim hatred rather than any oppression they encounter from their own men. Highlighting the importance of media as a part of the infrastructure for anti-Muslim politics, Sarkar suggests that Hindu nationalist women develop their religious identities not by responding to traditional devotional teachings but through a highly mediated version of Hinduism created by a high-tech modern media, a version in which women are avenging angels who restore a Hindu national order; a racial order comes into existence as a religious one.[26]

A racial project is no less perceptible, although coded differently, in the case of China's persecution of Muslims. The same genocidal impulses

188 Conclusion

as in the Indian case are narrated by the state as a project that is intended to contain a "terrorist" threat. In this way, as Sean R. Roberts put it, the colonizing nature of China's relationship with Muslim Uyghurs in their homeland is reimagined as a "war on terror."[27] Collaborating with other states claiming to be combating separatism, religious extremism, and international terrorism, the Chinese anti-Uyghur campaigns win the support of the Han Chinese majority on the strength of the argument that the state is protecting the population from a global enemy. As Roberts reminds us, the "war on terror" is not a war but a narrative about a people who carry the seeds of violence in their histories and cultures and who must be controlled if not annihilated.[28] Through an intensely politically motivated process, the People's Republic of China was eventually able to persuade the United States (who initially rejected the claim) that the Uyghurs should be classified as global "terrorists."[29] The narrative and classification enabled the Chinese government to recraft Uyghur anticolonial resistance as "Islamic terrorism."

The anti-Muslim campaign against the Uyghur Muslim minority bears all the hallmarks of a full-blown racial annihilation in actions ranging from mass incarceration in detention camps to disappearances, torture, forced sterilization, detention of small children in camps where they are not permitted to learn Uyghur, and organ harvesting. It is this last strategy that seemed to have finally caught the attention of the West. In late September 2019, *Business Insider* reported that the UN Human Rights Council received a complaint that China was engaged in widespread harvesting of human organs from detained Uyghur Muslims (and Falun Gong practitioners) whose homeland in Xinjiang province is China's western frontier.[30] The news was shocking, bringing to mind Kazuo Ishiguro's 2005 dystopian novel *Never Let Me Go*, in which a special class of human clones is bred to supply society with organs.[31] The extraction of value from humans declared to be waste became chillingly literal. As with so much news of this nature, outrage soon subsided, although the Western press continued to report on abuses against Uyghurs.

In November 2019 the *New York Times* reported that a cache of documents named the "China Cables" and leaked to fifteen media outlets[32] revealed China's plans to round up Muslim minorities in Xinjiang. The *Times* headlined their exposé with the directive issued by Chinese president Xi Jinping to officials, "Show absolutely no mercy," an offensive Xi described as one against "terrorism, infiltration and separatism" in a region that has long struggled for its autonomy.[33] The Sunday *Times* reader, perhaps reading this article over brunch, learned that Uyghur students arriving home at the end of the semester for the summer did so to empty houses. Although nearly a million people had been rounded up and detained in camps in the past three years, this latest offensive was nonetheless extreme.[34] The leaked memos advised government officials to manage the students' reactions to their absent family. The students were to be told that their parents and relatives had simply been sent for reeducation, having been exposed to "harmful influence in religious extremism and violent terrorist thoughts." China had earlier described the detention camps as job-training centers, something the memo clearly contradicted. The students were to be reassured, but also intimidated lest they felt inclined to spread the word about the detentions on social media. Citing civil war in Syria and the rise of ISIS, officials were instructed to explain to the students that "No matter what age, anyone who has been infected by religious extremism must undergo study."[35] The documents show that an accelerated crackdown on Uyghurs had begun in earnest in April 2014, two weeks after Uyghur militants stabbed more than 150 people in a train station, killing 31. Uyghurs also staged a suicide bombing injuring several and killing one on the occasion of President Xi's visit to Xinjiang. These antigovernment events were crude and linked to decades-long ethnic riots often sparked by repressive measures, such as the 1994 plan to transfer large numbers of the Han Chinese majority to Xinjiang and the creation of a massive system of electronic surveillance and in-person visits by Chinese officials to Uyghur homes. In a series of secret speeches, Xi emphasized his directive to show no mercy when rounding up Uyghurs. Referencing attacks by Muslims in Britain and the drawing out of U.S. troops in Afghanistan, he advised officials to emulate the United States after 9/11 in America's "war on terror." In this way, state and nonstate forms of terror would travel in a loop, endlessly reproducing itself.

Although President Xi once warned his party not to fan the flames between Uyghurs and the majority Han Chinese, in the memos he repeated his belief that those "captured by religious extremism—male or female—have their consciences destroyed, lose their humanity and murder without blinking an eye."[36] The cure was an ideological one: detention and reeducation, particularly of those displaying symptoms of radicalism evinced by the wearing of beards, studying Arabic, or praying. In a gendered targeting, the government launched a "Project Beauty" campaign in which Uyghur women were required to adopt less modest dress than traditional Uyghur clothing allowed. Uyghur women were sanctioned for their failure to dress accordingly. This campaign is an interesting parallel to French bans on the hijab and niqab and French insistence that Muslim girls should enjoy the right to wear short skirts.[37] In 2017, when this series of "de-extremification" measures were passed for the region, and Chen Quanguo was appointed party boss for the region, the detention of Uyghurs and forced relocations escalated. Officials did not always comply with the directive to round up Muslims, although in the case of discredited official Wang Yongzhi, who declared to his team that there was nothing wrong in having a Qur'an at home and who released seven thousand detainees, the government maintained that he had simultaneously engaged in the forced relocation of families. In 2020, Roberts reported that the mass incarceration of Uyghurs launched in 2017 had now transitioned into coerced and segregated forced labor camps, something accelerated under the conditions of a global Covid-19 pandemic. Although social media was increasingly shut down, GPS technology was used to document "large labor brigades with suitcases and wearing pandemic-mandated masks, presumably being transported to work in factories."[38]

Scholars, China policy analysts, and journalists who have continued to report abuses in the mass detention camps holding Xinjiang's Muslims point out that China's new Silk Road economic initiative cannot proceed without Uyghur participation. China has reason to engage in a Uyghur "final solution," warns Nuri Turkel, an American Uyghur lawyer.[39] As he and researcher Darren Byler show, the camps function as forced labor camps for the factories processing Xinjiang cotton goods (Chinese cotton goods amount to one-third of the world's cotton, of which 84 percent comes from Xinjiang). Scholars and journalists have documented arrests of Uyghurs for "crimes" as trivial as watching Turkish TV, soap operas that feature women wearing hijabs. More chillingly, researchers have documented the creation of "kindness centers" (nurseries) where

80 percent of Uyghur children are kept and are prohibited from speaking Uyghur. They confirm the removal of Uyghur leaders and the destruction of mosques and Uyghur burial grounds, a literal cleansing of the land of Uyghur presence. As other scholars also maintain, Byler does not hesitate to describe Chinese efforts in Xinjiang as cultural genocide.[40] Few seem able to contest the cultural genocide in progress, least of all through law and politics. Nations cannot protest the Chinese mass detention camps without risking the wrath of a powerful nation; some do so and are forced to retract a day later.[41] More chillingly, most don't want to unless there is something to be gained economically and politically. The United States, engaged in a trade war with China, condemned China's treatment of the Uyghurs in 2020.[42]

Notwithstanding its denunciation of the Chinese treatment of Uyghurs, the United States maintains a willful indifference to the torture and killing of Muslim people, even rewarding those who commit war crimes against Muslim populations. It is telling that President Trump intervened in a navy SEAL inquiry concerning indiscriminate shooting of civilians in Iraq, insisting that the review of Chief Petty Officer Edward R. Gallagher for his conduct be halted.[43] Gallagher had cut the throat of a captive Iraqi teenager who was receiving medical aid. He had earlier declared that he wanted to kill as many people as possible and had been reported several times for shooting at civilians.[44] Unable to prove the killings attested to by over a dozen soldiers under Gallagher's command, the navy settled for charging him with posing for pictures with an Iraqi corpse and stripping him of his military insignia. President Trump, already on record as pardoning soldiers convicted of war crimes in the Muslim world, insisted in a tweet that Gallagher not lose his Trident pin, the insignia that indicates membership in the elite SEAL community. Holding the line amid the objections of the president, Navy Secretary Richard Spencer was fired for refusing to comply with the president's request.[45] In contrast, architects of torture such as Gina Haspel, who oversaw secret torture and detention sites and who headed the CIA from 2018 until 2021, survive and thrive, while the full truth about the torture program remains officially buried.[46] For the parent outraged that his daughter had a homework assignment on Islam and who defended his desire to go to the school with a gun by referencing his military experience

192 Conclusion

killing Muslims, and for the soldier who engaged in torture without remorse, these presidential activities would seem entirely appropriate and necessary. These actions trade in white anti-Muslim feelings and endorse if not celebrate the disposability of Muslim populations.

Departure

After World War II, knowing that they confronted "international structures of unequal integration and racial hierarchy," Black anti-imperialists recognized that an end to colonialism could only be achieved by remaking the international order.[47] As Adom Getachew argues, these men were "world makers" who understood that empire would persist in other forms unless they could challenge white imperialism collectively and head-on. The global ambitions required collaboration. Eric Williams of Trinidad pursued a federation of Caribbean nations. Kwame Nkrumah, Ghana's first prime minister, saw the urgency of a union of African states. Both men failed in the plan to go beyond the nation-state. The Western world continued to view self-determination as a status few Black countries merited. The same recognition of the world-constituting force of European imperialism and the global white supremacy it inaugurated prompted the Black Panthers to understand that political engagement had to go beyond the nation-state. Their own grassroots activism for racial justice was always situated on a landscape of anticapitalist and anticolonial resistance.[48] Black thinkers and leaders have long seen that racial capitalism could not be dismantled unless its global reach was confronted.

Writing about the anti-imperialist vision of Malcolm X, Sohail Daulatzai notes the long-standing connections between Black radical thinkers and the Muslim third world.[49] For Malcolm and for Black Muslims, Islam was a way to reject the master narrative of slavery and of America itself. Proposing the term "Muslim International" to describe the shared histories and solidarities between Black Muslims, Black radicals, and the anticolonialism of the Muslim world, Daulatzai suggests that we resurrect this paradigm and remember that an international radical anti-imperialist challenge to American and European power is more than ever required. We are reminded of the urgency of the Muslim International and the connections between the Black freedom struggle and Muslims when we consider the persecution of Black Muslims as

Black criminals and "homegrown terrorists," a targeting Daulatzai reminds us results in the increased incarceration of Black Muslims. The argument for a return to internationalist politics practiced by the Black Panthers and Black leaders of the third world is compelling. Daulatzai makes the case that the way forward entails a careful mapping of how religious subjects become racial subjects and how anti-Muslim racism is "an operative and generative logic of white supremacy."[50] In its effort to map a global anti-Muslim racism, this book joins with scholars who argue that there is a global idea of race and who share in the conviction that the global whiteness that is made through the figure of the Muslim demands nothing less than a return to internationalist politics. The prospect is at once urgent and daunting.

In this book I have offered a contribution toward an internationalist politics through understanding anti-Muslim racism as embedded in a globalized white supremacy whose contours we can see when we follow the paths of phantom Muslims as they traverse Western law and politics. Although the liberatory projects of artists, intellectuals, social movements, and social actors are beyond the scope of this book, there is little doubt that it is in these artistic visions that many find direction for an internationalist politics. As Ronak Kapadia shows in *Insurgent Aesthetics* in his discussion of the "freedom dreams" of contemporary Arab, Muslim, and South Asian diasporic artists, a great "creativity and fugitive beauty [emanates] from the shadows of terrible violence incited by forever war."[51] Kenza Oumlil finds the same in the stand-up comedy of Mayzoon Zayid and the visual art and films of Shirin Neshat.[52]

Whether in art or politics, anti-Muslim violence and terror never go unresisted. As Tanika Sarkar reports, Muslim women in India have sat in protest day and night in New Delhi and through their words and songs refused their eviction.[53] Kashmiris engage in the politics of a general strike while finding ways to offer the essential services needed for everyday life.[54] Unable to protest within China, Uyghurs and their allies took to the streets of Washington, D.C., to call on the U.S. government to recognize China's policies of violence against them as a genocide.[55] If resistance can be hard to imagine against empires, in the wake of a deafening silence from the world community as genocides against Muslims unfold in various parts of the world, those who bear the brunt of the

194 Conclusion

violence have no option but to resist. There can be no standing outside of the currents of anti-Muslim feeling, particularly as they travel virtual pathways. As farmers discovered while participating in massive protests against the Indian government's new farming laws that suspend guaranteed prices for certain crops, protestors were depicted online (in a series of fake news plants) not as legitimate citizens engaging in protests but as "Islamic infiltrators."[56] When every perceived enemy of the state is collapsed into the category of "Islamic extremist," violence is authorized.

The work of American scholars such as Nadine Naber, Sunaina Maira, and Mayanthi Fernando, among others, disabuses anyone of the notion that Muslim communities do not resist. Clearly, a Muslim International is already well underway.[57] As the ethnographies of these feminist scholars show, resistance to racism and imperial wars has always demanded an analysis of global white supremacy and has required global solidarities. In several books and anthologies based on meticulous ethnographies of the leftist Arab movement in the United States, Naber has carefully traced the contours of Arab American women's resistance to racism and to the relentless attacks on their communities worldwide, charting the emergence of a "diasporic feminist anti-imperialism."[58] As the artists and activists she interviews respond to sanctions against Iraq, the continuing dispossession of Palestinians, and the wars and occupations in Syria and Yemen, they are as keenly aware as Black leaders were of the postwar period that what they confront is the making of a global color line with white nations and their partners (including some Arab nations) on one side and marginalized Muslim communities (among other racialized communities) on the other. Arab American feminist political action bears the hallmarks of a deep commitment to what, in the North American context, is typically described as an intersectional approach, the understanding of power as an intersection where imperialism, race, class, gender, and sexuality meet. As Naber shows, Arab American feminists operationalized an alternative to masculinist politics, turning to grassroots activism and cultural production and refusing singular articulations of Arabness premised on "compulsory heterosexuality, patriarchy and idealized concepts of biological reproduction within kin relations."[59] Significantly, Arab American feminists profoundly challenge the idea that Arab nations and their own diasporic communities are beyond critique, a position that Muslim feminists everywhere adopt.

In her work, Sunaina Maira shows that the intensified racial targeting that South Asian, Arab, and Afghan youth experienced after 9/11 yields an internationalist anti-imperialist Muslim politics that connects the surveillance, policing, and disciplining that youth experience domestically to the wars and occupations in their parents' communities of origin. In particular, the exceptional censorship and demonization of the Palestine solidarity movement within the United States since the 1980s deepened their criticisms of U.S. foreign policy in the Middle East and sharpened awareness of the transnational security regimes that target Muslims. The American state's own international and domestic collaborations, between Israel (who supplies surveillance technology), the FBI and Homeland Security in their "counterterrorism" pursuits, and local police and agencies of border enforcement give rise to a radical politics across constituencies, both domestically and internationally. The widely repeated phrase "From Ferguson to Gaza" is but one illustration of an internationalist and coalitional politics on the ground.[60]

Scholars examining Muslim political resistance often assume that an antiracist and anti-imperial politics can have little to do with religion. When the politics of pious Muslims is considered, it is common to assume that the pious Muslim is always politically conservative. Contesting this assumption, Mayanthi Fernando's ethnography of young Muslim people in France suggest that the Muslim French (French citizens of Muslim faith) in her study draw upon both Islamic and secular-republican traditions to craft an oppositional politics that insists on religious piety and, simultaneously, on staking a claim to membership in the nation. Muslim French practice "a publicly engaged religiosity"[61] that refuses their eviction from political community. There is no one shape to the politics of piety, however, just as there is no single version of secular politics. Whether religiosity provides the basis for an oppositional politics or not, those charting a global anti-Muslim racism and resistance in all its regional specificities know that it is important to attend to the translations and mistranslations that arise when anti-Muslim *and* antiracist discourses travel transnationally.[62] There can be no easy deployment of the categories religious or secular, "Muslim" and "non-Muslim," or Black and Muslim. As Zeynep K. Korkman argues in the case of Turkey, there are consequences for transnational feminist analysis and solidarity when we fail to see how the authoritarian and gender-conservative Turkish

196 Conclusion

regime deploys antiracist discourses where Black is an analogy to pious. At the same time that it boasts of its antiracist politics, Turkey pursues a repressive politics and a neoliberal agenda in the name of Islam, while simultaneously racializing Kurds and other minorities.[63] These various complexities must all be examined in oppositional politics, which is necessarily internationalist.

For many of us who arrive as Muslim, the challenge to think beyond the nation-state is a personal and perhaps an intuitive one that begins with our own crossing of borders and colonial histories. Ferruh Yilmaz writes: "I went to Denmark in 1979 as a young left-wing activist who had no idea what the term identity meant. Within two decades, I became a Muslim." He adds, "My 'conversion' had nothing to do with religion."[64] How does it feel to live in an anti-Muslim world when one is Muslim or presumed Muslim, newly arrived or not? In truth, I have not wanted to think about what it feels like to see people I recognize as sharing my culture detained in camps and bombed-out landscapes, a personal connection that Hage names.[65] Instead, I have wanted to insist that we must all care, not because the inmates of camps and the bodies on the ground are biologically or culturally related to us, but because the violence has been done in our name. Yet as a feminist, I know that the personal is political and that I find myself on the landscape of global anti-Muslim racism in intimate and familial ways that deeply inform my work and no doubt intensify and complicate my personal and scholarly responses. I felt fear when I first saw that fifteen-year-old Omar Khadr, tortured at Bagram and Guantánamo, looks like my son, is his age, and grew up close by, and that the men tortured at Abu Ghraib look like my brothers, uncles, and nephews. The Muslim congregants whom Alexandre Bissonette shot in Canada, and whom Brenton Tarrant killed in New Zealand, could easily have been my family and friends. On the day of my mother's funeral memorial, white supremacists gathered for an anti-Muslim rally in downtown Toronto. We took care to scan the exits of the mosque before the ceremony began. It seems that there are very few degrees of separation from violence of any kind, but only some violence can be acknowledged in public discourse. We are all implicated in these economies of violence, and as people whose origins are in places that are frequently connected to violence, we are never remote from it.[66] The

Conclusion **197**

mosque my parents helped to build in 1954 in our small Caribbean island town is now given a rating as a tourist site on Tripadvisor and described as having a *madrassa*, an Arabic word for "school" that I did not learn until the events of 9/11. Like so many people raised as Muslim outside of Muslim-majority countries, I have had to develop a vocabulary that includes words like *madrassa, hijab,* and *niqab.* In the post-9/11 period, there is no place for stumbling explanations either of secularism or that in our Islam men and women prayed beside each other, that we did not wear the hijab, and that we often went straight from the early morning prayer to enjoying family excursions to the beach already dressed in our swimsuits. These childhood memories are too easily conscripted in the game of good Muslim/bad Muslim.

It is not easy to avoid the snares of "fake news" and the strong emotions in which it trades. We often reach out to one another across the virtual circuits of propaganda and the waves of emotion on which it travels. My cousin tells me that she has read that ISIS is recruiting young men from my country of origin and in turn circulates on WhatsApp Indian government propaganda about Kashmir. "We Muslims" is not a phrase that comes easily either to her lips or to mine as we work out what we stand for and what we will not accept. Yassir Morsi describes how we are summoned as good Muslims and wonders how we live in what we know to be a trap.[67] "Islamland," the fantasy world of anti-Muslim racists, is an emotional place in which to dwell, a place where there is a constant pressure to prove that one is a good Muslim. My own response to the trap Morsi identifies is to pay attention to the circuits of affect into which we are drawn and through which we are produced, negotiating between the shoals of liberalism and fascism. Others have offered their own approaches. Houria Bouteldja offers the *WE* of an Indigenous revolutionary politics of love.[68] Ghassan Hage insists that we must all find a way to live in the world that is not about subordinating others in the name of extracting value, and he places his hopes in "the multiplicity of surviving forms of inhabitance and relationality."[69] It is clear that any attempt to confront anti-Muslim racism must recognize our place in its proximity and its function in global white supremacy.

Acknowledgments

This book began to take form shortly after the publication of *Casting Out* in 2008. I am indebted to the graduate students of the Department of Social Justice Education of the Ontario Institute for Studies in Education, University of Toronto, who offered their finest research skills. For their work on early drafts of some of the essays here, my thanks go to Nashwa Salem, Falak Mujtaba, Louise Tam, Nazira Mawji, and Corey Balsam. I have been having this conversation about Muslims as a race with Toronto friends and especially with Honor Ford Smith, Ramabai Espinet, Amina Jamal, and Sheryl Nestel for decades and depend on their insights more than they know. Thank you for never letting me go. Relocating to the United States in 2016, I would not have even begun putting together this book without the friendship and intellectual sustenance of American friends. I must start with Sohail Daulatzai and Junaid Rana, editors of the Muslim International book series and longtime interlocutors, who made this book much better than it would have been without their interventions. The challenge they issue to think about how Islam and Muslims are at the center of twenty-first-century global white supremacy is one that inspired this book. I thank them for the hours they spent reading drafts and providing critical feedback, an unstinting intellectual generosity that drove this project.

I finished the manuscript during a pandemic, a time when friends and intellectual nourishment are more necessary than ever. Laura Gomez was there every step of the way, offering crucial intellectual and emotional support and reminding me why we write as critical race scholars. I thank her for never letting me give up and for the inspiration of her own work. At UCLA, I found amazing friendship and community without which it is not easy to write. Co-conspirator Zeynep K. Korkman took me by the hand and quietly and with the maximum of warmth and tact helped me to move away from my North Americanist lens. Her own capacity to

199

200 Acknowledgments

understand anti-Muslim racism as it travels transnationally inspired my efforts to do the same. I also thank Purnima Mankekar, Aslı Bâli, Nadine Naber, and Nadera Shalhoub-Kevorkian for showing me what a transnational analysis looks like. They and the other participants of the Racial Violence Hub's 2019 workshop "Feminist Approaches to Understanding Global Anti-Muslim Racism" (Nadine Naber, Sherene Seikaly, Saree Makdisi, Saiba Varma, Elora Shehabuddin, Sohail Daulatzai, Junaid Rana, Minoo Moallem, Catherine Sameh, Khanum Shaikh, Azza Basarudin, Sherine Hafez, Sarah Gualtieri, Asma Sayeed, Ali Behdad, Fatima El-Tayeb, Evelyn Alsultany, and Sondra Hale) offered provocative debate warmly and with a deep commitment to the issue of anti-Muslim racism. Two students were the backbone of research assistance for this book in its final stages: Shawndeez Jadalizadeh and Bianca Beauchemin gave generously of their research skills and never minded the last-minute requests for help. Bianca made it possible to get to the finish line, and I can't thank her enough for sticking with this project with great dedication even when her own writing was at risk and for applying her stellar research skills with unvarying good humor. Toward the end of the writing Shaira Vadasaria organized a virtual manuscript workshop at the University of Edinburgh that proved to be immensely fruitful. I hope that Shaira and the participants of the workshop see how valuable their comments have been. I thank Nasar Meer, Giulia Liberatore, Nicola Perugini, Katucha Bento, Rashné Limki, Andrew Neal, Shadaab Rahemtulla, Sharon Cowan, Ibtihal Ramadan, Sophia Hoffinger, Nadine El-Enany, Laura Kwak, and Carmela Murdocca enormously for taking the time to offer their insights at a time when it could not have been easy to do so. I would like to thank Natasha Bakht, Shona Hunter, Anna Oriolo, and Anja Matwijkiw for their comments on specific chapters, and Yogita Goyal, Purnima Mankekar, and Inderpal Grewal for discussions about the Indian context.

Old friends have suffered through innumerable conversations about Muslims, race, and law, and even more about how to survive the writing process. It is one thing to have friends who respond unfailingly and another to be able to depend on their brilliance. Gada Mahrouse and Carmela Murdocca pulled me out of some very deep emotional and intellectual holes and were always willing to stop what they were doing to read a draft and provide intellectual and emotional support. Thank you for offering both to me and at a very critical time. Inderpal Grewal, Barbara Buckman, and Jeanie Lucas are always on standby mode, ready to jump in whenever they hear my cry for help. To Inderpal, who calmly explains race in America and India and waits patiently for me to catch up; to Barb, who reminds me that I am theorizing on Indigenous land; and to Jeanie, whose capacity for transnational friendship sustains me, I thank you all from the bottom of my heart.

The shadow of my late brother, Zai, to whom this book is dedicated, falls on every page. The most devout, the funniest, and the sincerest Muslim I have ever known, Zai would have got a kick out of the fact that his irreverent sister finally had to begin thinking seriously about what Islam means, albeit to white people rather than to Muslims themselves. Jokingly warning me to watch out where the lightning strikes if I denied Allah, his faith was often a reminder to live more mindfully and joyfully. I miss him greatly. My family are always conscripted into my writing projects and have reported for duty with unfailing love and good humor. My sister, Farida, my sister-in-law Narda, and my brothers Jameel, Billy, and Saleem and their partners and children have stood as close as is possible to me, keeping me in the circle of their love. My sons, Ilya and Benjamin, and my daughter-in-law, Sandy, make it possible not only to survive but to thrive; the bonus is that their sharp intellects have enriched every conversation we ever had about the topic of this book. To Ben I owe a special debt for reading the last draft of the Introduction and offering up acute insights and a good deal of emotional support when it was most needed. To Ilya, the son on parental watch in California, I owe daily conversations about surviving academic life during Covid and the readiness to find whatever source I needed online. To my grandchildren—Logan, who at three years old wondered what a Muslim was, and Max, who tried to share his toys virtually with me by dumping the phone in his toy truck—I can only send you my love again and hope that one day this book helps you to connect to your Caribbean and Muslim family heritage by thinking critically about the world we live in. Everyone who knows me understands that I couldn't do much without the love, not to mention the daily tangible support, of Larry Brookwell. To Larry, I hope you know that I never take this love and support for granted. To indulge in a bad pun, nothing makes any sense without your love.

Notes

Introduction

1 See, for example, https://www.redbubble.com/shop/charlie+hebdo+t-shirts.

2 Joseph Massad, *Islam in Liberalism* (Chicago: Chicago University Press, 2015), 19.

3 Daulatzai and Rana itemize anti-Muslim violence in a list that bears repeating: "targeted killing, assassination, collateral damage, drone strikes, detention, detainment, surveillance, infiltration, policing, torture, military capitalism, necropolitical calculation, death-making, war machines." Sohail Daulatzai and Junaid Rana, "Writing the Muslim Left: An Introduction to Throwing Stones," in *With Stones in Our Hands: Writings on Muslims, Racism, and Empire*, ed. Sohail Daulatzai and Junaid Rana (Minneapolis: University of Minnesota Press, 2018), ix.

4 Sherene Razack, *Casting Out: The Eviction of Muslims from Western Law and Politics* (Toronto: University of Toronto, 2008).

5 Darryl Li, *The Universal Enemy: Jihad, Empire, and the Challenge of Solidarity* (Stanford: Stanford University Press, 2019).

6 Natasha Bakht, *In Your Face: Law, Justice, and Niqab-Wearing Women in Canada* (Toronto: Irwin Law Inc, 2020).

7 Daulatzai and Rana, "Writing the Muslim Left," x.

8 Daulatzai and Rana, xvi.

9 Ghassan Hage, *Is Racism an Environmental Threat?* (Cambridge: Polity Press, 2017), 46–51.

10 Sophia Rose Arjana, *Muslims in the Western Imagination* (New York: Oxford University Press, 2015), 1.

11 Willie James Jennings, *The Christian Imagination: Theology and the Origins of Race* (New Haven, Conn.: Yale University Press, 2010).

203

204 Notes to Introduction

12 Matt Stefon, "The Rapture," *Encyclopaedia Britannica*, https://www.britannica.com/topic/Rapture-the.

13 Edward W. Said, *The Question of Palestine* (1979; New York: Vintage Books, 1992).

14 Barnor Hesse, "Im/Plausible Deniability: Racism's Conceptual Double Bind," *Social Identities* 10, no.1 (2004): 9.

15 Described as an anti-Muslim and gun-rights activist, Stachowiak is a well-known white supremacist who has posted a video of himself outside an Augusta mosque calling for "Death to Islam." As the *Augusta Chronicle* reported, his 2018 "online postings include a video of a vigil at the 'Silent Sam' Confederate monument in Chapel Hill, N.C., a call to implant 'microchips' in undocumented immigrants, who he terms 'animals,' a video of him burning a rainbow flag, the symbol of the lesbian, gay, bisexual and transgender community, and a video of 'proof' that Black Lives Matter is connected to an 'Islamic terrorist' organization. He's also posted videos calling Black Lives Matter protestors 'looters' who should be 'shot on sight.'" Kemp, elected to governor shortly after the photo was taken, was criticized for posing for a photograph with such an avowed white supremacist, a man who can be seen at demonstrations wearing Nazi insignia and who has a long history of violent social-media posts. The criticism of Kemp did little to hinder his political success and, given the white supremacist cast to Republican politics in the United States, likely enhanced it. See Susan McCord, "Candidates Defend Taking Photos with Local Extremist at Kemp Event," *Augusta Chronicle*, October 30, 2018, https://www.augustachronicle.com/news/20181029/candidates-defend-taking-photos-with-local-extremist-at-kemp-event. See also "Meet the 'Patriots,'" Intelligence Report in Southern Poverty Law Center, May 20, 2010, https://www.splcenter.org/fighting-hate/intelligence-report/2010/meet-patriots.

16 Rachel S. Mikva, "Christian Nationalism Is a Threat, and Not Just from Capitol Attackers Invoking Jesus," *USA Today*, January 31, 2021, https://www.usatoday.com/story/opinion/2021/01/31/christian-nationalism-josh-hawley-ted-cruz-capitol-attack-column/4292193001/

17 Roisin O'Connor, "Anti-Muslim Protester at 'Draw Mohamed' Rally Has Change of Heart after Arizona Mosque Visit," *Independent*, June 4, 2015, https://www.independent.co.uk/news/world/americas/anti-muslim-protester-draw-mohamed-rally-has-change-heart-after-arizona-mosque-visit-10297546.html.

18 Hesse, "Im/Plausible Deniability," 22.

19 Daulatzai and Rana, "Writing the Muslim Left," xi.

Notes to Introduction   205

20 Ayaan Hirsi Ali, *Infidel: My Life* (New York: Free Press, 2007).

21 See Ayaan Hirsi Ali, *Nomad: From Islam to America: A Personal Journey through the Clash of Civilizations* (New York: Free Press, 2010); Ayaan Hirsi Ali, *Heretic: Why Islam Needs a Reformation Now* (New York: HarperCollins, 2015); Ayaan Hirsi Ali, *Prey: Immigration, Islam, and the Erosion of Women's Rights* (New York: HarperCollins, 2021).

22 Razack, *Casting Out*, 83–106; Lila Abu-Lughod, *Do Muslim Women Need Saving?* (Cambridge: Harvard University Press, 2013)

23 Massad notes that the reasonableness of Christianity was a case made by Enlightenment philosophers, such as John Locke, who specifically excludes Islam from the category of reasonable religion (*Islam in Liberalism*, 21).

24 Abu-Lughod, *Do Muslim Women Need Saving?*, 47.

25 Elizabeth Mertz, *The Language of Law School: Learning to "Think Like a Lawyer"* (New York: Oxford University Press, 2007).

26 Sara Ahmed, *The Cultural Politics of Emotion* (New York: Routledge, 2004), 12.

27 Simon Clarke, "Thinking Psychoanalytically about Difference: Ethnicity, Community and Emotion," in *Emotion: New Psychosocial Perspectives*, ed. Shelley Slater, David Jones, Heather Price, and Candida Yates (London: Palgrave MacMillan, 2009), 111–22.

28 Shona Hunter, *Power, Politics, and the Emotions: Impossible Governance?* (New York: Routledge, 2015), 19.

29 See Ghassan Hage, *Against Paranoid Nationalism: Searching for Hope in a Shrinking Society* (Annandale, New South Wales: Pluto Press, 2003), 49. Hage writes: "'Paranoia' denotes here a pathological form of fear based on a conception of the self as excessively fragile, and constantly threatened. It also describes a tendency to perceive a threat where none exists or, if one exists, to inflate its capacity to harm the self. The core element of Australia's colonial paranoia is a fear of loss of Europeanness or Whiteness and of the lifestyle and privileges that are seen to emanate directly from that. It is a combination of the fragility of White European colonial identity in general and the Australian situation in particular."

30 Hunter, *Power, Politics, and the Emotions*, 180.

31 Hunter, 11.

32 Renée L. Bergland, *The National Uncanny: Indian Ghosts and American Subjects* (Hanover, N.H.: University Press of New England, 2000).

33 Bergland, 17.

34 Sohail Daulatzai, *Black Star, Crescent Moon: The Muslim International and*

206 Notes to Introduction

Black Freedom beyond America (Minneapolis: University of Minnesota Press, 2012).

35 Pascal Bruckner, *An Imaginary Racism: Islamophobia and Guilt,* trans. Steven Rendall and Lisa Neal (Cambridge: Polity Press, 2018).

36 Pankaj Mishra, "What Are the Cultural Revolution's Lessons for Our Current Moment?" *New Yorker,* January 25, 2021, https://www.newyorker.com /magazine/2021/02/01/what-are-the-cultural-revolutions-lessons-for-our -current-moment.

37 Junaid Rana and Diane C. Fugino, "Taking Risks, or The Question of Palestine Solidarity and Asian American Studies," *American Quarterly* 67, no. 4 (December 2015): 1032. The authors reference Junaid Rana, *Terrifying Muslims: Race and Labor in the South Asian Diaspora* (Durham: Duke University Press, 2011).

38 Namira Islam, "Soft Islamophobia," *Religions* 9, no. 9 (September 15, 2018): 1–16, https://doi.org/10.3390/rel9090280.

39 Daulatzai and Rana, "Writing the Muslim Left," xviii.

40 Melani McAlister, "A Virtual Muslim Is Something to Be," *American Quarterly* 62, no. 2 (June 2010): 228.

41 Angela Denker, *Red State Christians: Understanding the Voters Who Elected Donald Trump* (Minneapolis: Fortress Press, 2019).

42 James Baldwin, "The Price May Be Too High," *New York Times,* February 2, 1969.

43 Robert P. Jones, *White Too Long: The Legacy of White Supremacy in American Christianity* (New York: Simon and Shuster, 2020), 10 (emphasis added).

44 John W. Compton, *The End of Empathy: Why White Protestants Stopped Loving Their Neighbors* (New York: Oxford University Press, 2020).

45 Michael Powell, "'White Supremacy' Once Meant David Duke and the Klan: Now It Refers to Much More," *New York Times,* October 15, 2020, https://www .nytimes.com/2020/10/17/us/white-supremacy.html

46 Dylan Rodríguez, "White Supremacy as Substructure: Toward a Genealogy of a Racial Animus from 'Reconstruction' to 'Pacification,'" in *State of White Supremacy: Racism, Governance, and the United States,* ed. Moon-Kie Jung, João H. Costa Vargas, and Eduardo Bonilla-Silva (Stanford: Stanford University Press, 2011), 47–76. See also Dylan Rodríguez, *White Reconstruction: Domestic Warfare and the Logics of Genocide* (New York: Fordham University Press, 2020). See also the special section of the *American Anthropologist,* "Anthropology of White Supremacy," including the works of Aisha M. Beliso-De Jesús and Jemima Pierre, "Introduction: Special Section: Anthropology of White Supremacy," *American Anthropologist* 122, no. 1 (March 2020):

Notes to Introduction **207**

65–75, https://doi.org/10.1111/aman.13351; Shannon Speed, "The Persistence of White Supremacy: Indigenous Women Migrants and the Structures of Settler Capitalism," *American Anthropologist* 122, no. 1 (March 2020): 76–85, https://doi.org/10.1111/aman.13359; Jemima Pierre, "The Racial Vernaculars of Development: A View from West Africa," *American Anthropologist* 122, no. 1 (March 2020): 86–98, https://doi.org/10.1111/aman.13352; Junaid Rana, "Anthropology and the Riddle of White Supremacy," *American Anthropologist* 122, no. 1 (March 2020): 99–111, https://doi.org/10.1111/aman.13355; Shalini Shankar, "Nothing Sells Like Whiteness: Race, Ontology, and American Advertising," *American Anthropologist* 122, no. 1 (March 2020): 112–19, https://doi.org/10.1111/aman.13354; Jonathan Rosa and Vanessa Díaz, "Raciontologies: Rethinking Anthropological Accounts of Institutional Racism and Enactments of White Supremacy in the United States," *American Anthropologist* 122, no. 1 (March 2020):120–32, https://doi.org/10.1111/aman.13353; Laurence Ralph, "The Making of Richard Zuley: The Ignored Linkages between the US Criminal In/Justice System and the International Security State," *American Anthropologist* 122, no. 1 (March 2020): 133–42, https://doi.org/10.1111/aman.13356; Aisha M. Beliso-De Jesús, "The Jungle Academy: Molding White Supremacy in American Police Recruits," *American Anthropologist* 122, no.1 (March 2020): 143–56, https://doi.org/10.1111/aman.13357; Keisha-Khan Y. Perry, "The Resurgent Far Right and the Black Feminist Struggle for Social Democracy in Brazil," *American Anthropologist* 122, no.1 (March 2020): 157–62, https://doi.org/10.1111/aman.13358.

47 Cheryl I. Harris, "Whiteness as Property," *Harvard Law Review* 106, no. 8 (June 1993): 1707–91.

48 George Lipsitz, *The Possessive Investment in Whiteness: How White People Profit from Identity Politics* (Philadelphia: Temple University Press, 2006).

49 Kalpana Seshadri-Crooks, "The Comedy of Domination: Psychoanalysis and the Conceit of Whiteness," in *The Psychoanalysis of Race*, ed. Christopher Lane (New York: Columbia University Press, 1998), 355. It is useful to note here the distinction between *fantasmic* and *phantasmic* or *phantasmatic*, the former referring to the conscious mind, the latter referring to the unconscious mind. In common usage the two terms are often blurred. Blandy and Sibley discuss these two aspects in the work of Melanie Klein, who suggested that boundary separations constitute a defense against psychotic anxieties. See Sarah Blandy and David Sibley, "Law, Boundaries, and the Production of Space," *Social and Legal Studies* 19, no. 3 (August 2010): 279.

50 Ruth Frankenberg, *White Women, Race Matters: The Social Construction of Whiteness* (Minneapolis: University of Minnesota Press, 1993).

208 Notes to Introduction

51 Saidiya V. Hartman, *Scenes of Subjection: Terror, Slavery, and Self-Making in Nineteenth Century America* (New York: Oxford University Press, 1997), 19.

52 Rodríguez, "White Supremacy as Substructure," 51.

53 William F. Pinar, *The Gender of Racial Politics and Violence in America: Lynching, Prison Rape, and the Crisis of Masculinity* (New York: Peter Lang, 2001), 19.

54 Jennings, *The Christian Imagination*, 58.

55 Jennings, 93.

56 Michelle Fine, Lois Weis, Linda C. Powell, and L. Mun Wong, eds., *Off White: Readings on Race, Power, and Society* (New York: Routledge, 1997). More than twenty years ago, prompted by Du Bois's essay, the editors of the pathbreaking anthology *Off White* remark: "Rarely, however, is it acknowledged that whiteness demands and constitutes hierarchy, exclusion, and deprivation" (viii). Attention to the compelling interest of whiteness in subjugation, as Pinar puts it, remains one of its least acknowledged features.

57 W. E. B. Du Bois, "The Ethics of the Problem of Palestine, ca. 1948," W. E. B. Du Bois Papers (MS 312) (Special Collections and University Archives, University of Massachusetts Amherst Libraries, 1948), https://credo.library.umass.edu/view/full/mums312-b209-i090. I am grateful to Nasar Meer for bringing this to my attention.

58 W. E. B. Du Bois, "The Souls of White Folk," in *Darkwater: Voices from within the Veil* (1920; New York: Dover, 1999), 23.

59 Du Bois, 19.

60 Du Bois, 19.

61 Du Bois, 17.

62 Du Bois, 18.

63 Du Bois, 19.

64 bell hooks, *Black Looks: Race and Representation* (Boston: South End Press, 1992), 62.

65 Alistair Bonnett, "Who Was White? The Disappearance of Non-European White Identities and the Formation of European Racial Whiteness," *Ethnic and Racial Identities* 21, no. 6 (1998): 1039, https://doi.org/10.1080/01419879808565651.

66 Edward J. Blum, Tracy Fessenden, Prema Kurien, and Judith Weisenfeld, "Forum: American Religion and 'Whiteness,'" *Religion and American Culture: A Journal of Interpretation* 19, no. 1 (Winter 2009): 3.

67 Blum et al., 3

68 Blum et al., 5.

69 Fessenden in Blum et al., 14.

70 Jan Nederveen Pieterse, "The Aesthetics of Power: Time and Body Politics," *Third Text* 7, no. 22 (1993): 38.

Notes to Introduction **209**

71 David Theo Goldberg, "Militarizing Race," *Social Text* 34, no. 4 (129) (December 2016): 19, https://doi.org/10.1215/01642472-3680846.

72 Nasar Meer, "Racialization and Religion: Race, Culture, and Difference in the Study of Antisemitism and Islamophobia," in *Racialization and Religion: Race, Culture, and Difference in the Study of Antisemitism and Islamophobia*, ed. Nasar Meer (New York: Routledge, 2014), 5.

73 Michael Omi and Howard Winant, *Racial Formation in the United States from the 1960s to the 1990s*, 2nd ed. (New York: Routledge, 1994).

74 Nabil Matar, *Turks, Moors, and Englishmen in the Age of Discovery* (New York: Columbia University Press, 1999); James S. Shapiro, *Shakespeare and the Jews* (New York: Columbia University Press, 1996).

75 Anouar Majid, *We Are All Moors: Ending Centuries of Crusades against Muslims and Other Minorities* (Minneapolis: University of Minnesota Press, 2009).

76 François Soyer, "Faith, Culture, and Fear: Comparing Islamophobia in Early Modern Spain and Twenty-First-Century Europe," in *Racialization and Religion: Race, Culture, and Difference in the Study of Antisemitism and Islamophobia*, ed. Nasar Meer (New York: Routledge, 2014): 17–26.

77 See Sean R. Roberts, *The War on the Uyghurs: China's Internal Campaign against a Muslim Minority* (Princeton: Princeton University Press, 2020).

78 Pnina Werbner, "Folk Devils and Racist Imaginaries in a Global Prism: Islamophobia and Anti-Semitism in the Twenty-First Century," in *Racialization and Religion: Race, Culture, and Difference in the Study of Antisemitism and Islamophobia*, ed. Nasar Meer (New York: Routledge, 2014), 74.

79 Goldberg, "Militarizing Race," 20.

80 Goldberg, 32.

81 Jennings, *The Christian Imagination*, 146.

82 Ratna Kapur, *Gender, Alterity, and Human Rights: Freedom in a Fishbowl* (Cheltenham: Edward Elgar Publishing, 2018), 1.

83 Kapur, 3.

84 Kapur, 3.

85 Kapur, 3.

86 Massad, *Islam in Liberalism*.

87 See Irfan Ahmad, *Religion as Critique: Islamic Critical Thinking from Mecca to the Marketplace* (Chapel Hill: University of North Carolina Press, 2017).

88 Irfan Ahmad, "Islam and the Enlightenment," *Marginalia: Los Angeles Review of Books*, January 15, 2021, https://marginalia.lareviewofbooks.org/islam-and-the-enlightenment/.

89 Massad, *Islam in Liberalism*, 25.

210 Notes to Introduction

90 Mahmood Mamdani, *Good Muslim, Bad Muslim: America, the Cold War, and the Roots of Terror* (New York: Three Leaves Press, 2005).

91 Kapur, *Gender, Alterity, and Human Rights*, 11.

92 Massad, *Islam in Liberalism*, 237.

93 See, for example, Inderpal Grewal, *Home and Harem: Nation, Gender, Empire, and Cultures of Travel* (Durham: Duke University Press, 1996); Sherene H. Razack, *Looking White People in the Eye: Gender, Race, and Culture in Courtrooms and Classrooms* (Toronto: University of Toronto Press, 1998).

94 Marilyn Lake and Henry Reynolds, *Drawing the Global Colour Line: White Men's Countries and the International Challenge of Racial Equality* (Cambridge: Cambridge University Press, 2008), 6.

95 Lake and Reynolds, 7.

96 Lake and Reynolds, 9.

97 Lake and Reynolds, 11.

98 Jennings, *The Christian Imagination*, 241.

99 Nadine Suleiman Naber, "Imperial Whiteness and the Diasporas of Empire," *American Quarterly* 66, no. 4 (December 2014): 1107–15.

100 Daulatzai and Rana, "Writing the Muslim Left," xvii.

101 Roberts, *The War on the Uyghurs*.

102 Edward Said, "Edward Said, an American and an Arab, Writes on the Eve of the Iraqi-Soviet Peace Talks," *London Review of Books*, March 7, 1991, https://www.lrb.co.uk/the-paper/v13/n05/edward-said/edward-said-an-american-and-an-arab-writes-on-the-eve-of-the-iraqi-soviet-peace-talks. See also Edward Said, *Culture and Imperialism* (New York: Knopf, 1993).

103 Li, *The Universal Enemy*, 5.

104 Li, 6.

105 Li, 5.

106 Tendayi Achiume and Aslı Ü. Bâli, "Race and Empire: Legal Theory within, through and across National Borders," *67 UCLA Law Review*, UCLA School of Law, Public Law Research Paper No. 20-34 (November 18, 2020): 9, https://ssrn.com/abstract=3733164.

107 Aziz Rana and Aslı Ü. Bâli, "America's Imperial Unraveling," *Boston Review*, October 16, 2017, http://bostonreview.net/politics/asli-bali-aziz-rana-americas-imperial-unraveling.

108 Daulatzai, *Black Star, Crescent Moon*, 158.

109 Keith P. Feldman, *A Shadow over Palestine: The Imperial Life of Race in America* (Minneapolis: University of Minnesota Press, 2015), 161.

110 Feldman, 11.

111 Said, *The Question of Palestine*.

Notes to Introduction **211**

112 Minoo Moellem, *Between Warrior Brother and Veiled Sister: Islamic Fundamentalism and the Politics of Patriarchy in Iran* (Berkeley: University of California Press, 2005), 7.

113 Malinda S. Smith, "Africa, 9/11, and the Temporality and Spatiality of Race," in *At the Limits of Justice: Women of Colour on Terror,* ed. Suvendrini Perera and Sherene Razack (Toronto: University of Toronto Press, 2014), 394.

114 Nicholas De Genova, "The 'Migrant Crisis' as Racial Crisis: Do *Black Lives Matter* in Europe?," *Ethnic and Racial Studies* 41, no. 10 (August 2018): 1765–82.

115 Smith, "Africa, 9/11," 394.

116 Ju Hui Judy Han, "Shifting Geographies of Proximity: Korean-Led Evangelical Christian Missions and the U.S. Empire," in *Ethnographies of U.S. Empire,* ed. Carole McGranahan and John F. Collins (Durham: Duke University Press, 2018), 194–213.

117 Junaid Rana, "The Racial Infrastructure of the Terror-Industrial Complex," *Social Text 129* 34, no. 4 (December 2016): 111–38.

118 Sedef Arat-Koç, "New Whiteness(es), Beyond the Colour Line? Assessing the Contradictions and Complexities of 'Whiteness' in the (Geo)Political Economy of Capitalist Globalism," in *States of Race: Critical Race Feminism for the 21st Century,* ed. Sherene Razack, Malinda Smith, and Sunera Thobani (Toronto: Between the Lines, 2010), 153.

119 W. Paul Reeve, *Religion of a Different Color: Race and the Mormon Struggle for Whiteness* (New York: Oxford University Press, 2015).

120 Austin Ramzy and Chris Buckley, "'Show Absolutely No Mercy': Inside China's Mass Detentions," *New York Times,* November 17, 2019, A1, A8–A9.

121 See Hannah Ellis-Petersen, "India Strips Kashmir of Special Status and Divides It in Two," *Guardian,* October 31, 2019, https://www.theguardian.com /world/2019/oct/31/india-strips-kashmir-of-special-status-and-divides-it-in -two; Sameer Yasir, Suhasini Raj, and Jeffrey Gettleman, "Inside Kashmir, Cut Off from the World: 'A Living Hell' of Anger and Fear," *New York Times,* August 10, 2019, https://www.nytimes.com/2019/08/10/world/asia/kashmir -india-pakistan.html.

122 See Fiza Pirani, "Who Are the Rohingya Muslims? 7 Things to Know about the 'World's Most Persecuted Minority,'" *Atlanta Journal-Constitution,* March 13, 2018, https://www.ajc.com/news/world/who-are-the-rohingya -muslims-things-know-about-the-world-most-persecuted-minority /MzQMo6SjX8kohGKzot9cnM/; Al Jazeera Staff, "Who Are the Rohingya?," April 18, 2018, https://www.aljazeera.com/indepth/features/2017/08/rohingya -muslims-170831065142812.html.

212 Notes to Introduction

123 Li, *The Universal Enemy*, 10.

124 Li, 25.

125 Meera Seghal, "Defending the Nation: Militarism, Women's Empowerment, and the Hindu Right," in *Border Politics: Social Movements, Collective Identities, and Globalization*, ed. Nancy A. Naples and Jennifer Bickham Mendez (New York: New York University Press, 2015), 60–94.

126 Roberts, *The War on the Uyghurs*.

127 David Cole, *Enemy Alien: Double Standards and Constitutional Freedoms in the War on Terrorism* (New York: The New Press, 2003), xxiv.

128 Denise Ferreira da Silva, "No-Bodies: Law, Raciality, and Violence," *Griffith Law Review* 18, no. 2 (2009): 213, https://doi.org/10.1080/10383441.2009.10854638. See also Denise Ferreira da Silva, *Toward a Global Idea of Race* (Minneapolis: University of Minnesota Press, 2007).

129 Ferreira da Silva, "No-Bodies," 213.

130 Ferreira da Silva, 221.

131 Bergland, *The National Uncanny*, 8.

132 Bergland, 8.

133 Denise Ferreira da Silva, "Radical Praxis or Knowing (at) the Limits of Justice," in *At the Limits of Justice: Women of Colour on Terror*, ed. Suvendrini Perera and Sherene H. Razack (Toronto: University of Toronto Press, 2014), 526–37.

134 Bergland, *The National Uncanny*, 18.

135 Toni Morrison, *Birth of a Nation'hood: Gaze, Script, and Spectacle in the O.J. Simpson Case* (New York: Pantheon Books, 1997), ix.

136 Morrison, ix.

137 Colin Dayan, *The Law Is a White Dog: How Legal Rituals Make and Unmake Persons* (Princeton: Princeton University Press, 2011), 152.

138 Colin Dayan, *The Story of Cruel and Unusual* (Cambridge: MIT Press, 2007), 25.

139 See in this regard Angela Davis, *Abolition Democracy: Beyond Empire, Prison, and Torture* (New York: Seven Stories Press, 2005).

140 Dayan, *The Story of Cruel and Unusual*, 26.

141 Dayan, 60.

142 Samera Esmeir, *Juridical Humanity: A Colonial History* (Stanford: Stanford University Press, 2012), 3.

143 Anna M. Agathangelou, "Visual Colonial Economies and Slave Death in Modernity: Bin Laden's Terror?," in *At the Limits of Justice: Women of Colour on Terror*, ed. Suvendrini Perera and Sherene Razack (Toronto: University of Toronto Press, 2014), 436.

Notes to Introduction 213

144 Agathangelou, 444.

145 Agathangelou, 441.

146 Agathangelou, 436.

147 Werbner, "Folk Devils and Racist Imaginaries," 74.

148 Nasar Meer, "Semantics, Scales, and Solidarities in the Study of Antisemitism and Islamophobia," in *Racialization and Religion: Race, Culture, and Difference in the Study of Antisemitism and Islamophobia,* ed. Nasar Meer (New York: Routledge, 2014), 125. Meer cites Nabil Matar, "Britons and Muslims in the Early Modern Period: From Prejudice to (a Theory of) Toleration," *Patterns of Prejudice* 43, nos. 3–4 (2009): 215.

149 Hage, *Is Racism an Environmental Threat?*, 46–51.

150 Hage, 8–9.

151 Achille Mbembe, *Critique of Black Reason,* trans. Lauren Dubois (Durham: Duke University Press, 2017).

152 Mbembe, 31.

153 Mbembe, 32.

154 Mbembe, 10.

155 Trump v. Hawai'i—Petition for Writ of Certiorari (9th circuit, June 26, 2018), 585 U.S. (2018): 65–92, https://www.supremecourt.gov/opinions/17pdf/17-965 _h315.pdf#page=65.

156 Agathangelou, "Visual Colonial Economies," 435.

157 Meyda Yeğenoğlu, *Colonial Fantasies: Towards a Feminist Reading of Orientalism* (Cambridge: Cambridge University Press, 1998), 45.

158 I am grateful to Rashné Limki for reminding me of this point. See also Massad, "Pre-positional Conjunctions: Sexuality and/in 'Islam,'" in *Islam in Liberalism,* 213–74.

159 Jasbir K. Puar, *Terrorist Assemblages: Homonationalism in Queer Times* (Durham: Duke University Press, 2007) 37–61.

160 Klaus Theweleit, *Male Fantasies,* vol. 2, *Male Bodies: Psychoanalyzing the White Terror,* trans. Erica Carter, Chris Turner, and Stephen Conway (Minneapolis: University of Minnesota Press, 1989), 241.

161 Theweleit, *Male Fantasies,* 274.

162 Rey Chow, *The Protestant Ethnic and the Spirit of Capitalism* (New York: Columbia University Press, 2002). See also Razack, *Looking White People in the Eye.*

163 Rodríguez, "White Supremacy as Substructure," 72–73.

164 Sherene Razack, *Dying from Improvement: Inquests and Inquiries into Indigenous Deaths in Custody* (Toronto: University of Toronto Press, 2015).

165 Ahmed, *Cultural Politics of Emotion,* 12.

214 Notes to Introduction

166 Hage, *Is Racism an Environmental Threat?*, 13.
167 Arjana, *Muslims in the Western Imagination.*
168 Mamdani, *Good Muslim, Bad Muslim.*

1. "A New Phase of a Very Old War"

1 See https://gatesofvienna.net.
2 Richard Slotkin, *Gunfighter Nation: The Myth of the Frontier in Twentieth-Century America* (New York: University of Oklahoma Press, 1992), 8.
3 Wendy Brown, *In the Ruins of Neoliberalism: The Rise of Antidemocratic Politics in the West* (New York: Columbia University Press, 2019), 175.
4 Slotkin, *Gunfighter Nation,* 8. Also see Richard Slotkin, *Fatal Environment: The Myth of the Frontier in the Age of Industrialization, 1800–1890* (New York: University of Oklahoma Press, 1985), 28, where he highlights how the approach to mythmaking that centers the archetype and the collective unconscious is much too abstract, occluding historical processes.
5 Zionism is a movement for the establishment of a Jewish nation in Palestine.
6 Jan Nederveen Pieterse, "Aesthetics of Power: Time and Body Politics." *Third Text* 7, no. 22 (1993): 33–42.
7 See, for example, Tim Craig, "Proud Boys and Black Lives Matter Activists Clash in a Florida Suburb: Only One Side Is Charged." *Washington Post,* February 2, 2021, https://www.seattletimes.com/nation-world/proud-boys-and -black-lives-matter-activists-clashed-in-a-florida-suburb-only-one-side-was -charged/.
8 Rachel S. Mikva, "Christian Nationalism Is a Threat, and Not Just from Capitol Attackers Invoking Jesus," *USA Today,* January 31, 2021, https://www .usatoday.com/story/opinion/2021/01/31/christian-nationalism-josh-hawley -ted-cruz-capitol-attack-column/4292193001/.
9 Grant Wacker, "The Christian Right," Duke University Divinity School, National Humanities Center, 2000, http://nationalhumanitiescenter.org/tserve /twenty/tkeyinfo/chr_rght.htm.
10 For an account of Du Bois on this point see Edward J. Blum, *W. E. B. Du Bois, American Prophet* (Philadelphia: University of Pennsylvania Press, 2007).
11 Willie James Jennings, *The Christian Imagination: Theology and the Origins of Race* (New Haven, Conn.: Yale University Press, 2011), 24.
12 Steven Salaita, *The Holy Land in Transit: Colonialism and the Quest for Canaan* (Syracuse: Syracuse University Press, 2006), 13.
13 For accounts of white settler mythologies see Sherene H. Razack, ed., *Race, Space, and the Law: Unmapping a White Settler Society* (Toronto: Between the Lines, 2004).

Notes to Chapter 1   **215**

14 Salaita, *The Holy Land in Transit*, 25.

15 Edward W. Said, *The Question of Palestine* (New York: Vintage Books, 1979, 1992), 25.

16 Richard Cimino, "'No God in Common': American Evangelical Discourse on Islam after 9/11," *Review of Religious Research* 47, no. 2 (December 2005): 162–74.

17 For Hunt see The Berean Call, http://www.thebereancall.org; for Morey see Faith Defenders, http://www.faithdefenders.com; Ergun Mehmet Caner and Emir Caner, *Unveiling Islam* (Grand Rapids, Mich.: Kregel, 2002).

18 George Otis, *The Last of the Giants: Lifting the Veil on Islam and the End Times* (Grand Rapids, Mich.: Chosen Books, 1991).

19 Ann Burlein, *Lift High the Cross: Where White Supremacy and the Christian Right Converge* (Durham: Duke University Press, 2002), 86.

20 Burlein, 44.

21 Burlein, 195.

22 Sophie Bjork-James, "Training the Porous Body: Evangelicals and the Ex-Gay Movement," *American Anthropologist* 120, no. 4 (December 2018): 647–58. See also Sophie Bjork-James, *The Divine Institution: White Evangelicalism's Politics of the Family* (New Brunswick, N.J.: Rutgers University Press, 2021).

23 Victoria Clark, *Allies for Armageddon: The Rise of Christian Zionism* (New Haven, Conn.: Yale University Press, 2007).

24 Clark, 256.

25 Clark, 271.

26 Clark, 5.

27 Clark, 5.

28 Clark, 185.

29 Adam Laats, "Our Schools, Our Country: American Evangelicals, Public Schools, and the Supreme Court Decisions of 1962 and 1963," *Journal of Religious History* 36, no. 3 (September 2012): 319–34. The status of Christian evangelicals would not improve until President Ronald Reagan recognized the constituency as the "Moral Majority" in 1984. Christian evangelical leaders such as Jerry Falwell then obtained the kind of influence leaders such as Billy Graham had achieved decades earlier.

30 See, for example, AAR Religion in the Schools Task Force, "Guidelines for Teaching about Religion in K–12 Public Schools in the United States," American Academy of Religion, Chair Diane L. Moore, April 2010, https://www.aarweb.org/common/Uploaded%20files/Publications%20and%20News/Guides%20and%20Best%20Practices/AARK-12Curriculum GuidelinesPDF.pdf.

216 Notes to Chapter 1

31 AAR Task Force, "Guidelines for Teaching about Religion," ii.

32 For an example of this position see Aaron D. Pina, Congressional Research Service Report for Congress, *Palestinian Education and the Debate over Textbooks*, update May 3, 2005, Order Code RL32886, https://fas.org/sgp/crs/mideast/RL32886.pdf.

33 Terry Handy, *Islam: A Simulation of Islamic History and Culture, 610–1100* (El Cajon, Calif.: Interaction, 1991), https://eric.ed.gov/?id=ED419740.

34 "Enemy Judge: No. 1—Phyllis J. Hamilton," *Free Republic*, June 2, 2004, http://www.freerepublic.com/focus/f-news/1146555/posts.

35 Eklund v. Byron Union School District, 154 Fed. Appx. 648 (9th Circuit 2005), cert. denied, 549 U.S. 942 (2006), https://www.scribd.com/document/266923198/Eklund-v-Byron-Union-School-District.

36 "Thomas More (1478–1535)," http://www.bbc.co.uk/history/historic_figures/more_sir_thomas.shtml.

37 "About: About the Thomas More Law Center," Thomas More Law Center, https://www.thomasmore.org/about-the-thomas-more-law-center-1/.

38 "About: President and Chief Counsel," Thomas More Law Center, https://www.thomasmore.org/president-chief-counsel/.

39 See https://www.actforamerica.org/.

40 ACT for America, *Education or Indoctrination? The Treatment of Islam in 6th through 12th Grade American Textbooks*, 2011, http://d3n8a8pro7vhmx.cloudfront.net/themes/57365ca5cd0af55ea6000001/attachments/original/1483921270/Education_or_Indoctrination_Executive_Summary.pdf.

41 See "Issues," https://www.actforamerica.org/.

42 "Thomas More Law Center Uncovers Taxpayer-Funded Islamic Propaganda Forced on Teachers—A Special Investigative Report," Thomas More Law Center, August 22, 2019, https://www.thomasmore.org/news/thomas-more-law-center-uncovers-taxpayer-funded-islamic-propaganda-forced-on-teachers-a-special-investigative-report/.

43 "Thomas More Law Center."

44 Andrew Trotter, "Justices Decline Case about Public School's Islamic-Themed Unit," *Education Week*, October 10, 2006, https://www.edweek.org/ew/articles/2006/10/11/07scotus.h26.html.

45 "About Us: The Spirit of the American West," Mountain States Legal Foundation, https://mslegal.org/about/.

46 For documentation of Pipes's anti-Muslim activities see Christopher Bail, *Terrified: How Anti-Muslim Fringe Organizations Became Mainstream* (Princeton: Princeton University Press, 2015).

47 Daniel Pipes, "Become a Muslim Warrior," *Jerusalem Post*, July 3, 2002, http://www.danielpipes.or/430/become-a-muslim-warrior.

Notes to Chapter 1 **217**

48 Pipes.

49 Bail, *Terrified*, 11.

50 Bail, 102–3.

51 "Combating Bullying," https://www.cair-ny.org/bullying.

52 Bail, *Terrified*, 89–99.

53 "About Us: Mission and History," Freedom of Conscience Defense Fund, https://www.fcdflegal.org/about-us/about/mission/.

54 Rupa Shenoy, "San Diego School District and Parents Reach Settlement over Muslim Civil Rights Program," *PRI*, April 5, 2019, https://www.pri.org/stories/2019-04-05/san-diego-school-district-and-parents-reach-settlement-over-muslim-civil-rights.

55 Bail, *Terrified*, 70.

56 San Diego Unified School District, "5/16/17 Board of Education Meeting," May 16, 2017, YouTube video, 2:57:07, https://www.youtube.com/watch?v=rruP96vmDnQ.

57 Aaryn Belfer, "Hate Wins at SDUSD Meetings," *San Diego City Beat*, May 23, 2017, http://sdcitybeat.com/news-and-opinion/backwards-in-high-heels/hate-wins-at-sdusd-meetings/.

58 Eric Bartl, "Five White Men Walk into Chicano Park . . . ," *San Diego Reader*, November 19, 2017, https://www.sandiegoreader.com/news/2017/nov/19/stringers-five-white-men-walk-chicano-park/.

59 "Dad Takes on San Diego Unified School District!," May 5, 2017, YouTube video, 2:01, https://www.youtube.com/watch?v=zykvkTkFz5g; San Diego Unified School District, "5/16/17 Board of Education Meeting."

60 Burlein, *Lift High the Cross*, 6.

61 See, for example, Anarchist Federation, "Meet Kristopher Evan Wyrick, White Nationalist and Member of American Guard," https://www.anarchistfederation.net/meet-kristopher-evan-wyrick-white-nationalist-and-member-of-american-guard/.

62 Belfer, "Hate Wins at SDUSD Meetings."

63 Caleigh Wood v. Evelyn Arnold; Shannon Morris—Petition for Writ of Certiorari (3rd Circuit, May 13, 2019), https://www.thomasmore.org/wp-content/uploads/2019/05/Wood-Petition-to-Print.pdf. All subsequent references to the case refer to page numbers in the writ, which contains the petition submitted by Richard Thompson, counsel of record for the Thomas More Law Center, all court decisions, Wood's Memorandum Opinion, the homework assignment, teacher's notes, and the PowerPoint slides used in the course.

64 Wood v. Arnold, 52; references omitted.

65 Wood v. Arnold, 52–53.

66 Wood v. Arnold, 67.

218 Notes to Chapter 1

67 Wood v. Arnold, 84.

68 Wood v. Arnold, 82.

69 Wood v. Arnold, 85.

70 Wood v. Arnold, 84–85.

71 Wood v. Arnold, 36.

72 Wood v. Arnold, i.

73 Wood v. Arnold, 51.

74 Burlein, *Lift High the Cross,* 8.

75 Burlein, 8.

76 Burlein, 27.

77 Burlein, 183.

78 Wilson Dizard, "Arabic Calligraphy Fracas Closes Virginia School District," *Al Jazeera America,* December 18, 2015, http://america.aljazeera.com/articles /2015/12/18/shahada-islam-virginia.html.

79 Dizard.

80 Megan Williams, "Islamic Faith Statement Outrages County Parents," *News Leader,* December 18, 2015, https://www.newsleader.com/story/news/local /2015/12/15/augusta-county-riverheads-high-school-teacher-world -geography-islam-angry-parents/77374858/.

81 Channing Frampton, "Augusta Co. Parents Concerned over Islam-Related Assignment," *WHSV ABC 3,* December 15, 2015, modified November 17, 2016, https://www.whsv.com/content/news/Community-Meeting -About--362492691.html.

82 Williams, "Islamic Faith Statement Outrages County Parents."

83 Vernon Freeman Jr., "Augusta County Schools Closed Friday after Parental Outrage over Arabic Assignment," *CBS 6 News,* December 17, 2015, https:// wtvr.com/2015/12/17/augusta-county-schools-closed-friday-after-parental -outrage-over-arabic-assignment/.

84 Ed Mazza, "Virginia Schools Close after Uproar over Arabic Calligraphy Lesson," *Huffington Post,* December 18, 2015, https://www.huffingtonpost.ca /entry/arabic-calligraphy-shuts-schools_n_56737382e4b06fa6887cdc1f?ri18n =true.

85 Baron Bodissey, "How Did the Shahada Come to Augusta County?," *Gates of Vienna,* December 19, 2015, https://gatesofvienna.net/2015/12/how-did-the -shahada-come-to-augusta-county/#more-38228.

86 Bail reports that the Donors Capital Fund donated $17 million to the Clarion Fund, which then financed the making of several films that promoted its anti-Muslim message widely. The Clarion Fund's advisory board includes prominent anti-Muslim ideologues such as Daniel Pipes and Frank Gaffney. See Bail, *Terrified,* 83.

Notes to Chapter 1 **219**

87 Dan Miller, "Why Is the Dept. of Education Promoting Islam to School Kids?," *The Clarion Project*, April 13, 2017, https://clarionproject.org/u-s-dept-of -education-promoting-islam-to-schoolchildren/.

88 Stoyan Zaimov, "Virginia Parents Angry after Students Told to Write 'There Is No God but Allah,'" *Christian Post,* December 16, 2015, https://www .christianpost.com/news/virginia-parents-students-write-there-is-no-god -but-allah.html.

89 Allison Pries, "Chatham Mother Sues School District for Allegedly Trying to Convert Her Son to Islam," New Jersey Advance Media for NJ.com, January 27, 2018, modified January 30, 2019, https://www.nj.com/morris/2018/01 /chatham_mother_sues_school_district_saying_that_tr.html.

90 Tucker Carlson, "Tucker Carlson: New Jersey Parents Concerned about Teaching Islam in Middle School: 2/20/2017," *Tucker Carlson Tonight,* Fox News, February 21, 2017, YouTube video, 4:55, https://www.youtube.com /watch?v=4A7FA5Y8–0Y.

91 Chatham High School, "SDOC BOE Meeting 3/6/17," March 8, 2017, You-Tube video, 2:17:48, https://www.youtube.com/watch?v=ZkHadG3Plis&list =PLtSqyQYTViIy6G-Bpc8toxsoCjmzvCsgI&index=4.

92 "Chatham Middle School Students Are Taught That Islam Is the True Faith; Two Mothers Pilloried for Making It Public; Must See Video," Thomas More Law Center, https://www.thomasmore.org/press-releases/chatham-middle -school-students-taught-islam-true-faith-two-mothers-pilloried-making -public-must-see-video/.

93 See, for example, Michael Patrick Leahy, "Middle School Mothers with Objections to Islamic Curriculum Hire Law Firm," *Breitbart News,* March 30, 2017, https://www.breitbart.com/politics/2017/03/30/middle-school-mothers -with-objections-to-islamic-curriculum-hire-law-firm/.

94 "Chatham Middle School Students."

95 Susan Brinkmann, "Parents Lay Down the Law about Islamic Indoctrination in Public Schools," Women of Grace, June 21, 2018, https://www.womenofgrace .com/blog/?p=64877#more-64877.

96 Dr. Susan Berry, "U.S. Education Department Asked to Eliminate Lesson Plans on Islam," *Breitbart News,* March 31, 2017, https://www.breitbart.com/politics /2017/03/31/u-s-education-department-asked-to-eliminate-lesson-plans-on -islam/.

97 Anugrah Kumar, "New Jersey School Sued for Showing Islamic Video Praising Muhammad for Killing Christians," *The Christian Post,* January 27, 2018, https://www.christianpost.com/news/new-jersey-school-sued-showing -islamic-video-praising-muhammad-killing-christians-jews-215355/.

220 Notes to Chapter 1

98 "The Islamization of the Public Schools," *The Jackson Press*, May 22, 2018, http://thejacksonpress.org/?p=83371.

99 Robert Spencer, "New Jersey: Parents Sue Public School District for Teaching 'Islam Is the True Faith,'" Jihad Watch, June 21, 2018, https://www.jihadwatch .org/2018/06/new-jersey-parents-sue-public-school-district-for-teaching -islam-is-the-true-faith.

100 Anita Carey, "Classrooms Pushing Islamic Propaganda," Church Militant, June 26, 2018, https://www.churchmilitant.com/news/article/islamic -indoctrination-in-schools-subverts-constitution.

101 "Thomas More Law Center Agrees to Help Father in Fight with School over Islamic Indoctrination of 13-Year-Old Daughter," Thomas More Law Center, June 19, 2018, https://www.thomasmore.org/news/thomas-more-law-center -agrees-to-help-father-in-fight-with-school-over-islamic-indoctrination-of -13-year-old-daughter/.

102 "Chatham Middle School Students."

103 Hilsenrath v. SCHOOL DISTRICT OF THE CHATHAMS et al, No. 2:2018cv00966—Document 22 (D.N.J. 2018), https://law.justia.com/cases /federal/district-courts/new-jersey/njdce/2:2018cv00966/365028/22/.

104 https://www.thomasmore.org.

105 https://aclj.org.

106 https://www.fcdflegal.org.

107 https://clarionproject.org.

108 Caroline Glenn, "Residents Clash over Textbook's Chapter on Islam," *Florida Today*, May 10, 2017, https://www.floridatoday.com/story/news /education/2017/05/10/brevard-residents-clash-over-textbooks-chapter -islam/101463030/.

109 Czarina Ong, "Angry Parents Object to Islamic Lessons, Quizzes Given to their Kids in US Schools," *Christian Today*, October 2, 2015, https:// www.christiantoday.com/article/angry-parents-object-to-islamic-lessons -quizzes-given-to-their-kids-in-us-schools/66269.htm.

110 John Griffing, "Students Made to Wear Burqas—in Texas," *WND*, February 24, 2013, https://www.wnd.com/2013/02/students-made-to-wear-burqas-in-u-s -state/#r7kp2RCwtFKFoRkk.99.

111 "School Writing Assignment: 'Pretend You Are a Muslim,'" *Fox News Insider*, April 15, 2015, https://insider.foxnews.com/2015/04/15/high-school-writing -assignment-pretend-you-are-muslim; see also "TMLC Uncovers Tax-Payer Funded Islamic Propaganda Forced on Teachers: A Special Investigative Report," Thomas More Law Center, August 22, 2019, https://www.thomasmore .org/press-releases/tmlc-uncovers-tax-payer-funded-islamic-propaganda -forced-on-teachers/.

Notes to Chapter 2 **221**

112 Ismat Sarah Mangla, "Fearing 'Indoctrination,' Parents in One US State Are Succeeding in Removing Islam from a School Curriculum," *Quartz*, September 29, 2016, https://qz.com/796141/tennessee-school-board-removes-section-on-islam-from-social-studies-curriculum/.

113 David Horowitz, *Dark Agenda: The War to Destroy Christian America* (West Palm Beach, Fla.: Humanix Books, 2018).

114 Erica L. Green, "U.S. Orders Duke and U.N.C. to Recast Tone in Mideast Studies," *New York Times*, September 19, 2019, https://www.nytimes.com/2019/09/19/us/politics/anti-israel-bias-higher-education.html; see also Michael Arria, "Education Dept Says Middle East Studies Program Has to Advance the Security Interests of the United States in Order to Receive Further Funding," *Mondoweiss*, September 18, 2019, https://mondoweiss.net/2019/09/education-security-interests/; Joshua Leifer, "The Trump Administration's Crackdown on Campus Criticism of Israel Is Orwellian," *Guardian*, September 23, 2019, https://www.theguardian.com/commentisfree/2019/sep/23/the-trump-administrations-crackdown-on-campus-criticism-of-israel-is-orwellian.

115 A 2012 poll by the Brookings Institution cited in Bail, *Terrified*, 113.

116 Bail, 1–5.

117 Sindre Bangstad, *Anders Breivik and the Rise of Islamophobia* (London: Zed Books, 2014).

118 Brown, *In the Ruins of Neoliberalism*, 177–78.

119 Brown, 178.

2. "I Can Never Tell If You're Responding to My Smile"

1 "Australian Man Verbally Abuses Muslim Woman Wearing Niqab," *Daily Mail Online*, http://www.dailymail.co.uk/video/news/video-1418411/Australianman-verbally-abuses-Muslim-woman-wearing-hijab.html.

2 Meyda Yeğenoğlu, *Colonial Fantasies: Towards a Feminist Reading of Orientalism* (Cambridge: Cambridge University Press, 1998), 39.

3 Frantz Fanon, *A Dying Colonialism* (New York: Grove Press, 1967), 45–46.

4 Fanon, 42.

5 Rey Chow, *The Protestant Ethnic and the Spirit of Capitalism* (New York: Columbia University Press, 2002), 168.

6 For a discussion of the relationship between recognition and norms see Judith Butler, *Undoing Gender* (New York: Routledge, 2004), 1–16.

7 Sianne Ngai, *Ugly Feelings* (Cambridge: Harvard University Press, 2005), 1.

8 I do not pursue a detailed psychoanalytic reading of fantasy, and explore instead only the anxiety that the niqab provokes that bans seek to dispel. This chapter blurs the fantasmic, referring to the conscious mind, and the phantasmic or phantasmatic, referring to the unconscious mind. As I noted

222 Notes to Chapter 2

in the Introduction, Blandy and Sibley discuss these two aspects in the work of Melanie Klein, who suggested that boundary separations constitute a defense against psychotic anxieties. See Sarah Blandy and David Sibley, "Law, Boundaries, and the Production of Space," *Social and Legal Studies* 19, no. 3 (August 2010): 279.

9 Jan Nederveen Pieterse, "Aesthetics of Power: Time and Body Politics," *Third Text* 7, no. 22 (1993): 33.

10 For a discussion of this point, see the Introduction and Denise Ferreira da Silva, "No-Bodies: Law, Raciality, and Violence," *Griffith Law Review* 18, no. 2 (2009): 213.

11 Figure 3a is based on the following sources: Open Society Justice Initiative, "Briefing Papers: Restrictions on Muslim Women's Dress in the 28 EU Member States: Current Law, Recent Legal Developments, and the State of Play," *Open Society Foundations,* July 2018, 17, https://www.justiceinitiative.org /uploads/dffdb416-5d63-4001-911b-d3f46e159acc/restrictions-on-muslim -womens-dress-in-28-eu-member-states-20180709.pdf; and the following:

Austria: "Austria: Full-Face Veil Ban Enters into Force," Global Legal Monitor, November 3, 2017, https://www.loc.gov/law/foreign-news/article /austria-full-face-veil-ban-enters-into-force/; for full description of the law, see also Bundesgesetz über das Verbot der Verhüllung des Gesichts in der Öffentlichkeit (Anti-Gesichtsverhüllungsgesetz— AGesVG) StF: BGBl. I Nr. 68/2017 (NR: GP XXV RV 1586 AB 1631 S. 179. BR: AB 9800 S. 868), https://www.ris.bka.gv.at/GeltendeFassung.wxe ?Abfrage=Bundesnormen&Gesetzesnummer=20009892.

Belgium: 1er JUIN 2011.—Loi visant à interdire le port de tout vêtement cachant totalement ou de manière principale le visage (1), http://www .ejustice.just.fgov.be/eli/loi/2011/06/01/2011000424/moniteur.

Bulgaria: Open Society Justice Initiative, "Briefing Papers," 26; for full description of the law, see also Wearing Clothing Covering or Hiding the Face Act (project) (Проект на Закон за носенето на облекло прикриващо или скриващо лицето), Signature 654-01-58 from 20 April 2016, http://www.parliament.bg/bills/43/654-01-58.pdf.

Denmark: Open Society Justice Initiative, "Briefing Papers," 32; for full description of the law, see also Folketinget [National Parliament], 3. Behandling af L 219: Om et tildækningsforbud. Endelig vedtagelse 2017–18 L 219 [3. Reading of L 219: Ban to Cover. Final Adoption], 31 May 2018, https://www.retsinformation.dk/eli/ft/201713L00219.

France: Open Society Justice Initiative, "Briefing Papers," 38; for full description of the law, see also FRENCH BAN ON FACE COVERING:

Notes to Chapter 2 **223**

LOI no. 2010–1192 du 11 octobre 2010 interdisant la dissimulation du visage dans l'espace public (1), https://beta.legifrance.gouv.fr/jorf/id/JORFTEXT000022911670.

Netherlands: Open Society Justice Initiative, "Briefing Papers," 61; for full description of the law, see also Eerste Kamer der Staten-Generaal, "Wet gedeeltelijk verbod gezichtsbedekkende kleding" https://www.eerstekamer.nl/wetsvoorstel/34349_wet_gedeeltelijk_verbod.

Germany: Open Society Justice Initiative, "Briefing Papers," 54–55; for full description of the law, see also Veneto Regional Regulation no. 2 of 4 July 2017, https://bur.regione.veneto.it/BurvServices/pubblica/DettaglioRegolamento.aspx?id=34924.

Hungary: Open Society Justice Initiative, "Briefing Papers," 51.

Italy: Open Society Justice Initiative, "Briefing Papers," 54–55; for full description of the law, see also Veneto Regional Regulation no. 2 of 4 July 2017, https://bur.regione.veneto.it/BurvServices/pubblica/DettaglioRegolamento.aspx?id=34924.

Norway: Jon Sharman, "Norway's Parliament Votes to Ban Burqa in Schools and Universities," *The Independent*, June 7, 2018, https://www.independent.co.uk/news/world/europe/norway-burqa-ban-schools-universities-parliament-vote-niqab-latest-a8387826.html.

Spain: Open Society Justice Initiative, "Briefing Papers," 68, 69; for full description of the law, see also Ley Orgánica 4/2015, de 30 de marzo, de protección de la seguridad ciudadana, "gag law," https://www.boe.es/boe/dias/2015/03/31/pdfs/BOE-A-2015-3442.pdf.

Switzerland: Nick Squires, "Burkas and Niqabs Banned from Swiss Canton," *The Telegraph*, September 23, 2013, https://www.telegraph.co.uk/news/worldnews/europe/switzerland/10327534/Burkas-and-niqabs-banned-from-Swiss-canton.html.

Turkey: "Türkiye'de başörtüsü yasağı: Nasıl başladı, nasıl çözüldü?," *Al Jazeera Turk*, December 30, 2013, http://www.aljazeera.com.tr/dosya/turkiyede-basortusu-yasagi-nasil-basladi-nasil-cozuldu.

Proposed ban: Estonia: Open Society Justice Initiative, "Briefing Papers," 34.

Proposed ban: Latvia: Open Society Justice Initiative, "Briefing Papers," 56; see also Tieslietu ministrija, "Ministru kabinets atbalsta Sejas aizsegšanas ierobežojuma likumprojektu," Ministru Kabinets, August 22, 2017, https://www.mk.gov.lv/lv/aktualitates/ministru-kabinets-atbalsta-sejas-aizsegsanas-ierobezojuma-likumprojektu.

Hijab ban: Bosnia and Herzegovina: "Bosnia Mulls Courtroom Headscarf Ban for Muslim Women," *DW*, February 28, 2016, https://www.dw.com

224 Notes to Chapter 2

/en/bosnia-mulls-courtroom-headscarf-ban-for-muslim-women
/a-19080860.

Hijab ban: Kosovo: Mark Lowen, "Headscarf Ban Sparks Debate over Kosovo's Identity," *BBC News*, August 24, 2010, https://www.bbc.com /news/world-europe-11065911.

Hijab ban: Russia: "The Islamic Veil across Europe," *BBC News*, May 31, 2018, https://www.bbc.com/news/world-europe-13038095.

Hijab ban: Sweden: Open Society Justice Initiative, "Briefing Papers," 71–72.

12 Bill no. 94: *An Act to Establish Governing Accommodation Requests within the Administration and Certain Institutions*, National Assembly of Quebec, 1st Sess., 39th Leg. (2010), http://www.assnat.qc.ca/en/travaux-parlementaires /projets-loi/projet-loi-94-39-1.html?appelant=MC.

Bill no. 60: *Charter Affirming the Values of State Secularism and Religious Neutrality and of Equality between Women and Men, and Providing a Framework for Accommodation Requests*, National Assembly of Quebec, 1st Sess., 42nd Leg. (2013), https://web.archive.org/web/20140124205655 /http://www.nosvaleurs.gouv.qc.ca/medias/pdf/Charter.pdf.

Bill no. 491: *An Act Respecting the Religious Neutrality of the State and the Fight against Religious Fundamentalism and to Amend the Charter of Human Rights and Freedoms and the Act Respecting the Ministère du Conseil Exécutif*, National Assembly of Quebec, 1st Sess., 40th Leg. (2014), http://www.assnat.qc.ca/en/travaux-parlementaires/projets-loi/projet -loi-491-40-1.html.

Bill no. 62: *An Act to Foster Adherence to State Religious Neutrality and, in Particular, to Provide a Framework for Accommodations on Reli- gious Grounds in Certain Bodies*, SQ 2017, c 19, http://www.assnat .qc.ca/en/travaux-parlementaires/projets-loi/projet-loi-62-41-1.html ?appelant=MC.

Bill no. 21: *An Act Respecting the Laicity of the State*, National Assembly of Quebec, 1st Sess., 42nd Leg. (2019), http://www.assnat.qc.ca/en/travaux -parlementaires/projets-loi/projet-loi-21-42-1.html.

13 Feliks Garcia, "US State Bill Could Make Hijabs and Niqabs Illegal in Public," November 17, 2016, *Independent*, https://www.independent.co.uk/news/world /americas/georgia-hijab-niqab-ban-illegal-bill-islam-muslims-law-a7423441 .html; Lindsay Bever, "After Outcry, Georgia Lawmaker Abandons Bill That Would Have Banned Muslims from Wearing Veils," *Washington Post*, Novem- ber 18, 2016, https://www.washingtonpost.com/news/acts-of-faith/wp/2016/11 /18/after-outcry-georgia-lawmaker-abandons-bill-that-would-have-banned

Notes to Chapter 2   225

-muslims-from-wearing-veils/. See also Daniel Patrick Shaffer, "Why the United States Cannot Ban Burqas and Niqabs," *Morocco World News*, December 25, 2016. https://www.moroccoworldnews.com/2016/12/204457/united-states-cannot-ban-burqas-niqabs. For an account of cases of discrimination against niqab and hijab wearers see American Civil Liberties Union, "Discrimination against Muslim Women—Fact Sheet," https://www.aclu.org/other/discrimination-against-muslim-women-fact-sheet.

14 See Natasha Bakht, *In Your Face: Law, Justice, and Niqab-Wearing Women in Canada* (Toronto: Irwin Law Inc, 2020), 121, for a map of global legal projects targeting niqab-wearing women.

15 Katharine Murphy, "Brandis Stands Up for Decency after Burqa Stunt—But That's Exactly What Hanson Wanted," *Guardian*, August 17, 2017, https://www.theguardian.com/australia-news/2017/aug/17/george-brandis-decency-burqa-stunt-senate-pauline-hanson.

16 Colby Itkowitz and John Wagner, "Trump Says He Has No Regrets about Sharing Ilhan Omar Video," *Washington Post*, April 16, 2019, https://www.washingtonpost.com/politics/trump-no-regrets-about-sharing-ilhan-omar-video/2019/04/16/71070d7c-6044-11e9-bfad-36a7eb36cb60_story.html?noredirect=on&utm_term=.328730ddc73f.

17 Glenn Greenwald and Murtaza Hussain, "Suspect in Quebec Mosque Attack Quickly Depicted as a Moroccan Muslim. He's a White Nationalist," *The Intercept*, January 30, 2017, https://theintercept.com/2017/01/30/suspect-in-quebec-mosque-attack-quickly-depicted-as-a-moroccan-muslim-hes-a-white-nationalist/.

18 Lisa Martin and Ben Smee, "What Do We Know about the Christchurch Attack Suspect?," *Guardian*, March 15, 2019, https://www.theguardian.com/world/2019/mar/15/rightwing-extremist-wrote-manifesto-before-livestreaming-christchurch-shooting; Joey Garrison, "'Violent Terrorist': Who Is the White Supremacist Suspected in New Zealand Mosque Shootings?," *USA Today*, March 15, 2019, https://www.usatoday.com/story/news/nation/2019/03/15/new-zealand-christchurch-mosque-shootings-who-brenton-tarrant/3172550002/.

19 Alexandre Bissonnette, "Quebec Mosque Gunman Explains Motives in Interrogation Video," The Canadian Press, April 16, 2018, YouTube video, 2:17, https://www.youtube.com/watch?v=lCOfaUsP5nU.

20 Bakht, *In Your Face*, 130; Bill no. 94: *An Act to Establish Governing Accommodation Requests within the Administration and Certain Institutions*, Assemblée Nationale du Québec, 1st Sess., 39th Leg. (2010), http://www.assnat.qc.ca/en/travaux-parlementaires/projets-loi/projet-loi-94-39-1.html?appelant=MC.

226 Notes to Chapter 2

21 Bakht, *In Your Face*, 130–32; Bill no. 62: *An Act to Foster Adherence to State Religious Neutrality and, in Particular, to Provide a Framework for Accommodations on Religious Grounds in Certain Bodies*, SQ 2017, c 19, http://www.assnat.qc.ca/en/travaux-parlementaires/projets-loi/projet-loi-62-41-1.html ?appelant=MC; Bill no. 21: *An Act Respecting the Laicity of the State*, National Assembly of Quebec, 1st Sess., 42nd Leg. (2019) http://www.assnat.qc.ca/en/travaux-parlementaires/projets-loi/projet-loi-21-42-1.html.

22 Jonathan Montpetit and Benjamin Shingler, "Quebec Superior Court Upholds Most of Religious Symbols Ban, but English-Language Schools Exempt," April 20, 2021, *CBC News*, https://www.cbc.ca/news/canada/montreal/bill-21-religious-symbols-ban-quebec-court-ruling-1.5993431.

23 Amanda Connolly, "Quebec's Bill 21 Again Faces Questions amid Outrage over London, Ont. Vehicle Attack," June 9, 2021, *Global News*, https://globalnews.ca/news/7934352/bill-21-quebec-secularism-criticism/.

24 See the contributors to Leila Celis, Dia Dabby, Dominique Leydet, and Vincent Romani, eds., *Modération ou extrémisme? Regards critiques sur la loi 21* (Québec: Presses de l'Université Laval, 2020), especially Dalie Giroux, "La question nationale et de la laïcité au Québec: Psychopolitique d'une intrication"; Catherine Larochelle, "Petite histoire de nationalisme québécois et de ses racines orientalistes"; and Vincent Romani, "La loi 21 québécoise et l'indicible mot en R—Réfuter le racisme pour mieux dominer."

25 Étienne Balibar, *We, the People of Europe? Reflections on Transnational Citizenship*, trans. James Swenson (Princeton: Princeton University Press, 2004), 36.

26 Bakht, *In Your Face*, 137.

27 Bakht, 115.

28 Bakht, 115.

29 R. v. N.S., 2012 SCC 72, [2012] 3 SCR 726, https://scc-csc.lexum.com/scc-csc/scc-csc/en/item/12779/index.do.

30 R. v. N.S., para. 4.

31 I participated in one such intervention, that of the Women's Legal Education and Action Fund. The Supreme Court of Canada decided the case on December 20, 2012.

32 Natasha Bakht, "In Your Face: Piercing the Veil of Ignorance about Niqab-Wearing Women," *Social and Legal Studies* 24, no. 3 (2015): 419.

33 Bakht, 423.

34 Sherene Razack, *Casting Out: The Eviction of Muslims from Western Law and Politics* (Toronto: University of Toronto Press, 2008).

35 Bakht, "In Your Face," 423–25.

Notes to Chapter 2 **227**

36 *Lie to Me* is an American crime drama television series (2009–11) in which the protagonist is a deception researcher who studies facial expression, body language, and tone of voice to determine when a person is lying and why. His "insights" assist law enforcement to uncover the truth. https://www.imdb.com/title/tt1235099/.

37 Bakht, "In Your Face," 424–25.

38 Bakht, 425.

39 Bakht, 429.

40 Bakht, 430.

41 LeBel quoted in Bakht, 429.

42 Charles Mills, "Liberalism and the Racial State," in *State of White Supremacy: Racism, Governance, and the United States*, ed. Moon-Kie Jung, João H. Costa Vargas, and Eduardo Bonilla-Silva (Stanford: Stanford University Press, 2011), 35.

43 Bakht, "In Your Face," 434.

44 Jason Kenney, "On the Value of Canadian Citizenship," Government of Canada, December 12, 2011, https://www.canada.ca/en/immigration-refugees-citizenship/news/archives/speeches-2011/jason-kenney-minister-2011-12-12.html.

45 Kenney.

46 Kenney.

47 George C. Grinnell, "Veiling and Other Fantasies of Visibility," *New Centennial Review* 13, no. 3 (Winter 2013): 244, https://doi.org/10.1353/ncr.2013.0032.

48 Gada Mahrouse, "Minimizing and Denying Racial Violence: Insights from the Quebec Mosque Shooting," *Canadian Journal of Women and the Law* 30, no. 3 (December 2018): 471, https://doi.org/10.3138/cjwl.30.3.006.

49 Canada (Citizenship and Immigration) v. Ishaq, 2015 FCA 194 (CanLII), https://canlii.ca/t/gl64o.

50 Phil Lord, "What Is the True Purpose of Quebec's Bill 21?," *CRRF Directions* 9, no. 3 (March 2020): 1–9, https://ssrn.com/abstract=3516964. See also Celis et al., *Modération ou Extrémisme?*, 3.

51 Joan Wallach Scott, *The Politics of the Veil* (Princeton: Princeton University Press, 2007).

52 Ratna Kapur, *Gender, Alterity, and Human Rights: Freedom in a Fishbowl* (Cheltenham: Edward Elgar Publishing, 2018), 128.

53 Kapur, 128.

54 Kapur, 129.

55 Peter Baehr and Daniel Gordon, "From the Headscarf to the Burqa: The Role

228 Notes to Chapter 2

of Social Theorists in Shaping Laws against the Veil," *Economy and Society* 42 no. 2 (March 2013): 253, https://doi.org/10.1080/03085147.2012.718620.

56 Baehr and Gordon, 253.

57 See, for example, Anne Norton, *On the Muslim Question* (Princeton: Princeton University Press, 2013), 23.

58 Mayanthi L. Fernando, *The Republic Unsettled: Muslim French and the Contradictions of Secularism* (Durham: Duke University Press, 2014), 9.

59 S.A.S. v. France, European Court of Human Rights, Application no. 43835/11 (2014).

60 "Joint Partly Dissenting Opinion of Judges Nussberger and Jäderblom," S.A.S. v. France, 61.

61 "Joint Partly Dissenting Opinion," 63.

62 This argument has been made by Joan Wallach Scott, *Sex and Secularism* (Princeton: Princeton University Press, 2017); Lila Abu-Lughod, *Do Muslim Women Need Saving?* (Cambridge: Harvard University Press, 2013); and Norton, *On the Muslim Question.*

63 André Gerin, Assemblée Nationale, *Rapport d'information au nom de la mission d'information sur le territoire national,* January 26, 2010, available at http://www.assemblee-nationale.fr/13/pdf/rap-info/i2262.pdf [hereinafter cited as Gerin Report].

64 Chow, *The Protestant Ethnic,* 173.

65 Kirsten M. Yoder Wesselhoeft, "Gendered Secularity: The Feminine Individual in the 2010 Gerin Report," *Journal of Muslim Minority Affairs* 31, no. 3 (September 2011): 399–410. The references to the Gerin Report discussed here are drawn from Wesselhoeft and are her translations of the Gerin Report. There are some discrepancies on the naming of the Gerin Report (sometimes referred to as Guerin), the proper spelling is in fact Gerin as indicated in the report itself.

66 Wesselhoeft, 400.

67 Wesselhoeft, 401.

68 Wesselhoeft, 401.

69 Wesselhoeft, 402.

70 Chow, *The Protestant Ethnic,* 173. Chow's remarks are made in the context of her analysis of the race and gender scripts of the film *Hiroshima mon amour* (and the novel by Marguerite Duras on which the film is based). In the film, the protagonist is the sexually experienced and knowledgeable French woman who has an affair with a Japanese man in Hiroshima, where she has gone to make a film about the effects of the bomb on the city.

71 Wesselhoeft, "Gendered Secularity," 406.

Notes to Chapter 2 **229**

72 Wesselhoeft, 403.

73 Sherene Razack, "Policing the Borders of a Nation: The Imperial Gaze in Gender Persecution Cases," in *Looking White People in the Eye: Gender, Race, and Culture in Courtrooms and Classrooms* (Toronto: University of Toronto Press, 1998), 88–129.

74 Chow, *The Protestant Ethnic*, viii.

75 Fanon, *A Dying Colonialism*, 44.

76 Bidar quoted in Baehr and Gordon, "From the Headscarf to the Burqa," 260.

77 Blandy and Sibley, "Law, Boundaries, and the Production of Space," 279.

78 See Samira Kawash, "The Homeless Body," *Public Culture* 10, no. 2 (May 1998), https://doi.org/10.1215/08992363-10-2-319, for a brilliant illustration of how the exclusion of the homeless from public space is the constitutive violence that defines the boundaries of public space and the contours of the normative citizen as property owner. See also Sherene Razack, *Dying from Improvement: Inquests and Inquiries into Indigenous Deaths in Custody* (Toronto: University of Toronto Press, 2015), for a discussion of how the eviction of Indigenous people from settler spaces constitutes white settlers as the only owners of public space.

79 Lauren Berlant, *The Queen of America Goes to Washington City: Essays on Sex and Citizenship* (Durham: Duke University Press, 1997), 195.

80 Berlant, 195–96.

81 Susan Schweik, *The Ugly Laws: Disability in Public* (New York: New York University Press, 2009), vii.

82 Quoted in Schweik, 1–2.

83 Schweik, 1–2. Although they had mainly ceased by World War I, the last documented arrest occurred in 1974 in Omaha, Nebraska. A police officer arrested a homeless man and took him into custody on the grounds that he had marks and scars on his body. The city prosecutor declined to file the charge on the grounds that the man did not fit the bill of the law.

84 Schweik, 6.

85 Bill S-7: *An Act to Amend the Immigration and Refugee Protection Act, the Civil Marriage Act and the Criminal Code and to Make Consequential Amendments to Other Acts*, 2nd Session, 41st Parliament, Statutes of Canada, 2015, http://www.parl.ca/DocumentViewer/en/41-2/bill/S-7/royal-assent. This act was repealed by the Liberal government of Justin Trudeau in 2016.

86 Bakht, *In Your Face*, 43.

87 Schweik, *The Ugly Laws*, 111.

88 Schweik, 163.

89 Schweik, 208.

230 Notes to Chapter 2

90 See Miriam Ticktin, "Sexual Violence as the Language of Border Control: Where French Feminist and Anti-immigration Rhetoric Meet," *Signs: Journal of Women in Culture and Society* 33, no. 4 (Summer 2008), https://doi.org /10.1086/528851.

91 William Ian Miller, *The Anatomy of Disgust* (Cambridge: Harvard University Press, 1997), 177.

92 Miller, 9.

93 Douglas Husak, "Disgust: Metaphysical and Empirical Speculations," in *Incivilities: Regulating Offensive Behaviour*, ed. A. P. Simester and Andreas von Hirsch (Portland: Hart Publishing, 2006), 92.

94 Ngai, *Ugly Feelings*, 337.

95 Ngai, 335.

96 Grinnell, "Veiling and Other Fantasies of Visibility," 250.

97 Grinnell, 256.

98 Grinnell, 248. At the Hagia Sophia mosque (previously a Greek Orthodox church), even as she sees the beauty and watches people praying, she thinks that this mode of worship is convenient for plots. (Note that this is 1789, not 2016!) She reduces those she sees to threats forever lurking in the shadows.

99 Ghassan Hage, *White Nation: Fantasies of White Supremacy in a Multicultural Society* (New York: Routledge, 1998).

100 Chloe Patton, "Defacing Levinas: Vision, Veiling, and the Ethics of Republican Citizenship in France," *Social Identities* 20, nos. 2–3 (February 2014): 188, https://doi.org/10.1080/13504630.2013.878990.

101 Patton, 189.

102 Patton, 195.

103 Anne Anlin Cheng, *Second Skin: Josephine Baker and the Modern Surface* (New York: Oxford University Press, 2010), 21.

104 Saba Mahmood, *The Politics of Piety: The Islamic Revival and the Feminist Subject* (Princeton: Princeton University Press, 2004).

105 For interviews with women who wear the niqab see Bakht, *In Your Face*; and Anna Piela, *Wearing the Niqab: Muslim Women in the U.K. and the U.S.* (London: Bloomsbury Visual Arts, 2021).

106 Bakht, *In Your Face*, 61.

107 Asad quoted in Razack, *Casting Out*, 161.

108 Schweik, *The Ugly Laws*, 205.

109 A crucial point that is unexplored here is whether Levinas is mistakenly assumed to conflate knowing and seeing. The glance is not the measure of recognition.

110 Schweik, *The Ugly Laws*, 287.

111 Schweik, 287.

Notes to Chapter 3   231

112 Alia Al-Saji, "The Racialization of Muslim Veils: A Philosophical Analysis," *Philosophy and Social Criticism* 36, no. 8 (October 2010): 875, https://doi.org/10.1177/0191453710375589.

113 Schweik, *The Ugly Laws*, 286.

114 Patton, "Defacing Levinas," 194.

115 Patton, 194.

116 Ariella Azoulay, *The Civil Contract of Photography* (New York: Zone Books, 2008).

117 As the *New York Times* reported in April 2018, a French court denied citizenship to an Algerian woman who refused to shake hands with male officials at a French naturalization ceremony. Aurelien Breedene, "No Handshake, No Citizenship, French Court Tells Algerian Woman," *New York Times*, April 21, 2018, https://www.nytimes.com/2018/04/21/world/europe/handshake-citizenship-france.html.

118 Henk van Houtum, "Waiting before the Law: Kafka on the Border," *Social and Legal Studies* 19, no. 3 (August 2010): 285–97, https://doi.org/10.1177/0964663910372180.

119 Agence France-Presse, "French City Shuts Down Public Pools after Two Women Wear Burkinis," *Guardian*, June 27, 2019, https://www.theguardian.com/world/2019/jun/27/france-city-shuts-down-public-pools-after-two-women-wear-burkinis.

120 Ralph Grillo and Prakash Shah, "The Anti-burqa Movement in Western Europe," in *The Burqa Affair across Europe: Between Public and Private Space*, ed. Alessandro Ferrari and Sabrina Pastorelli (New York: Routledge, 2016), 202.

121 Toni Morrison, *The Source of Self-Regard: Selected Essays, Speeches, and Meditations* (New York: Knopf, 2019), 70.

3. "Terrorism in Their Genes"

1 Sherene Razack, *Casting Out: The Eviction of Muslims from Western Law and Politics* (Toronto: University of Toronto Press, 2008), 34–36.

2 François Soyer, "Faith, Culture, and Fear: Comparing Islamophobia in Early Modern Spain and Twenty-First-Century Europe," in *Racialization and Religion: Race, Culture, and Difference in the Study of Antisemitism and Islamophobia*, ed. Nasar Meer (New York: Routledge, 2014), 18–20.

3 Ana Echevarria, *The Fortress of Faith: The Attitude towards Muslims in Fifteenth Century Spain* (Leiden: Brill, 1999). See also Robert I. Burns, S.J., "Christian-Islamic Confrontation in the West: The Thirteenth-Century Dream of Conversion," *American Historical Review* 76, no. 5 (December 1971): 1386–1434.

232 Notes to Chapter 3

4 Michael Welner, "Testimony at Omar Khadr's Sentencing Hearing in Guantánamo Bay, Cuba" (2010), 4361–4614, accessed July 18, 2019, https://upload.wikimedia.org/wikipedia/commons/c/c6/Dr_Michael_Welner%27s_testimony_at_Omar_Khadr%27s_sentencing_hearing.PDF.

5 Hannah Arendt, "Race-thinking before Racism," *Review of Politics* 6, no. 1 (January 1944): 36–73. See also Arendt, *On the Origins of Totalitarianism* (New York: Harcourt, Brace, Jovanovich, 1975), 159.

6 Razack, *Casting Out*, 25–54.

7 David Theo Goldberg, *The Racial State* (Malden, Mass.: Blackwell, 2002), 26.

8 Netanyahu quoted in Edward W. Said, "The Essential Terrorist," review of *Terrorism: How the West Can Win*, by Benjamin Netanyahu, *Arab Studies Quarterly* 9, no. 2 (Spring 1987): 199.

9 Netanyahu quoted in Said, 199.

10 Nicole R. Fleetwood, *Marking Time: Art in the Age of Mass Incarceration* (Cambridge: Harvard University Press, 2020), 39.

11 Zygmunt Bauman, *Society under Siege* (Cambridge: Polity Press, 2002), 114.

12 Dorothy Roberts, *Fatal Invention: How Science, Politics, and Big Business Re-create Race in the Twenty-First Century* (New York: The New Press, 2011), 28.

13 Sherene H. Razack, "The Manufacture of Torture as Public Truth: The Case of Omar Khadr," in *At the Limits of Justice: Women of Colour Theorize Terror*, ed. Suvendrini Perera and Sherene Razack (Toronto: University of Toronto Press, 2014), 70–71.

14 "As Trial Looms, Little Change in How Canadians Feel about Omar Khadr," Angus Reid Institute, http://angusreid.org/as-trial-looms-little-change-in-how-canadians-feel-about-omar-khadr/.

15 Peter Jan Honigsberg, *Our Nation Unhinged: The Human Consequences of the War on Terror* (Berkeley: University of California Press, 2009), 160.

16 Scholars rightly question whether Agamben's argument about the space of exception captures the space where the racialized reside. Guantánamo, a prison established outside the bounds of U.S. law and territory, is a space of exception but the treatment of prisoners there, including torture, has its origin and parallel in U.S. domestic prisons where the prisoner, the embodiment of the slave in law, is civilly dead. See Colin Dayan, *The Law Is a White Dog: How Legal Rituals Make and Unmake Persons* (Princeton: Princeton University Press, 2011); Denise Ferreira da Silva, "No-Bodies: Law, Raciality and Violence," *Griffith Law Review* 18, no. 2 (2009): 212–36; Alexander G. Weheliye, *Habeas Viscus: Racializing Assemblages, Biopolitics, and Black Feminist Theories of the Human* (Durham: Duke University Press,

Notes to Chapter 3 **233**

2014); Junaid Rana, *Terrifying Muslims: Race and Labor in the South Asian Diaspora* (Durham: Duke University Press, 2011).

17 See Nathan Lean, *The Islamophobia Industry: How the Right Manufactures Fear of Muslims* (London: Pluto Press, 2012); Stephen Sheehi, *Islamophobia: The Ideological Campaign against Muslims* (Atlanta: Clarity Press, 2011).

18 Arun Kundnani, *The Muslims Are Coming! Islamophobia, Extremism, and the Domestic War on Terror* (London: Verso, 2014), 11.

19 Minister of Public Safety, press release, "In the Matter of Omar Ahmed Khadr and the *International Transfer of Offenders Act*," September 28, 2012, Ottawa, Canada. Omar Khadr was released on bail in May 2015 to live with his Canadian lawyer, Denis Edney, and in March 2019 a Canadian judge ruled that his sentence for war crimes had expired, and Khadr was freed.

20 Michelle Shephard, "Omar Khadr's Lawyers Question Pentagon's Star Witness," *Toronto Star,* April 18, 2011, http://www.thestar.com/news/world/2011 /04/18/omar_khadrs_lawyers_question_pentagons_star_witness.html.

21 Joshua Dratel, "No Laughing Matter," in *The Guantánamo Lawyers: Inside a Prison Outside the Law*, ed. Mark P. Denbeaux and Jonathan Hafetz (New York: New York University Press, 2009), 131.

22 Amy Davidson Sorkin, "At Guantánamo, Are Even the Judges Giving Up?," *New Yorker,* February 21, 2018, https://www.newyorker.com/news/daily-comment /at-guantanamo-are-even-the-judges-giving-up.

23 Lisa Stampnitzky, *Disciplining Terror: How Experts Invented "Terrorism"* (Cambridge: Cambridge University Press, 2013), 13.

24 Welner, "Testimony," 4490.

25 Michael Friscolanti, "Was Omar Khadr Sexually Abused?," *Maclean's,* August 31, 2012, https://www.macleans.ca/news/canada/was-omar-khadr -sexually-abused/.

26 I put terms such as "jihadi" in quotation marks to emphasize that they are used in this context by Welner and have no apparent connection to Islamic theology. The same is true for the phrase "radical Islam."

27 Michael Welner, "The Depravity Standard," *Forensic Panel,* accessed July 31, 2019, https://depravitystandard.org.

28 Welner, "Testimony," 4392.

29 Kundnani, *The Muslims Are Coming!,* 115.

30 Kundnani, 117.

31 Walter Laqueur, *The Terrible Secret: Suppression of the Truth about Hitler's "Final Solution"* (New York: Penguin Books, 1982).

32 Kundnani, *The Muslims Are Coming!,* 120.

33 Kundnani, 122.

234 Notes to Chapter 3

34 Razack, *Casting Out*, 25–58.

35 Welner, "Testimony," 4393.

36 Welner, 4394.

37 See, for example, Nicolai Sennels, "Among Criminal Muslims," interview by Jamie Glazov, *Frontpage Mag*, May 4, 2010, http://www.frontpagemag.com /2010/jamie-glazov/among-criminal-muslims/; "Nicolai Sennels," *Gates of Vienna*, accessed July 31, 2019, http://gatesofvienna.blogspot.ca/p/nicolai -sennels.html; Nicolai Sennels, "Muslims and Westerners: The Psychological Differences," *New English Review*, May 2010, https://www.newenglishreview .org/Nicolai_Sennels/Muslims_and_Westerners%3A_The_Psychological _Differences/; "Writings by Nicolai Sennels," *Islamist Watch*, accessed July 31, 2019, http://www.islamist-watch.org/author/Nicolai+Sennels; Nicolai Sennels, "Nicolai Sennels: Psychology: Why Islam Creates Monsters," *Jihad Watch*, September 27, 2013, http://www.jihadwatch.org/2013/09 /nicolai-sennels-psychology-why-islam-creates-monsters.

38 Sennels, "Among Criminal Muslims"; Sennels, "Muslims and Westerners."

39 Sennels, "Among Criminal Muslims."

40 Sennels.

41 Welner, "Testimony," 4403.

42 Welner, 4457.

43 Welner, 4559.

44 Welner, 4559.

45 Welner, 4408–9.

46 Sennels, "Muslims and Westerners."

47 Andres Leighton, "Camp Delta Four in the Guantánamo Bay Naval Station, Cuba," *Encyclopedia.com*, July 6, 2005, https://www.encyclopedia.com/history/ legal-and-political-magazines/camp-delta-four-guantanamo-bay-naval -station-cuba.

48 Welner, "Testimony," 4420.

49 Welner, 4421.

50 Welner, 4421.

51 Welner, 4437.

52 Welner, 4446.

53 Jessie Daniels, *White Lies: Race, Class, Gender, and Sexuality in White Supremacist Discourse* (New York: Routledge, 1997), 107.

54 Welner, "Testimony," 4458.

55 Welner, 4406.

56 Welner, 4408.

57 Welner, 4570.

Notes to Chapter 3 **235**

58 Welner, 4600–4601.

59 Ghassan Hage, *Is Racism an Environmental Threat?* (Cambridge: Polity Press, 2017), 8.

60 For an analysis of the how narratives about Khadr travel from the media to political and legal spaces, see Razack, "The Manufacture of Torture."

61 Welner, "Testimony," 4490.

62 Welner, 4541.

63 Welner, 4545.

64 Shephard, "Omar Khadr's Lawyers."

65 Welner, "Testimony," 4600.

66 Welner, 4603–5.

67 Stephen N. Xenakis, "Radical Jihadism Is Not a Mental Disorder," *Washington Post,* December 5, 2010, http://www.washingtonpost.com/wp-dyn/content /article/2010/12/10/AR2010121006997.html.

68 The term "pre-crime" is widely attributed to the prolific science fiction writer Phillip K. Dick (1928–82), whose novels have inspired films such as *Minority Report.* "Phillip K. Dick," *Encyclopedia Britannica,* https://www .britannica.com/biography/Philip-K-Dick.

69 María Elena Martínez, *Genealogical Fictions: Limpieza de Sangre, Religion, and Gender in Colonial Mexico* (Stanford: Stanford University Press, 2008), 16.

70 Martínez, 47.

71 Pamela Geller, *Stop the Islamization of America: A Practical Guide to the Resistance* (Washington, D.C.: WND Books, 2011); Steven Emerson, *American Jihad: The Terrorists Living among Us* (New York: Simon & Schuster, 2003); Robert Spencer, *The History of Jihad: From Muhammad to ISIS* (New York: Post Hill Press, 2018); Daniel Pipes, *Militant Islam Reaches America* (New York: Norton Paperback, 2003); Frank Gaffney Jr., *Shariah: The Threat to America: Abridged* (Washington, D.C.: Center for Security Policy Press, 2016).

72 François Debrix, "Tabloid Realism and the Revival of American Security Culture," *Geopolitics* 8, no. 3 (October 2003): 151–90, https://doi.org/10.1080 /14650040412331307752.

73 Colleen Flaherty, "Unwelcome Guest," *Inside Higher Ed,* December 19, 2018, https://www.insidehighered.com/news/2018/12/19/northwestern-students -want-controversial-scholar-their-campus.

74 Satoshi Kanazawa, "The Savanna Principle: What the Human Brain Can and Cannot Comprehend, and Why," *Psychology Today,* February 28, 2010, https:// www.psychologytoday.com/us/blog/the-scientific-fundamentalist/201002 /the-savanna-principle.

236 Notes to Chapter 3

75 Satoshi Kanazawa, "The Evolutionary Psychological Imagination: Why You Can't Get a Date on Saturday Night and Why All Suicide Bombers Are Muslim," *Journal of Social, Evolutionary, and Cultural Psychology* 1, no. 2 (January 2007): 12, http://dx.doi.org/10.1037/h0099090.

76 Nancy Hartevelt Kobrin, *The Banality of Suicide Terrorism: The Naked Truth about the Psychology of Islamic Suicide Bombing* (Washington, D.C.: Potomac Books, 2010); Nancy H. Kobrin, *Penetrating the Terrorist Psyche* (New York: MultiEducator Inc., 2013); Nancy H. Kobrin, *The Maternal Drama of the Chechen Jihadi* (New York: MultiEducator Inc., 2014); Nancy H. Kobrin, *The Jihadi Dictionary: The Essential Intel Tool for the Military, Law Enforcement, Government, and the Concerned Public* (New York: MultiEducator Press, 2016).

77 See Kobrin's introduction to Sennels's "Muslims and Westerners."

78 Nancy Hartevelt Kobrin, "Nobody Born a Terrorist, but Early Childhood Matters: Explaining the Jihadis' Lack of Empathy," *Perspectives on Terrorism* 10, no. 5 (October 2016): 108–11.

79 Phyllis Chesler, *Women and Madness* (New York: Avon, 1972) and *The New Anti-Semitism and What We Must Do about It* (New York: Jossey-Bass, 2003). For a discussion of Chesler's anti-Muslim racism see Razack, *Casting Out*, 95–98.

80 Phyllis Chesler, "Foreword: The Psychoanalytic Roots of Islamic Suicide Terrorism," in *The Banality of Suicide Terrorism: The Naked Truth about the Psychology of Islamic Suicide Bombing*, ed. Nancy H. Kobrin (Washington, D.C.: Potomac Books, 2010), ix.

81 Jasbir Puar has insightfully observed that explanations about the family as the incubator of violent tendencies are premised on the Western heterosexual nuclear family. She reminds us that feminist and queer-inspired accounts of the terrorist family that aim to contest the script of normative gender in the above accounts argue instead that it is patriarchy that causes damage to the terrorist psyche. This argument shares a terrain with the cultural racism of the writers above; the universalism on which it is premised obscures how race, gender, and sexuality work through each other to form a hierarchical world. The Muslim/Arab terrorist remains a monstrous figure in feminist and queer accounts that suggest that the lives of Muslim boys and men are shaped by the same-sex intimacy of the terrorist world, a world in which homosexuality cannot be expressed. All such explanations foreclose "any kind of political, economic, or material critique immanent to terrorist motivations." Jasbir K. Puar, *Terrorist Assemblages. Homonationalism in Queer Times* (Durham: Duke University Press, 2007), 57.

Notes to Chapter 3 237

82 Kobrin, "Nobody Born a Terrorist."

83 Kobrin, 110.

84 Anat Berko, *The Path to Paradise: The Inner World of Suicide Bombers and Their Dispatchers* (Westport, Conn.: Praeger Security International, 2007), 10.

85 Berko, 16.

86 Farhad Khosrokhavar, "The Psychology of Global Jihadists," in *The Fundamentalist Mindset: Psychological Perspectives on Religion, Violence, and History*, ed. Charles B. Strozier, David M. Terman, James W. Jones, and Katherine A. Boyd (New York: Oxford University Press, 2010), 144.

87 Kobrin, "Nobody Born a Terrorist"; Kanazawa, "The Evolutionary Psychological Imagination"; Khosrokhavar, "The Psychology of Global Jihadists"; Berko, *The Path to Paradise*.

88 Tom Griffin, David Miller, and Tom Mills, "The Neoconservative Movement: Think Tanks as Elite Elements of Social Movements from Above," in *What Is Islamophobia? Racism, Social Movements, and the State*, ed. Narzanin Massoumi, Tom Mills, and David Miller (London: Pluto Press, 2017), 218.

89 See in this regard the work of Arun Kundnani in *The Muslims Are Coming!* See also Asim Qureshi, "The UK Counter-terrorism Matrix: Structural Racism and the Case of Mahdi Hashi," in *What Is Islamophobia? Racism, Social Movements, and the State*, ed. Narzanin Massoumi, Tom Mills, and David Miller (London: Pluto Press, 2017), 74–96. See also Hilary Aked, "Islamophobia, Counter-extremism, and the Counterjihad Movement," in *What Is Islamophobia? Racism, Social Movements, and the State*, ed. Narzanin Massoumi, Tom Mills, and David Miller (London: Pluto Press, 2017), 163–85.

90 Jonathan Githens-Mazer, "The Rhetoric and Reality: Radicalization and Political Discourse," *International Political Science Review* 33, no. 5 (November 2012): 556–67.

91 Sarah Marusek, "The Transatlantic Network: Islamophobia and Israeli Settlements," in *What Is Islamophobia? Racism, Social Movements, and the State*, ed. Narzanin Massoumi, Tom Mills, and David Miller (London: Pluto Press, 2017), 186–214.

92 Clarion Project, https://clarionproject.org.

93 See, for example, the funding profile assembled by the Centre for American Progress, https://islamophobianetwork.com/organization/clarion-project/.

94 See, for example, Canary Mission, https://canarymission.org.

95 Nathan C. Lean, "Mainstreaming Anti-Muslim Prejudice: The Rise of the Islamophobia Industry in American Electoral Politics," in *What Is Islamophobia? Racism, Social Movements, and the State*, ed. Narzanin Massoumi, Tom Mills, and David Miller (London: Pluto Press, 2017), 123–36.

238 Notes to Chapter 3

96 Angela Saini, *Superior: The Return of Race Science* (Boston: Beacon Press, 2019), xiii.

97 Bo Winegard and Noah Carl, "*Superior: The Return of Race Science*—A Review," review of *Superior: The Return of Race Science*, by Angela Saini, *Quillette*, June 5, 2019, https://quillette.com/2019/06/05/superior-the-return-of-race-science-a-review/.

98 Saini, *Superior*, xi.

99 Roberts, *Fatal Invention*, 297.

100 Roberts, x.

101 Roberts, 305.

102 Roberts, 298.

103 Roberts, 299.

104 Richard J. Hernstein and Charles Murray, *The Bell Curve: Intelligence and Class Structure in American Life* (New York: Free Press Paperbacks, 1994).

105 Kyla Schuler, *The Biopolitics of Feeling: Race, Sex, and Science in the Nineteenth Century* (Durham: Duke University Press, 2018).

106 Israel Rosenfield and Edward Ziff, "Epigenetics: The Evolution Revolution," *New York Review of Books*, June 7, 2018, https://www.nybooks.com/articles/2018/06/07/epigenetics-the-evolution-revolution.

107 Tanya Titchkosky, personal email communication, October 29, 2014.

108 Linda Gordon, "The Original Wall," *New York Times*, July 7, 2019, BR14.

109 Katherine McKittrick, "Axis, Bold as Love: On Sylvia Wynter, Jimi Hendrix, and the Promise of Science," in *Sylvia Wynter: On Being Human as Praxis*, ed. Katherine McKittrick (Durham: Duke University Press, 2015), 150.

110 McKittrick, 151.

111 McKittrick, 152, 155.

112 McKittrick, 155.

4. "We Didn't Kill 'em, We Didn't Cut Their Heads Off"

1 Dionne Brand, "Dionne Brand: On Narrative, Reckoning, and the Calculus of Living and Dying," *Toronto Star*, July 4, 2020, https://www.thestar.com/entertainment/books/2020/07/04/dionne-brand-on-narrative-reckoning-and-the-calculus-of-living-and-dying.html.

2 Gwen Shuni D'Arcangelis, *Bio-Imperialism: Disease, Terror, and the Construction of National Fragility* (Newark, N.J.: Rutgers University Press, 2020) 58.

3 Jay Winter, "Remembering War: The Great War between Memory and History in the Twentieth Century," in *The Collective Memory Reader*, ed. Jeffrey K. Olick, Vered Vinitzky-Seroussi, and Danie Levy (Oxford: Oxford University Press, 2011), 426.

Notes to Chapter 4 **239**

4 Winter, 428.

5 Anupama Rao and Steven Pierce, "Discipline and the Other Body: Humanitarianism, Violence, and the Colonial Exception," in *Discipline and the Other Body: Correction, Corporeality, Colonialism,* ed. Anupama Rao and Steven Pierce (Durham: Duke University Press, 2006), 22.

6 Angela Davis, *Abolition Democracy: Beyond Empire, Prisons, and Torture* (New York: Seven Stories Press, 2005), 59.

7 Davis, 79.

8 D'Arcangelis, *Bio-Imperialism,* 12.

9 For a discussion of these two films that reveals their endorsement of torture, see Sadia Abbas, *At Freedom's Limit: Islam and the Postcolonial Predicament* (New York: Fordham University Press, 2014).

10 Errol Morris, dir., *Standard Operating Procedure* (Participant Productions and Sony Pictures Classics, 2008), film.

11 Barack Obama, State of the Union Address, February 24, 2009, https://obamawhitehouse.archives.gov/the-press-office/remarks-president-barack-obama-address-joint-session-congress.

12 "Bush Says U.S. 'Does Not Torture People,'" NBC News, October 5, 2007, https://www.nbcnews.com/id/wbna21148801.

13 A. Naomi Paik, "Representing the Disappeared Body: Videos of Force-Feeding at Guantánamo," *Humanity: An International Journal of Human Rights, Humanitarianism, and Development* 9, no. 3 (Winter 2018): 423–48. http://doi.org/10.1353/hum.2018.0021.

14 Laura Briggs, "Making Race, Making Sex: Perspectives on Torture," *International Feminist Journal of Politics* 17, no. 1 (2015): 31, https://doi.org/10.1080/14616742.2013.855089.

15 Mark Denbeaux, Stephanie Moreno Haire, Tatiana Laing, Kristopher Guldner, Danera Pope-Ragoonanan, "How America Tortures," *Seton Hall Public Law Research,* November 27, 2019, http://dx.doi.org/10.2139/ssrn.3494533; see also Michael Conte, "Newly Released Illustrations Depict Post-9/11 Torture Techniques," *CNN,* December 6, 2019, https://www.cnn.com/2019/12/06/politics/torture-techniques-report/index.html; "Abu Zubaydah," *The Rendition Project,* https://www.therenditionproject.org.uk/prisoners/zubaydah.html, accessed August 27, 2020.

16 National Public Radio, "The Supreme Court Considers Whether the CIA's Black Sites Are State Secrets," October 6, 2021, *Morning Edition,* https://www.npr.org/2021/10/06/1043484190/supreme-court-considers-whether-cias-black-sites-are-state-secrets; Supreme Court, Docket 20-827, United States, Petitioner v. Zayn al-Abidin Muhammed Husayn, aka Abu Zubaydah, et al.,

240 Notes to Chapter 4

https://www.supremecourt.gov/docket/docketfiles/html/public/20-827
.html.

17 Robert M. Pallitto, ed., *Torture and State Violence in the United States* (Baltimore: John Hopkins University Press, 2011); Rebecca Gordon, *Mainstreaming Torture: Ethical Approaches to the Post-9/11 United States* (New York: Oxford University Press, 2014); W. Fitzhugh Brundage, *Civilizing Torture: An American Tradition* (Cambridge: Belknap Press of Harvard University Press, 2018).

18 Brundage, *Civilizing Torture*, 334.

19 Shampa Biswas and Zahi Zalloua, "Introduction: Torture, Democracy, and the Human Body," in *Torture: Power, Democracy, and the Human Body*, ed. Shampa Biswas and Zahi Zalloua (Seattle: University of Washington Press, 2011), 11.

20 Sherene Razack, *Casting Out: The Eviction of Muslims from Western Law and Politics* (Toronto: University of Toronto Press, 2008), 59–80.

21 I use the term *race pleasure* here in the same way that Anthony Farley does, as a pleasure in one's own superiority and the other's abjection. Anthony Paul Farley, "The Black Body as Fetish Object," *Orlando Law Review* 76 (1997): 457–535.

22 Shawn Michelle Smith, *American Archives: Gender, Race, and Class in Visual Culture* (Princeton: Princeton University Press, 1999), 50.

23 Michael Taussig, *Shamanism, Colonialism, and the Wild Man: A Study in Terror and Healing* (Chicago: University of Chicago Press, 1987), 27.

24 Achille Mbembe, "Aesthetics of Superfluity," *Public Culture* 16, no. 3 (2004): 373–405, https://doi.org/10.1215/08992363-16-3-373.

25 Marnia Lazreg, *Torture and the Twilight of Empire: From Algiers to Baghdad* (Princeton: Princeton University Press, 2008), 7.

26 Lazreg, 121.

27 Lazreg, 184.

28 I offer this example from my own experience.

29 Joshua Dratel, "The Curious Debate," in *The Torture Debate in America*, ed. Karen J. Greenberg (New York: Cambridge University Press, 2006), 113.

30 Stephen Holmes, "Is Defiance of Law a Proof of Success? Magical Thinking in the 'War on Terror,'" in *The Torture Debate in America*, ed. Karen J. Greenberg (New York: Cambridge University Press, 2006), 127.

31 See Samuel P. Huntington, *The Clash of Civilizations and the Remaking of World Order* (New York: Touchstone Press, 1997).

32 John Gray, "Power and Vainglory," in *Abu Ghraib: The Politics of Torture*, ed. Meron Benvenisti and Barbara Ehrenreich (Berkeley: North Atlantic Books, 2004), 50.

Notes to Chapter 4 **241**

33 Mark Danner, "The Logic of Torture," in *Abu Ghraib: The Politics of Torture,* ed. Meron Benvenisti and Barbara Ehrenreich (Berkeley: North Atlantic Books, 2004), 31.

34 Danner, 32.

35 Heather MacDonald, "How to Interrogate Terrorists," in *The Torture Debate in America,* ed. Karen J. Greenberg (New York: Cambridge University Press, 2006), 86.

36 Andrew McCarthy, "Thinking about the Unthinkable," in *The Torture Debate in America,* ed. Karen J. Greenberg (New York: Cambridge University Press, 2006), 96.

37 Timothy M. Jones and Penelope Sheets, "Torture in the Eye of the Beholder: Social Identity, News Coverage, and Abu Ghraib," *Political Communication* 26, no. 3 (August 2009): 278–95. https://doi.org/10.1080/10584600903053460.

38 Paul Gronke, Darius Rejali, Dustin Drenguis, James Hicks, Peter Miller, and Bryan Nakayama, "U.S. Public Opinion on Torture, 2001–2009," *Political Science and Politics* 43, no. 3 (July 2010): 437–44. https://doi.org/10.1017/S1049096510000697.

39 David Cole, "What to Do about the Torturers?," review of *Torture Team: Rumsfeld's Memo and the Betrayal of American Values,* by Philippe Sands, *The Trial of Donald Rumsfeld: A Prosecution by Book,* by Michael Ratner and the Center for Constitutional Rights, and *Administration of Torture: A Documentary Record from Washington to Abu Ghraib and Beyond,* by Jameel Jaffer and Amrit Singh, *New York Review of Books,* January 15, 2009, https://www.nybooks.com/articles/2009/01/15/what-to-do-about-the-torturers/.

40 Cole.

41 Karen J. Greenberg, "Introduction: The Rule of Law Finds Its Golem: Judicial Torture Then and Now," in *The Torture Debate in America,* ed. Karen J. Greenberg (New York: Cambridge University Press, 2008), 1.

42 See, for example, the 1,249-page collection *The Torture Papers: The Road to Abu Ghraib,* ed. Karen J. Greenberg and Joshua L. Dratel (New York: Cambridge University Press, 2005).

43 Mark Danner, "US Torture: Voices from the Black Sites," review of *ICRC Report on the Treatment of Fourteen "High Value Detainees" in CIA Custody,* by the International Committee of the Red Cross, *New York Review of Books,* April 9, 2009, https://www.nybooks.com/articles/2009/04/09/us-torture-voices-from-the-black-sites.

44 Danner.

45 Veterans of the conflict in Iraq adopted the term "Winter Soldier" from Vietnam Veterans Against the War, who sponsored a media event called the Winter Soldier investigation from January 31 to February 2, 1971, to publicize

242 Notes to Chapter 4

the war crimes of the United States armed forces in Vietnam. See Andrew E. Hunt, *The Turning: A History of Vietnam Veterans Against the War* (New York: New York University Press, 1999); and Richard Stacewicz, *Winter Soldiers: An Oral History of the Vietnam Veterans Against the War* (New York: Twayne, 1997).

46 Richard Weisman asks this question in "Showing Remorse at the TRC: Towards a Constitutive Approach to Reparative Discourse," *Windsor Yearbook of Access to Justice* 24, no. 2 (2006): 221–40.

47 Sherene Razack, *Dark Threats and White Knights: The Somalia Affair, Peacekeeping, and the New Imperialism* (Toronto: University of Toronto Press, 2004).

48 Errol Morris, "Errol Morris with Philip Gourevitch," interview by Philip Gourevitch., *New Yorker,* October 5, 2007, video, https://video.newyorker.com/watch/errol-morris-with-philip-gourevitch.

49 Morris, *Standard Operating Procedure*; Philip Gourevitch and Errol Morris, *Standard Operating Procedure* (New York: Penguin Press, 2008).

50 Joanne Laurier, "*Standard Operating Procedure*: Images from a Neo-colonial War," *World Socialist Website,* June 17, 2008, http://www.wsws.org/articles/2008/jun2008/sop-j17.shtml.

51 Amy Goodman, "'The Ghosts of Abu Ghraib'—Doc Traces Path to Torture of Prisoners at Infamous Iraqi Prison," *Democracy Now!,* March 21, 2007, http://www.democracynow.org/2007/3/21/the_ghosts_of_abu_ghraib_doc.

52 Pierre Nora, "Between Memory and History," in *The Collective Memory Reader,* ed. Jeffrey K. Olick, Vered Vinitzky-Seroussi, and Danie Levy (Oxford: Oxford University Press, 2011), 8.

53 Nora, 8.

54 Amy Goodman, "Winter Soldier: US Vets, Active-Duty Soldiers from Iraq and Afghanistan Testify about the Horrors of War," *Democracy Now!,* March 17, 2008, https://www.democracynow.org/2008/3/17/winter_soldier_us_vets_active_duty.

55 Goodman.

56 Amy Goodman, "Winter Soldier: Hundreds of Veterans of Iraq and Afghanistan Gather to Testify in Echo of 1971 Vietnam Hearings," *Democracy Now!,* March 14, 2008, https://www.democracynow.org/2008/3/14/hundreds_of_veterans_of_iraq_and.

57 Weisman, "Showing Remorse at the TRC."

58 Lazreg, *Torture and the Twilight of Empire,* 2 (emphasis added).

59 Razack, *Dark Threats and White Knights.*

60 Ridley quoted in Razack, 58.

Notes to Chapter 4   **243**

61 Gourevitch and Morris, *Standard Operating Procedure,* 273.

62 Gourevitch and Morris, 277.

63 D'Arcangelis, *Bio-Imperialism,* 95.

64 The lesbian relationship is casually inserted and unremarked upon in the story, communicating that we are watching a film and reading a book made by progressive people. Unlike the Fox News commentators, for whom the label of homosexual for Arabs marks Arab barbarism, the mark of lesbianism in the soldiers' narratives places Americans in modernity.

65 Gourevitch and Morris, *Standard Operating Procedure,* 112.

66 Gourevitch and Morris, 117.

67 Gourevitch and Morris, 160.

68 Gourevitch and Morris, 164.

69 Gourevitch and Morris, 164.

70 Morris quoted in Omar P. L. Moore, "In American Torture and Terror, Errol Morris Finds Shades of Black, White, and Gray," *The Popcorn Reel,* March 1, 2008, http://www.popcornreel.com/htm/errolmorris.htm.

71 Ian Buruma, "Ghosts," review of *Standard Operating Procedure,* by Philip Gourevitch and Errol Morris, and *Standard Operating Procedure,* by Errol Morris, *New York Review of Books,* June 26, 2008, https://www.nybooks.com/articles/2008/06/26/ghosts/.

72 Peter Goddard, "Images of Abu Ghraib," *Toronto Star,* June 1, 2008, https://www.thestar.com/entertainment/books/2008/06/01/images_of_abu_ghraib.html.

73 Goddard.

74 Michael S. Roth, "Framed," review of *Standard Operating Procedure,* by Philip Gourevitch and Errol Morris, *Los Angeles Times,* May 25, 2008, https://www.latimes.com/archives/la-xpm-2008-may-25-bk-roth25-story.html.

75 Michael Chaiken, "Review: *Standard Operating Procedure,*" review of *Standard Operating Procedure,* by Philip Gourevitch and Errol Morris, *Film Society of Lincoln Center,* May 8, 2008, https://www.filmcomment.com/article/standard-operating-procedure-review/.

76 Cynthia Fuchs, "Fraction of a Second," review of *Standard Operating Procedure,* by Philip Gourevitch and Errol Morris, *Pop Matters,* May 2, 2008, https://www.popmatters.com/standard-operating-procedure-2496155154.html.

77 Laurier, "Standard Operating Procedure."

78 Lazreg, *Torture and the Twilight of Empire,* 3.

79 Lazreg, 118.

80 Borzou Daragahi and Raheem Salman, "Blackwater Shooting Highlights a

244 Notes to Chapter 4

U.S., Iraq Culture Clash," *Los Angeles Times*, May 4, 2008, http://articles
.latimes.com/2008/may/04/world/fg-blackwater4.

81 Daragahi and Salman.

82 Associated Press, "Trump Pardons Military Personnel Accused of Crimes
Overseas," *Guardian*, November 15, 2020, https://www.theguardian.com/us
-news/2019/nov/15/trump-military-pardons-afghanistan; see also Richard
Luscombe, "Navy Seal Pardoned of War Crimes by Trump Described by
Colleagues as 'Freaking Evil,'" *Guardian*, December 27, 2019, https://www
.theguardian.com/us-news/2019/dec/27/eddie-gallagher-trump-navy
-seal-iraq.

83 Jinee Lokaneeta, *Transnational Torture: Law, Violence, and State Power in
the United States and India* (New York: New York University Press, 2011).

84 Dunya Mikhail, "An Urgent Call," in *The War Works Hard*, trans. Elizabeth
Winslow (New York: New Directions, 2005), 13.

Conclusion

1 See, for example, Pascal Bruckner, *An Imaginary Racism: Islamophobia and
Guilt*, trans. Steven Rendall and Lisa Neal (Cambridge: Polity Press, 2018).

2 Lila Abu-Lughod, *Do Muslim Women Need Saving?* (Cambridge: Harvard
University Press, 2013), 68–69.

3 Richard Slotkin, *Gunfighter Nation: The Myth of the Frontier in Twentieth-
Century America* (New York: University of Oklahoma Press, 1992), 658.

4 European Council on Refugees and Exiles, *ECRE Weekly Bulletin*, "Italy: Officials of the Italian Coast Guard Prosecuted for Shipwreck in 2013," September 20, 2019, https://ecre.org/italy-officials-of-the-italian-coast-guard
-persecuted-for-a-shipwreck-in-the-mediterranean-sea-in-2013/.

5 Walter Johnson, "Racial Capitalism and Human Rights," *Boston Review*,
February 21, 2018, http://bostonreview.net/forum/remake-world-slavery
-racial-capitalism-and-justice/walter-johnson-racial-capitalism-and
-human.

6 Genesis 9:3 quoted in Ghassan Hage, *Is Racism an Environmental Threat?*
(Cambridge: Polity Press, 2017), 83.

7 Sophia Rose Arjana, *Muslims in the Western Imagination* (New York: Oxford University Press, 2015), 1.

8 Arjana, 49.

9 Junaid Rana, "The Racial Infrastructure of the Terror Industrial Complex,"
Social Text 129 34, no. 4 (December 2016): 111–38.

10 Peter Gottschalk and Gabriel Greenberg, "Common Heritage, Uncommon
Fears: Islamophobia in the United States and British India, 1687–1947," in

Notes to Conclusion **245**

Islamophobia in America: The Anatomy of Intolerance, ed. Carl W. Ernst (New York: Palgrave, 2013), 39.

11 Hage, *Is Racism an Environmental Threat?,* 17–51.

12 Achille Mbembe, *Critique of Black Reason,* trans. Lauren Dubois (Durham: Duke University Press, 2017), 3.

13 Sedef Arat-Koç, "Power in/through Speaking of Terror: The Geopolitics and Anti-politics of Discourses on Violence in Other Places," in *At the Limits of Justice: Women of Colour on Terror,* ed. Suvendrini Perera and Sherene Razack (Toronto: University of Toronto Press, 2014), 356–79.

14 Sean R. Roberts, *The War on the Uyghurs: China's Internal Campaign against a Muslim Minority* (Princeton: Princeton University Press, 2020), 65.

15 Ben Emmerson, foreword to Roberts, *The War on the Uyghurs,* x.

16 "Myanmar Rohingya: What You Need to Know about the Crisis," *BBC News,* January 23, 2020, https://www.bbc.com/news/world-asia-41566561.

17 "Yemen: Events of 2019," Human Rights Watch: World Report 2020, https://www.hrw.org/world-report/2020/country-chapters/yemen#.

18 Sui-Lee Wee and Paul Mozur, "China Uses DNA to Map Faces," *New York Times,* December 10, 2019, https://www.nytimes.com/2019/12/03/business/china-dna-uighurs-xinjiang.html?auth=login-email&login=email. See also Roberts, *The War on the Uyghurs;* and Raffi Khatchadourian, "Ghost Walls," *New Yorker,* April 12, 2021, 30–54.

19 "Genetically Indian Story of Indian Muslims," *Radiance Weekly,* https://www.radianceweekly.com/57/407/draught-of-character-in-the-high-ups/2007-05-06/science-amp-technology/story-detail/genetically-indianstory--of-indian-muslims.html.

20 Bilal Kuchay, "India Police Stop Interfaith Marriage Citing 'Love Jihad' Law," *Al Jazeera,* December 4, 2020, https://www.aljazeera.com/amp/news/2020/12/4/india-police-stop-interfaith-marriage-citing-love-jihad-law.

21 Arundhati Roy, "India: Intimations of an Ending," *Nation,* November 22, 2019, https://www.thenation.com/article/archive/arundhati-roy-assam-modi/. This text was adapted from her address "India, Portents of an Ending: Modi, the RSS, and the Rise of the Hindu Far Right" for the Jonathan Schell Memorial Lecture on the Fate of the Earth on November 12, 2019, in New York City.

22 Roy.

23 Roy.

24 Sikata Banerjee, "Armed Masculinity, Hindu Nationalism, and Female Political Participation in India," *International Feminist Journal of Politics* 8, no. 1 (2006): 62–83; see also Amrita Basu, "Feminism Inverted: The Real Women

246 Notes to Conclusion

and Gendered Imagery of Hindu Nationalism," *Bulletin of Concerned Asian Scholars* 25, no. 4 (1993): 25–37.

25 Sucheta Mazumdar, "Women on the March: Right-Wing Mobilization in Contemporary India," in "Feminist Politics: Colonial/Postcolonial Worlds," special issue of *Feminist Review*, no. 49 (Spring 1995): 1.

26 Tanika Sarkar, "The Women of the Hindutva Brigade," *Bulletin of Concerned Asian Scholars* 25, no. 4 (1993): 16–24. See also Manisha Sethi, "Avenging Angels and Nurturing Mothers: Women in Hindu Nationalism," *Economic and Political Weekly*, April 20–26, 2002, 1545–52.

27 Roberts, *The War on the Uyghurs*, 21.

28 Roberts, 64.

29 Roberts, 63.

30 Will Martin, "China Is Harvesting Thousands of Human Organs from Its Uighur Muslim Minority, U.N. Human-Rights Body Hears," *Business Insider*, September 25, 2019, https://www.businessinsider.com/china-harvesting -organs-of-uighur-muslims-china-tribunal-tells-un-2019-9. See also Nabila Ramdani, "While China Harvests Human Organs from Its Persecuted Minorities, Britain Is Staying Silent to Protect Free Trade," *Independent*, September 25, 2019, https://www.independent.co.uk/voices/china-religious-ethnic -minorities-organ-harvesting-uighur-muslims-falun-gong-brexit-a9120146 .html; and Hataru Nomura, "Proof of China's Organ Harvesting Found in Xinjiang," The Liberty Web, September 21, 2018, http://eng.the-liberty.com /2018/7286/.

31 Kazuo Ishiguro, *Never Let Me Go* (New York: Vintage Books, 2005).

32 Emma Graham-Harrison and Juliette Garside, "'Allow No Escapes': Leak Exposes Reality of China's Vast Prison Camp Network," *Guardian*, November 24, 2019, https://www.theguardian.com/world/2019/nov/24/china-cables -leak-no-escapes-reality-china-uighur-prison-camp.

33 Austin Ramzy and Chris Buckley, "'Show Absolutely No Mercy': Inside China's Mass Detentions," *New York Times*, November 17, 2019, A8.

34 Ramzy and Buckley, A8.

35 Ramzy and Buckley, A8.

36 Ramzy and Buckley, A8.

37 Roberts, *The War on the Uyghurs*, 167.

38 Roberts, xiv.

39 Nury A. Turkel, "The Uyghur Crisis in China: Adversity, Advocacy, Activism" (panel discussion, UCLA Center for Near Eastern Studies, UCLA, Los Angeles, November 16, 2019).

40 Darren Byler, "The Uyghur Crisis in China: Adversity, Advocacy, Activism"

Notes to Conclusion 247

(panel discussion, UCLA Center for Near Eastern Studies, UCLA, Los Angeles, November 16, 2019).

41 Editorial Board, "Muslim Countries Joined China in Defending Its Cultural Genocide of Uighurs: Aren't They Ashamed?," *Washington Post,* July 20, 2019, https://www.washingtonpost.com/opinions/global-opinions/muslim -countries-joined-china-in-defending-its-cultural-genocide-of-uighurs -arent-they-ashamed/2019/07/20/0a7d62b4-aa3f-11e9–86dd-d7f0e60391e9 _story.html.

42 Sophie Richardson interviewed by Audie Cornish, "How the U.S. Is Responding to China's Mass Detention of Uighurs, Hong Kong Protests," *NPR,* November 18, 2019, https://www.npr.org/2019/11/18/780563138/how-the-u-s -is-responding-to-chinas-mass-detention-of-uighurs-hong-kong-protests. See also "US Bars China Officials over Uighur Crackdown in Xinjiang," *AlJazeera,* October 8, 2019, https://www.aljazeera.com/news/2019/10/bars -china-officials-xinjiang-crackdown-191009025000362.html.

43 Doyle Hodges, "Trump Said the Navy Can't Take Away Eddie Gallagher's SEAL Qualification. That Could Be a Problem," *Washington Post,* November 22, 2019, https://www.washingtonpost.com/politics/2019/11/22/trump -said-navy-cant-take-away-eddie-gallaghers-seal-qualification-that-could -be-problem/.

44 Dave Phillips, Peter Baker, Maggie Haberman, and Helene Cooper, "How a Navy Seal Gained the Favor of the President," *New York Times,* December 1, 2019, https://www.nytimes.com/2019/11/30/us/politics/trump-seals-eddie -gallagher.html.

45 Hodges, "Trump Said."

46 Hina Shamsi, "Opinion: We Need the Full Truth about CIA's Torture Program," *Los Angeles Times,* November 21, 2019, https://www.latimes.com /opinion/story/2019-11-21/torture-cia-senate-investigation-secret.

47 Adom Getachew, *Worldmaking after Empire: The Rise and Fall of Self-Determination* (Princeton: Princeton University Press, 2019), 2.

48 Sohail Daulatzai, *Black Star, Crescent Moon: The Muslim International and Black Freedom beyond America* (Minneapolis: University of Minnesota Press, 2012), 45–51.

49 Daulatzai.

50 Daulatzai, xviii.

51 Ronak K. Kapadia, *Insurgent Aesthetics: Security and the Queer Life of the Forever War* (Durham: Duke University Press, 2019), 9.

52 Kenza Oumlil, *North American Muslim Women Artists Talk Back: Assertions of Intelligibility* (Oxford: Routledge, Taylor Francis, forthcoming).

248 Notes to Conclusion

53 Tanika Sarkar, "Citizenship Protests in India: Possibilities and Challenges of Opposition to Hindu Nationalism," Berkley Center for Religion University Peace and World Affairs at Georgetown, March 9, 2020, https://berkleycenter .georgetown.edu/responses/citizenship-protests-in-india-possibilities-and -challenges-of-opposition-to-hindu-nationalism.

54 Nishita Trisal, "How to Sustain a Strike: Rules, Routines, and Logistics in Kashmir" (presentation, UCLA Department of Anthropology, Zoom, February 18, 2021).

55 Asim Kashgarian, "Washington, New York Protesters Call for Recognition of Uighur Abuses as Genocide," *VOA News*, August 29, 2020, https://www .voanews.com/east-asia-pacific/washington-new-york-protesters-call -recognition-uighur-abuses-genocide.

56 Alexandre Capron, "Why Are Protesting Farmers in India Being Labelled 'Violent Muslim Infiltrators'?," *The Observers*, January 28, 2021, https:// observers.france24.com/en/asia-pacific/20210128-farmers-india-protests -fake-news-social-media.

57 See Nadine Naber, *Arab America: Gender, Cultural Politics, and Activism* (New York: New York University Press, 2012); Mayanthi Fernando, *The Republic Unsettled: Muslim French and the Contradictions of Secularism* (Durham: Duke University Press, 2014); Sunaina Maira, *Boycott! The Academy and Justice for Palestine* (Oakland: University of California Press, 2017); Rabab Abdulhadi, Evelyn Alsultany, and Nadine Naber, eds., *Arab and Arab American Feminisms: Gender, Violence, and Belonging* (Syracuse: Syracuse University Press, 2011); and Amaney Jamal and Nadine Naber, *Race and Arab Americans before and after 9/11: From Invisible Citizens to Visible Subjects* (Syracuse: Syracuse University Press, 2008).

58 Naber, *Arab America*, 204.

59 Naber, 220.

60 Sunaina Maira, "Coming of Age under Surveillance: South Asian, Arab, and Afghan American Youth and Post-9/11 Activism," in *Activists and the Surveillance State: Learning from Repression*, ed. Aziz Choudry (London: Pluto Press, 2018): 79–96; see also Sunaina Maira, *The 9/11 Generation: Youth, Rights, and Solidarity in the "War on Terror"* (New York: New York University Press, 2016).

61 Lara Deeb cited in Fernando, *The Republic Unsettled*, 13. See also Lara Deeb, *An Enchanted Modern: Gender and Public Piety in Shi'i Lebanon* (Princeton: Princeton University Press, 2006).

62 Sherene H. Razack and Zeynep K. Korkman, eds., special issue, "Transnational Approaches to Anti-Muslim Racism," *Meridians* 20, no. 2 (2021).

Notes to Conclusion   249

63 Zeynep K. Korkman, "(Mis)Translations of Anti-Muslim Racism Discourse and the Repercussions or Transnational Feminist Solidarities," *Meridians* (forthcoming).

64 Ferruh Yilmaz, *How the Workers Became Muslims: Immigration, Culture, and Hegemonic Transformation in Europe* (Ann Arbor: University of Michigan Press, 2016), 3.

65 Hage, *Is Racism an Environmental Threat?*, 5.

66 Suvendrini Perera and Sherene H. Razack, "Introduction: At the Limits of Justice: Women of Colour Theorize Terror," in *At the Limits of Justice: Women of Colour on Terror*, ed. Suvendrini Perera and Sherene H. Razack (Toronto: University of Toronto Press, 2014), 3–15.

67 Yassir Morsi, *Radical Skin, Moderate Masks: De-radicalising the Muslim and Racism in Post-racial Societies* (London: Rowman and Littlefield International, 2017).

68 Houria Bouteldja, *Whites, Jews, and Us: Toward a Politics of Revolutionary Love*, Semiotext(e)/Intervention Series 22 (Cambridge: MIT Press, 2016).

69 Hage, *Is Racism an Environmental Threat?*, 133.

Index

Abella, Justice Rosalie, 94

abortion, 45, 63, 64, 70

Abu Ghraib, 39, 47, 152, 171, 177, 196; discussions of, 160, 161, 175; documentary on, 146, 149–50, 159–60; releasing photos from, 154; remembering, 164, 175; torture at, 35, 48, 140, 145–49, 151, 156, 157, 158, 159–62, 165, 166, 170, 172, 173, 179, 184; war on terror and, 168

Abu-Lughod, Lila, 177

abuse, 147, 151, 159, 163, 167, 188, 189; documenting, 166, 170; prisoner, 146

accumulation, 182; capitalist, 14, 34, 48; racial project of, 20, 39, 180

Achiume, Tendayi, 29

ACLJ. *See* American Center for Law and Justice

ACT for America (ACT), 64, 65, 67

affect: anti-Muslim, 6, 8, 13, 45, 46, 52, 63, 81, 86, 160; colonial, 183; definition of, 13; whiteness as, 13

African Americans, 58, 68–69, 129

Agamben, Giorgio, 232n16

Agathangelou, Anna, 39–40, 43

aggrievement: harnessing, 60–80; white Christian, 80–83

Ahmad, Irfan, 25

Ahmed, Sara, 13

Algerians, 162, 172, 173

Allah, 3, 8; God and, 11, 12, 48

al-Qaeda, 2, 63, 124, 130, 132, 148

Ambuhl, Megan, 159, 164, 166

American Academy of Religion, 60

American Center for Law and Justice (ACLJ), 76–77, 79

animus: anti-Muslim, 2, 3, 9, 15–16, 53, 63; racial, 2, 4, 18, 19, 34; white-supremacist, 45

anti-bullying programs, 66, 67, 68, 69

Anti-Defamation League (ADL), 68

anti-immigrant agenda, 4, 112, 181

anti-Muslim actors, 3, 6, 11, 53, 64, 78, 79, 81, 119, 139

anti-Muslim feelings, 2, 17, 46, 52, 54, 60, 125, 178, 180, 182, 186, 192, 194

anti-Muslim interests, 55, 70, 178, 188

anti-Muslim movements, 33, 45, 66, 68

anti-Muslim projects, 6, 82, 138, 187

anti-Semitism, 32, 61, 64, 68, 79, 137

apologies, function of, 158, 161

Arab-Israeli War (1967), 30

Arat-Koç, Sedef, 32, 183

Arendt, Hannah, 117

Arjana, Sophia Rose, 5, 177, 178, 181

Arnold, Evelyn, 71, 72

Asad, Talal, 109

Asian Americans, concerns of, 67–68

Assamese Indians, 185, 186

assassination, targeted, 4, 35, 203n3

251

252 Index

Augusta County, school conflict in, 74–75, 75–76
Aung San Suu Kyi, 33
Azoulay, Ariella, 111–12

Badinter, Elizabeth, 101, 102
Baehr, Peter, 98
Bagram, 116, 119, 146, 147, 196
Bail, Christopher, 66, 218n86
Baker, Josephine, 108
Bakht, Natasha, 85, 91, 93–94, 105, 109
Baldwin, James, 16
Bâli, Aslı, 29
Balibar, Étienne, 90
bans, 3, 46, 51, 86, 95, 103, 112, 113; anti-Muslim, 22, 47, 178, 183, 190; citizenship, 97; clothing, 22, 26, 47, 86, 91, 98, 105–6, 111, 112, 183; impact of, 90, 91; implementing, 87; legal, 6, 107; logic of, 91; niqab/burqa/hijab/in Europe/North America map, 84; refusing, 110–11; religious symbol, 89, 98; sexuality and, 109; spatial analysis of, 102; travel, 42, 88, 89, 178; whiteness and, 182–83
Baruma, Ian, 170
Belfer, Aaryn, 69, 70
Bellotto (il Canaletto), Bernardo: painting by, 50
Bergland, Renée L., 1, 3, 13, 14
Berko, Anat, 137
Berlant, Lauren, 103
Bharatiya Janata Party, 186
Bidar, Abdennour, 102
bin Laden, Osama, 40, 44, 128, 177
biology, as destiny, 139–43
biopolitics, 141
Bissonnette, Alexandre, 88–89, 196

Bjork-James, Sophie, 58
Black bodies, 19, 37, 45
Black freedom struggles, 14, 192–93
Black Lives Matter, 1, 17, 54, 55, 204n15
Black Muslims, 14; anticolonialism and, 192; persecution of, 192–93
Black Panthers, 192, 193
Black peoples, 14, 38, 47; police brutality and, 140
Blackwater, 174
Blandy, Sarah, 207n49, 222n8
Blum, Edward, 21
Bouteldja, Houria, 197
Brahmins, 185
Brand, Dionne, 146
Breitbart News, 76, 79
Breivik, Anders, 81
Brondage, W. Fitzhugh, 151
Brown, Nicole, 37
Brown, Wendy, 53, 81, 82
Brown peoples, 17, 38
brutality, 35, 140, 142, 145, 149
bullying, 2, 66, 67–69
Burlein, Ann, 57, 58, 69, 73, 74
burqas: bans on, 84, 98; wearing, 85, 88
Bush, George W., 172; torture and, 148, 150, 157, 158, 173
Business Insider, 188
Butler, Judith, 111
Byler, Darren, 190, 191

CAIR. *See* Council on American-Islamic Relations
calligraphy, Arabic, 12, 46, 61, 62, 74, 75, 76, 80, 82, 178, 184
Cameron, David, 132
Camp Delta, 156
Camp 4: 127, 128, 129

Index   253

Campus Watch, 76, 77
Camp X-Ray, 156
Canadian Charter of Rights and Freedoms, 89
Caner, Emir and Ergun, 57
capitalism, 40; global, 32, 34; racial, 6, 22
Carl, Noah, 139–40
Carlson, Tucker, 77, 78
Casting Out: The Eviction of Muslims from Western Law and Politics (Razack), 4, 93, 115, 124
Catherine of Aragon, 63
Catholicism, 25, 54, 67
Chaiken, Michael, 171
Charles County, school conflict in, 70–71
Charlie Hebdo, 1, 30
Chatham School Board, 77, 79
Cheng, Anne Anlin, 85, 108
Chen Quanguo, Uyghurs and, 190
Chesler, Phyllis, 136–37, 141, 236n79
"China Cables," 188
Chinese Communist Party, 184
Chow, Rey, 44, 100, 228n70
Christian Action Network, 76, 79
Christian Europe, 10, 51; defending, 41, 81
Christian evangelicals, 16, 46, 53, 54, 55, 57, 59, 60, 81, 183; of color, 31; Korean, 31; sexual politics of, 58; white, 82
Christianity, 2, 6, 8, 15, 24, 25, 33, 46, 52, 55, 57, 59, 60, 65, 66, 77, 82; authority of, 56; colonialism and, 23; defending, 51, 58, 61, 79; fears of, 83; fundamentalist, 72; hegemony of, 61; Islam and, 22, 40–41, 49, 182; jihad against, 54; as normative, 61;

Other and, 21; positive imagery of, 80; rationality and, 10, 61; white, 16, 181; whiteness and, 17, 19, 20–21, 56; white supremacy/subjectivity and, 7
Christian Post, 76, 79
Christian right, 54, 55, 66, 76; blogs of, 41, 50, 51; interventions by, 80; leadership of, 73; politics of, 52
Christians: African American, 31; conservative, 55, 57, 61, 67, 70, 78; Muslims and, 69–70, 130; as normative citizens, 42. *See also* Christian evangelicals
Christian women: Islamic indoctrination and, 78; leadership of, 73–80
CIA, 151, 155, 191
Cimino, Richard, 57
Citizens for Quality Education, 67
citizenship, 100, 110, 112, 120; ban on, 97; enactments of, 107; oath, 96, 97, 99; racialized, 91–92
civility, 66, 97, 99, 150; codes of, 95
civilization, 31, 61, 100, 125, 152, 173; European, 6, 10; Judeo-Christian, 55, 81; liberal foundation of, 120; Muslims and, 3; superior, 183; Western, 12; white, 55
Clarion Fund, 76, 218n86
Clarion Project, 79, 139
Clark, Victoria, 58, 59, 81
clothing: bans on, 22, 26, 47, 86, 91, 98, 105–6, 111, 112, 183; Muslim, 3, 22, 108; Uyghur, 190
Cole, David, 35, 157
colonialism, 5, 6, 7, 15, 16, 22, 40, 41, 43, 86, 188, 192; Christianity and, 23; French, 90; progress/rationality and, 56; settler, 29, 45; slavery and,

254 Index

38; Spanish, 115; white supremacy and, 9–10

color line, cracks in, 31–35, 183–84

communism, 118, 120, 154

Compton, John, 16–17

concentration camps, 4, 118, 185, 186

Congress for Cultural Freedom, 123

Conrad, Joseph, 162

Contra Costa County, role-playing assignments in, 62

Copé, Jean-François, 107–8

Council on American-Islamic Relations (CAIR), 66, 70; ADL and, 68; bullying and, 67; curriculum issues and, 69, 78

countermemories, 73, 74

counterterrorism, 29, 123, 136, 184, 195

Craven, Lucy, 106–7, 108

Cromwell, John, 58

Crusades, 22, 41, 51, 52, 57, 59, 182

cultural developments, 25, 30, 194

cultural practices, 47, 104, 146

culture, 25, 99, 115, 173; Algerian, 86; dysfunctional, 138; European, 31; honor, 137; imperial, 29, 45; Muslim, 62, 64, 66, 76, 120, 125, 127, 129, 134, 137; national, 53; Oriental, 24; race and, 15, 117; religion and, 62, 136; torture, 157; Western, 11, 100, 179. See also popular culture

curriculum: deciding on, 73, 77–78; on Islam, 52, 55, 60, 61, 64, 69, 75, 77, 78, 79, 81; multicultural, 61, 62–63

Dahlab v. Switzerland, 105

Dallaire, Romeo, 119

Danner, Mark, 155, 158

D'Arcangelis, Gwen, 148, 164

Darwin, Charles, 139

Darwinism, 140

Daulatzai, Sohail, 4, 5, 10, 192, 193, 203n3

Davis, Angela, 147

Davis, Javal, 159, 164, 166

Dayan, Colin, 38, 39

De Genova, Nicholas, 30

democracy, 2, 3, 24, 47, 93, 100, 103, 151; liberal, 96; political, 25; Western, 25

demons, 1, 3, 7, 36, 52, 195

Dershowitz, Alan, 156

detention, 2, 34, 182; camps, 190, 191; indefinite, 35

DeVos, Betsy, 80

Diaz, Anthony, 167

Dick, Philip K., 235n68

difference, 35, 111; civilizational, 154; colonial, 43; cultural, 155, 173; psychological, 140; racial, 87, 141; sexual, 43, 87

disability, 103, 104, 141

discourse: anti-Muslim, 52, 55, 57, 183; antiracist, 195, 196; emotional, 111; far-right, 67; gendered, 100; nationalism, 90; public, 100, 196; racial, 33, 135; settler, 57; sexualized, 47; terrorism, 118; Zionist, 122

disposability, 33, 40, 47, 179, 184, 186, 192

dispossession, 17, 56, 186

Dobson, James, 57, 58, 73, 74

Donors Capital Fund, 218n86

Dratel, Joshua, 154

Du Bois, W. E. B., 32, 42, 208n56; Christianity and, 20–21; Islam, Palestinians and, 20; whiteness and, 19, 20–21

Index   255

Dugan, Tim, 168–69
Duke, David, 17, 69
Duras, Marguerite, 228n70

Eason, Chris, 128
economic crisis, 32, 53, 73–74, 181
Edney, Denis, 233n19
education, 60, 141; multicultural approach of, 52; religious, 55, 78; secular, 70, 78; sex, 69, 73
Eighth Amendment, 38
Eklund, Jonas and Tiffany, 62–63, 64, 65, 66, 75
Emmerson, Ben, 184
emotions, 6–7, 11, 37, 52, 86, 95, 111; anti-Muslim, 3, 7, 46, 55, 178; biopolitics of, 141; identity and, 13; racism and, 7
England, Lynndie, 156, 159, 169, 171–72, 175; Abu Ghraib lessons and, 16; described, 167–68; prisoner abuse and, 151; torture and, 149
entitlement, 14, 18, 24; Christian, 43, 153; racial threat to, 3; white, 16–17, 43, 53, 82
epigenetics, 117, 138, 141, 142
Esmeir, Samera, 39
Essa, Huda, 65
Establishment Clause, 60, 79
ethnic cleansing, 33, 81
European Court of Human Rights (ECHR), 99
European Union, 40, 132
evolutionary psychology, 119, 135–36, 138
Evolutionary Psychology, 142, 182
exceptionalism, 7, 29, 44, 146, 148
extremism, 27, 47, 87, 89, 117, 139; religious, 28, 188, 189–90

Falwell, Jerry, 58, 215n29
Fanon, Frantz, 32, 39, 40, 85, 86, 102, 108, 180
fantasmic, 207, 221n8
fantasy: colonial, 43, 107, 152, 154; imperial, 11; Orientalist, 40, 149; racial, 11, 40, 91; war, 171
Farley, Anthony Paul, 240n21
fascism, 7, 120, 197
FBI, counterterrorism and, 195
FCDF. *See* Freedom of Conscience Defense Fund
fears, 5, 15, 24, 34, 43, 45, 62, 63, 75, 80, 81, 83, 97, 112, 180, 196; amalgam of, 45, 56; fascist, 44; generalized, 82; ugly laws and, 103; voice and, 42; white, 14, 40
Feldman, Keith, 29
femininity, 100, 102, 111; normative, 101; white, 173
feminism: Arab American, 194; French, 100; liberal, 1; Muslim, 178, 194; niqabs and, 109; transnational, 195
Fernando, Mayanthi, 99, 194, 195
Ferreira da Silva, Denise, 35, 36
First Amendment, 60, 73
folk devils, 22, 40
foreign policy, 29, 46; God's, 59, 82
Fox News, 54, 64, 66, 76, 77, 78, 88, 155
Frederick, Ivan, 159, 169
freedom, 25, 67, 187, 193; academic, 73, 80; immigrant women and, 103; liberal, 23
Freedom Fighter Radio, 8
Freedom of Conscience Defense Fund (FCDF), 67, 79
Frost, Jeffrey, 167
Fuchs, Cynthia, 171–72

256 Index

Fugino, Diane, 15
fundamentalism, 27, 30–31, 137;
  Christian, 73; Islamic, 59, 73

Gabriel, Brigitte, 64
Gaddafi, Muammar, 29
Gaffney, Frank, 218n86
Gallagher, Edward R., 191
Gates of Vienna (website), 41, 50, 51,
  76
Gaza, 80, 139, 181, 195
gender, 26, 58, 182, 194; notion of, 100,
  101–2, 104
gender equality, 3, 24, 31, 47, 90, 93,
  109
gene pools, 134, 142, 185; damaged, 12,
  47, 133
genetics, 117, 119, 138, 141, 184; politics
  and, 185; racial knowledge about,
  42–43; violence and, 118, 179
Geneva Convention, 12, 155
genocide, 34, 148, 183–92; cultural, 33,
  65, 184, 191; Muslim, 183, 193–94
geopolitics, 7, 48, 177
Gerin Commission, 100, 101, 102
Gerin Report, 101, 102, 228n65
Getachew, Adom, 192
ghosts, 1, 14, 36
Ghosts of Abu Ghraib (film), 157,
  159–60
Githens-Mazer, Jonathan, 138
global North, 31, 186; anti-Muslim
  projects of, 34
global South, 31, 32, 33, 178, 186; anti-
  Muslim projects of, 34
global war on terror (GWOT), 10, 27
God, 42, 61, 74, 81; Allah and, 11, 12,
  48; foreign policy of, 59, 82
Goddard, Peter, 171

Goldberg, David, 21, 23, 117
Goodman, Amy, 160–61
Good News Ministries, 75
Gordon, Daniel, 98
Gordon, Linda, 142
Gourevitch, Philip, 159, 161, 162, 165,
  168, 169, 170
governance: Christian Zionist, 58–60;
  racial, 8, 35, 92, 112, 113; techniques
  of, 27
Graham, Billy, 215n29
Graner, Charles, 159, 164, 167, 169, 170,
  171, 175
Greek Orthodox church, 230n98
Griffin, Tom, 138
Griffin, Virgil, 73
Grillo, Ralph, 112
Grinnell, George, 96–97, 106, 107,
  110, 111
Guantánamo, 12, 31, 116, 119, 121, 124,
  127, 130, 134, 142, 146, 147, 177, 196;
  brutality at, 35; prisoner treatment
  at, 232n16; sentencing hearing at,
  47; torture at, 150, 156, 157, 158, 184
Gulf War, 30, 152
GWOT. *See* global war on terror

Hage, Ghassan, 13, 41, 107, 181, 196,
  197; on paranoia, 205n29; racism
  and, 131
Hagia Sophia mosque, 230n98
Hamas, 54, 69, 70, 139
Han, Judy, 31
Han Chinese, Uyghurs and, 34, 188,
  189–90
Hanson, Pauline, 88
Harman, Sabrina, 159, 163, 164, 169,
  171; molestation and, 165; narrative
  of, 166; torture by, 170

Harper, Stephen, 95–96, 104
Harris, Cheryl, 18
Hartman, Saidiya, 18
Haspel, Gina, 191
hegemony, 14, 92, 148; colonial, 153;
    white, 2–3, 6
heritability, 115–16, 134, 135
Herndon, Kimberly, 74, 75–76
Hesse, Barnor, 7–8
heterosexuality, 44, 236n81
Hezbollah, 58
hierarchy, 208n56; citizenship, 85;
    power, 140; racial, 92, 97, 141
hijabs, 11, 24, 197; bans on, 47, 84, 87,
    98, 112, 183, 190; wearing, 2, 37, 99,
    190
Hilsenrath, Libby, 77, 78, 79
Hinduism, 33, 186, 187
Hirsi Ali, Ayaan, 10, 177
Hochberg, Gil, 164
Holmes, Stephen, 154
Holocaust, 7, 22, 123
homeless, 105, 229n78, 229n83
homosexuality, 152, 155–56
hooks, bell, 20
Horowitz, David, 79
humanity, 111, 117, 120, 172; biometric
    model of, 142; division of, 185; evo-
    lutionary scale of, 142; superfluous,
    182
human rights, 2, 10–11, 23–24, 25, 27,
    99, 179
humiliation, 53, 82, 138, 169, 171; tor-
    ture and, 53, 164, 165, 166, 167
Hunt, David, 57
Hunter, Shona, 13
Hurt Locker, The (film), 149
Husak, Douglas, 106
Hussein, Saddam, 152

identity, 155, 180; Christian, 19, 53;
    countermemories and, 74; emo-
    tions and, 13; European, 55, 205n29;
    imperial, 153–54; Jewish, 23; phan-
    tasmatic, 18; racial, 15; religious, 15,
    187; torture and, 153–54; white, 21,
    22, 27, 205n29
immigration, 96, 125; clampdowns on,
    26, 45; reform, 64
imperialism, 5, 6, 14–15, 20, 22, 31, 82,
    177, 186, 194; white supremacy and,
    7, 9–10
inclusion, politics of, 61, 82–83
incoherence, 40, 41; miasma of, 37, 38
Indigenous peoples, 6, 14, 17, 21, 38,
    47, 54, 56, 181
individualism, 25, 101
indoctrination, Islamic, 75, 76, 79
infrastructure, 11, 80; economic/
    political/social, 27; media, 186; ra-
    cial, 182, 184
interrogation, 154; manual on, 155;
    Orientalist, 155; techniques, 39; tor-
    ture and, 156
Iran-Iraq War, 152
Ishiguro, Kazuo, 188
ISIS, 2, 74, 151, 179, 189, 197
Islam: banning of, 3, 46, 51, 53, 183;
    curriculum on, 52, 55, 60, 61, 75, 77,
    78, 79, 81; foundational role of, 24,
    55; fundamentalist, 71, 72; irrational,
    61; portrayal of, 62–63; presence
    of, 55, 61; progressive/conservative
    views of, 52; radical, 55, 67, 76, 91,
    123, 128, 139; rationality and, 25; re-
    jecting, 10; satanic, 61, 80; teaching,
    64; threat of, 29; traditional, 123;
    white supremacy and, 5
Islam, Namira, 15

258 Index

Islamic enemy, 4, 28, 34, 51, 52, 55, 62, 63, 98, 146, 147, 150, 151, 152, 166, 173, 175
Islamic Revolution (1979), 30
Islamization, 52, 79, 125
Islamland, 177, 178, 197
Islamophobia, 15, 46, 66, 78, 132, 138–39. *See also* fears
Israel, 29, 45, 58, 117, 118, 135, 195; criticism of, 57, 64, 79, 137, 139; foundational narrative of, 56, 61, 82; Islamic enemy and, 55; support for, 45, 53, 54, 59, 65, 81, 183

Jackson Press, 79
Jacobs, Harriet, 20
Jennings, Willie, 19, 23, 56
Jerusalem Post, 66
Jews, 19, 20, 22, 44, 46, 54, 56, 64, 65, 67, 68, 129, 181; gassing of, 186–87; Zionist, 70
jihad, 54, 57, 65, 120, 124, 125, 127
jihadis, 27, 34, 65, 120, 122, 124, 127, 129, 130, 136, 137; deradicalization of, 132; radical, 123, 125, 126
Jihad Watch, 77, 79
Johnson, Lyndon B., 138
Johnson, Walter, 181
Jones, Robert P., 16
Jones, Terry, 80
Jones, Timothy, 156
Judaism, 65, 66, 80; Catholicism and, 25

Kant, Immanuel, 25
Kapadia, Ronak, 193
Kapur, Ratna, 23, 24, 98
Kashmir, 33, 186, 193, 197
Kemp, Brian, 9, 204n15

Kennedy, Rory, 159–60
Kenney, Jason, 96, 99
Khadr, Ahmed, 128
Khadr, Omar, 116, 119–20, 126, 127; acculturation and, 129–34; assessment of, 122–23; behavior/rationality and, 128; culture/religion of, 129–30; non-Muslims and, 129; racial science and, 119; sentencing of, 121, 133; Sharia law and, 131; Speers and, 124; torture of, 146, 179, 196; Welner and, 124, 129–34
Khosrokhavar, Farhad, 137–38
killings: extrajudicial, 179; honor, 64, 179; targeted, 203n3
kindness centers, 190–91
King, Rodney, 37
KKK, 17, 73
Klein, Melanie, 207n49, 222n8
Kobrin, Nancy Hartevelt, 136–37, 139, 140, 141
Korkman, Zeynep K., 195
Kundnani, Arun, 120, 123
Kurdi, Aylan, 30
Kurds, 196

Lake, Marilyn, 26
Laqueur, Walter, 123, 124
Laurier, Joanne, 172
law, 47; anti-Muslim, 45; civil, 130; politics and, 46, 178; popular culture and, 142; rule of, 172, 173; Sharia, 80, 130, 131; whiteness and, 35, 185–86
law enforcement, 123–24, 227n36
Lazreg, Marnia, 153, 154, 162, 172, 173
League of Nations, Covenant of, 26–27
Lean, Nathan, 139

Index **259**

LeBel, Justice Louis, 94, 95, 96
legal cases, phantasmic scenes in, 92–102
Levinas, 107, 110, 111, 230n109
LGBTQ, organizations/programs, 69
Li, Darryl, 28, 34
liberalism, 7, 39, 45, 52, 90, 197;
  Muslims and, 23–26, 27
LiMandri, Charles, 67
Lindt, John Walker, 66
Lipsitz, George, 18
Locke, John, 36, 205n23
Lokaneeta, Jinee, 175
London School of Economics, 135
Long, Edwin, 115; painting by, 114

MacDonald, Heather, 155, 156
Mack, David, 174
Mahmood, Saba, 109
Mahrouse, Gada, 97
Maira, Sunaina, 194, 195
Majid, Anouar, 22
Malcolm X, 192
Mandela, Nelson, 130
Martínez, Maria Elena, 135
Marusek, Sarah, 138–39
Massad, Joseph, 24, 25, 205n23
Matar, Nabil, 22, 40
Mayer, Jane, 157
Mayer, Nancy, 77, 78, 79
Mbembe, Achille, 41, 42, 182–83
McCarthy, Andrew, 156
McKittrick, Katherine, 142, 143
McNulty, Kevin, 79
Meer, Nasar, 21, 40
memory: childhood, 197; cultural, 22, 145, 146, 148, 149, 173; history and, 146; national, 47; post-torture, 160–70; violence and, 146

Merkel, Angela, 133
Middle East Forum, 65
Middle East Studies, remaking, 80
Mikhail, Dunya, 175
Milgram, Stanley, 157–58, 160
Military Intelligence, 166–67
Miller, Dan, 76
Miller, David, 138
Miller, William, 106
Mills, Charles, 95
Mills, Tom, 138
Minority Report (film), 135, 235n68
Mishra, Pankaj, 14
misogyny, 1, 5, 60, 37, 155
modernity, 4, 11, 39, 41, 43, 45, 99;
  emergence of, 24–25; European, 40; metanarratives of, 22; violence and, 44
Modi, Narendra, 33, 187
Mongols, 25
monsters: Muslim, 5, 182; sexualized images of, 181–82
Moorish Proselytes of Archbishop Ximenes, Granada, 1500, The (Long), 114
moral community, 48, 149, 150, 159, 161–62
Moral Majority, 215n29
Morey, Robert, 57
Mormons, 33, 54, 67
Morris, Errol, 48, 149, 159, 160, 161, 162, 165, 168, 169, 170, 171, 172
Morris, Shannon, 71
Morrison, Toni, 36–37, 113
Morsi, Yassir, 197
Mountain States Legal Foundation, 65
Moynihan, Daniel Patrick, 138
Muhammad, Prophet, 25, 71, 74, 137;
  as pedophile, 43; sex slavery and, 69

260 Index

multiculturalism, 58, 60, 70, 73, 75, 96

Muslim bodies, 40, 42, 173; as targets, 45; violation of, 48

Muslim Brotherhood, 76

Muslim International, 192, 194

Muslim men: imagined, 46; marking of, 44; patriarchal, 87; as universal enemy, 4

Muslimness, 32, 104

Muslim phantoms, 3, 5, 7, 14, 42

Muslims: arriving as, 178–83; Black American, 82; Blacks and, 41; cartoon, 82; Chinese campaign against, 28; Christians and, 69–70, 130; dialogue with, 77; European antipathy for, 21–22; foreignness and, 61; French, 101–2, 172; good/bad, 8, 15, 71, 197; Indian, 185; legal abandonment of, 120; liberalism and, 23–26; marginalization of, 43, 194; military experience with, 72; protecting, 70; protests by, 80–81; racialized, 27, 28–29; Rohingya, 33, 184; settler subjects and, 55–60; Shia, 185; simulating, 62–63; stigmatization of, 120; strikes against, 59; Sunni, 185; surveillance/control of, 184–85; targeting of, 68; as terrorists, 34, 42, 61, 142, 150, 236n81; tolerance of, 52; Western civilization and, 3; Westernized, 116; white evangelicals and, 53

Muslim women, 42, 137; attacks on, 187; attention for, 104; choices for, 91; civic life and, 102; civilizing projects and, 26; colonial fantasy of, 106; controlling, 91, 98; criminalization of, 90, 107; desire for, 85; discrimination against, 88; feminism

and, 178; freedom/democracy and, 103; memoirs by, 10; patriarchs and, 11; property rights for, 24; protection of, 44–45; racialization of, 110; sovereignty over, 88

Muslim youth, 42, 68, 137

Myanmar, ethnic cleansing in, 33, 184

mythology, 53, 214n4; cultural, 179; national, 52, 54; settler, 56; unbounded, 153

Naber, Nadine Suleiman, 29–30, 194

narratives: anti-Muslim, 183; antitorture, 149–50, 156–60, 164; blood, 134; Christian evangelical, 54, 55; civilizational, 98; redemptive, 150; settler-colonial, 61; soldier, 166; torture, 152, 154; Zionist, 55

nationalism, 9, 13, 14, 90; English, 87; French, 87; white, 3, 4, 88, 89

National Register of Citizens, 185

nation-states, 17, 192, 196

neoliberalism, 33, 82, 196

Neshat, Shirin, 193

Netanyahu, Benjamin, 118

New York Review of Books, 141, 170

New York Times, 17–18, 189, 231n117; "China Cables" and, 188

Ngai, Sianne, 106

Nietzsche, Friedrich, 81, 145–46

9/11, 62, 66, 71, 122, 189, 195, 197

niqabs, 11, 24, 197; bans on, 47, 84, 87, 91, 96, 98, 100, 102, 103, 105–6, 111, 112, 183, 190; French core values and, 99–100; gender inequality and, 109; liberal democracy and, 96; removing, 86, 93, 94; wearing, 2, 37, 42, 85, 86, 88, 90, 91, 92, 94, 95, 96, 97, 101, 103–9, 178

Index **261**

Nkrumah, Kwame, 192
Nora, Pierre, 160

Obama, Barack, 76, 130, 150, 173
Ogden, Roger, 69
Omar, Ilhan, 88, 139
Omi, Michael, 21
Operation Desert Storm, 72
Orientalism, 25, 30, 32, 40, 52, 55, 107,
128, 130
Other, 24, 36, 43, 110, 182; atavistic, 3;
Christianity and, 21; constitution of,
42; dehumanization of, 158; differ-
ence of, 111; face of, 102; humanity
of, 108; Islamic, 3–4, 41, 52; Orien-
talizing, 32; racial, 2, 19, 21, 23, 27,
29, 42, 44, 45, 56, 101, 117, 148, 152,
163; self and, 23, 44; ungovernable, 5
Otis, George, 57
Ottoman empire, 40, 116, 181
Oumlil, Kenza, 193

Pack, Brent, 169, 172
Palestine, 20, 29, 30, 135; Jewish state
in, 23, 54, 56, 57; occupation of, 53
Palestinians, 5, 61, 112, 117–18, 137; dis-
possession of, 81, 180, 183, 194
Paris Peace Conference, 26
patriarchy, 11, 57, 93, 104, 109, 139
Patriot Fire, 69
Patton, Chloe, 107, 110, 111
Penkoski, Richard, 79
personhood, 23, 35, 39, 173
Peters, Pete, 57, 58, 73, 74
phantom Muslims, 36, 59–60, 62, 87,
122, 180
Pierce, Steven, 145, 151
Pinar, William, 18, 208n56
Pipes, Daniel, 65–66, 76, 77, 218n86

Planned Parenthood, 67, 70
political community, 13, 95, 112, 195;
Muslims and, 46, 47, 109, 142, 162
political projects, 7, 9, 180
politics, 6, 86, 115, 123, 151, 183, 192;
antidemocratic, 81; anti-imperialist,
195; anti-Muslim, 9, 27, 45, 46, 55,
82, 87, 187; antiracist, 196; Arab
American feminist, 194; Christian,
60; Christian Zionist, 58–60; coalitional, 195; of death, 138; far-right,
2; genetic research and, 185; global,
2, 27, 193; law and, 46, 178; liberal, 2,
8, 45, 61, 82–83; nationalist, 55, 60;
oppositional, 186, 196; racial, 20, 70;
radical, 195; science and, 122; sexual,
58; white, 4, 9, 52, 55, 60, 70, 185–86
popular culture, 1, 73, 98, 142, 146, 170
populist movements, 32, 82
Porterfield, Kate, 122
possession, 47, 65, 86, 91, 104; act of,
108; dreams of, 108, 113; erotics of,
43
power, 11, 153; aesthetics of, 86;
cultural, 16; governmental, 13;
imperial, 40, 45, 146, 148, 179, 180;
Ottoman, 24; political, 16, 24; racial,
45, 86, 100, 102, 148; sovereign, 23;
white, 86
predispositions, 38; cultural, 118, 119,
120; genetic, 141–42
prejudice, 15, 17, 18, 98, 141
"Project Beauty" campaign, 190
propaganda: anti-Muslim, 47, 121;
Indian government, 197; Islamic,
64–65
Protestantism, 16, 25, 67
Proud Boys, 54, 69
pseudoscience, 133, 134

262 Index

psychology, 120, 140; evolutionary, 19, 135–36, 138; pathological, 184; theology and, 123

Psychology Today, 135

Puar, Jasbir, 43–44, 236n81

public space, 110, 229n78; Muslim women and, 85–86, 91, 99, 102–3, 105; preserving, 104, 107; reimagining, 111

Putamayo Indians, 153

Quebec City mosque, attack at, 88–89, 97

Quebec Superior Court, Bill 21 and, 89

queers, 44, 59, 236n81

Qur'an, 62, 129, 190; burning, 80–81; memorizing, 126–27

race, 115, 194; culture and, 15; dysfunctional, 138; ideology of, 140; reason and, 42; religion and, 17, 33; torture and, 151–52, 172

race making, 7, 11, 34, 142, 184

race-thinking, 117–34

racial equality clause, 26

racial feeling, 33, 180

racial harm, 17, 37, 68

racialization, 28, 33, 36, 45, 47, 55, 86, 110, 117, 129, 142, 185, 186; Muslim, 29, 60; psychological, 123; religion and, 21

racial science, 37, 44, 116, 118, 140, 142; anti-Muslim, 117; coherency and, 122; war on terror and, 119

racism, 4, 16, 41–42, 69, 121, 129, 131, 155, 160, 194; anti-Muslim, 2, 5, 6–7, 7–14, 15, 24, 28, 29–30, 31, 32, 33, 43–44, 47, 51–52, 63, 68, 81, 82, 83,

88, 97, 99, 120, 177, 178, 180, 183, 184, 186, 193, 195, 196, 197; biological, 117; cultural, 26; double bind of, 8; emotional/affective registers of, 7–14; modern, 21–22; resistance to, 194; scientific, 117; targets of, 15, 83; varieties of, 9, 117

radicalism, 28, 125, 129, 190; Islamic, 64, 118, 182, 233n26; roots of, 138

Rajputs, 185

Rana, Junaid, 4, 10, 15, 182, 203n3; racial infrastructure and, 32

Rao, Anupama, 145, 151

rape, issue of, 30, 34, 39, 92, 101, 187

rationality, 10, 11, 12, 36, 56, 61, 117, 147; behavior and, 128; Islam and, 25

Razzaq, Abdul, 174

Reagan, Ronald, 215n29

Red Cross, 155, 158

refugees, 2, 4, 6, 31, 34, 85, 118, 181, 183

religion, 61, 72, 115, 129–30; culture and, 62, 136; race and, 17, 21, 33; terrorist, 91, 116

religiosity, 98, 109, 117–34, 195

religious symbols, bans on, 89, 98

remembrance, 146, 147

Rendition, 157

resentment, mobilizing, 62–68

"ressentiment," concept of, 81

Reynolds, Henry, 26

Ridley, Hugh, 163

Rippberger, Carl, 161

Roberts, Dorothy, 119, 140

Roberts, Sean R., 28, 142, 188, 190

Rodríguez, Dylan, 18, 45

Rohingya Muslims, ethnic cleansing of, 33, 184

Rosenfield, Israel, 141

Rossinot, André, 101

Index **263**

Roth, Michael, 171
Roy, Arundhati, 186
Rubaie, Haitham, 174–75
Rumsfeld, Donald, 158, 163
R. v. N.S., 92, 93, 94

Sageman, Marc, 133
Sahin v. Turkey, 105
Said, Edward W., 5, 24, 28, 30, 115, 118, 138
Saini, Angela: criticism of, 139–40
Salaita, Steven, 56
San Diego Asian Americans for Equality, 67, 68
San Diego City Beat, 69
San Diego Unified School District Board of Education, 66, 68–69
San Francisco, school conflict, in, 62–63, 75
Saracens, 48, 181
Sarkar, Tanika, 187, 193
S.A.S. v. France, 99
savagery, 48, 119, 154, 163
Scarry, Elaine: torture and, 173
Schlesinger, James, 159
Schuler, Kyla, 141
Schumer, Chuck, 79
Schwartz, Matthew: Welner and, 132
Schweik, Susan, 105; ugly laws and, 103, 104, 110, 111
science: politics and, 122. *See also* racial science
Scott, Joan, 98
secularism, 3, 23, 24, 31, 47, 60, 90, 95, 99, 109, 110, 180
security, 80, 111, 124, 135; national, 29, 31, 35; threat to, 134; transnational, 195
self, 12; Other and, 23, 44

self-determination, 28, 36, 192
Sennels, Nicolai, 32, 121, 126, 127; Muslim inbreeding and, 132–33; psychological differences and, 140; radicalization and, 125
separatism, 188, 189
settler projects, 54, 56, 57
sexual assault, 92, 93, 94, 104, 111
sexual availability, 104, 105, 106
sexuality, 101, 102, 109, 155, 182, 194
Shah, Prakash, 112
Shahada, 71, 72, 74, 79, 80, 82, 787
Shapiro, James, 22
Sharia law, 80, 126, 130, 131
Sheets, Penelope, 156
Shephard, Michelle, 133
Seshadri-Crooks, Kalpana, 18
Sibley, David, 207n49, 222n8
Sikhs, 177
Silverblatt, Irene, 115
Simpson, O. J., 37, 40
Sivits, Jeremy, 159, 164
slavery, 14–15, 41, 48, 40, 146; abolition of, 21; aura of, 39; colonialism and, 38; dynamics of, 20; narrative of, 192
Slotkin, Richard, 52, 179
Smith, Malinda, 31
social interaction, 12, 98, 102, 106
social problems, 53, 96, 158
sociobiology, 119
socioeconomics, 7, 32
Somalis, 31; abuses of, 159, 163
Sontag, Susan, 170, 171
Souls of Black Folk, The (Du Bois), 19
Souls of White Folk, The (Du Bois), 19
Southern Poverty Law Center, 8
Spanish Inquisition, 115, 134–35
Speers, Christopher, 116, 120, 124

264 Index

Spencer, Richard, 69, 79, 191

Spencer, Robert, 77

Stachowiak, James J., 8–9, 204n15

Stampnitzky, Lisa, 122

Standard Operating Procedure (film),
146, 147, 148, 149–50, 157, 159, 162

subjectivity, 101; countermemories
and, 74; white, 7, 134

suicide bombers, 136, 137

Suleiman the Magnificent, 51

superiority: abjection and, 240n21;
cultural, 107, 173; European, 12, 39;
French, 100; racial, 11, 91, 100, 107;
Western, 7, 100

supremacy, 5, 14, 88, 96; Hindu, 34,
186, 187; white, 24

Supreme Court of Canada, 89, 92–93,
94

surveillance, 2, 184, 189, 195, 203n3

Syria, civil war in, 189

Tarrant, Brenton, 196

Taussig, Michael, 153, 154

technology, 40, 182, 190, 195

Temple of the Mount, 57, 81

Tenbroek, Jacobus, 110

Terin Commission, 100

terrorism, 4, 26, 27, 28, 29, 35, 36, 42,
46, 48, 61, 62, 80, 82, 118, 133, 142,
172, 179, 182, 189; commitment to,
44; explanation for, 122, 123; images
of, 40; Islamic, 30, 31, 39, 48, 51, 67,
120, 123, 138, 184, 188; jihadi, 137;
prevention of, 138; rational actors
and, 122; risk of, 124; roots of, 120,
123; simulation exercises and, 66;
state, 47; suicide, 135, 136, 137; threat
from, 116

terrorists, 14, 80, 139; attack by, 89;

development of, 136; global, 184,
188; homegrown, 116; Muslim, 34,
61, 67, 89, 117–18, 119, 122, 129, 135,
142, 150, 187

Theweleit, Klaus, 44

Thirteenth Amendment, 38

Thomas More Law Center, 66, 67, 78,
79; goals of, 63–64; petition by, 73;
report by, 64–65

Thompson, Richard, 64, 66, 79, 217n63

372nd Military Police, 162

Titchkosky, Tanya, 141

Toronto Star, 133

torture, 2, 31, 34, 35, 38, 39, 47, 48, 145,
156–60, 168, 173, 182, 184; acceptability of, 148, 154; authorization of,
158; beatings and, 167; blame for,
159; charting, 181; concealing, 170;
criticism of, 149–50, 154, 156, 157,
159, 162, 175; culturally different enemies and, 151–56; cultural memory
of, 146, 148, 149; discussing, 152, 173;
end of, 150, 158; historical review
of, 151; humiliation and, 53, 164, 165,
166, 167; identity and, 153–54, 158;
interrogation and, 156; morality
and, 148, 159; pardons for, 175; practices of, 148, 156, 157, 169; psychological explanations for, 158; race
and, 151–52, 172; responsibility for,
160, 161; scenes of, 159, 162; sexualized, 47, 152–53, 154, 155, 168, 179;
sights of, 147, 191; transformation
of, 164; trauma and, 146

torturers, 146, 147, 149, 160, 162

Trump, Donald, 9, 54, 73, 187; Omar
and, 88; pardons by, 175; war crimes
and, 191; white nationalist politics
of, 55

Index **265**

T-shirts: anti-Muslim, viii, 1, 2, 3, 8, 9, 12, 13, 24; pedagogical operation of, 1, 8
Tucker Carlson Tonight, 77, 78
Turkel, Nuri, 190
Turks, 22, 107, 181
Turner, Jon Michael, 161

ugly laws, 105, 110, 111; civic contagion and, 103–4
Ugly Laws, The (Schweik), 103
United Nations Human Rights Council, 188
United Nations International Criminal Tribunals for Rwanda and the former Yugoslavia, 184
United Nations Security Council, 29
Universal Declaration of Human Rights, 27
U.S. Capitol, attack on, 9
U.S. Court of Appeals for the Fourth Circuit, 72
U.S. Court of Appeals for the Ninth Circuit, 63
U.S. Department of Defense, torture and, 156–57
U.S. Department of Education, 80, 81
U.S. Department of Homeland Security, 195
U.S. District Court for the District of Maryland, 72
U.S. Navy SEALs, inquiry by, 191
U.S. Supreme Court, 60, 75, 151; terror and, 35; travel bans and, 42; Wood case and, 73
Uyghurs, 33, 193; abuses of, 188, 189; campaign against, 22, 28, 187–88, 190, 191; genocide against, 184, 185; Han Chinese and, 34, 188, 189–90

Van Houtum, Henk, 112
veils, 104, 110; bans on, 112; removing, 86, 87, 107; wearing, 99, 101
Velazquez, Jose, 67
Vienna, siege of, 41
Vienna Viewed from the Belvedere Palace (Bellotto), 50
Vietnam Veterans Against the War, 160
violence, 4, 12, 27, 28, 37, 43, 47, 54, 86, 105, 117, 119, 121, 141, 147–48, 155, 187; against women, 44; anti-Black, 17; anti-Muslim, 31, 80, 86, 90, 145, 183, 187, 193; authorization of, 35–36, 186; confronting, 158–59; constitutive, 102; economics of, 196; genetics and, 118, 179; imperial, 149, 151–52; intimate partner, 101; Islamic extremist, 65, 194; law-preserving, 41; memory and, 146; modernity and, 44; Palestinian, 54; patriarchal, 109; of peacekeepers, 162–63; police, 17; political, 34; racial, 2, 7, 48, 90, 109, 145, 152, 186; religious, 126; state, 4, 158–59, 164; torture and, 146; whiteness and, 21, 152–53
Virginia Board of Education, 76
Voltaire, 25

Wang Yongszhi, 190
war crimes, 121, 191, 233n19, 242n45
war on terror, 36, 38, 116, 149, 154, 157, 168, 175, 188, 189; excesses of, 147; racial science and, 119. *See also* global war on terror
Washington Post, 134
Weber, Jill Critchley, 78
Weisman, Richard, 161

266 Index

Welner, Michael, 115, 116, 126, 127, 128; assessment by, 122, 123; on deracialization, 129; jihad and, 125; Khadr and, 122, 124, 129–34; psychological differences and, 140; terrorism and, 133; testimony of, 121, 132

Werbner, Pnina, 22, 40

Wesselhoeft, Kirsten, 100, 101, 111, 228n65

white masculinity: aggressive, 68–73; Christian rage and, 70–71

whiteness, 10, 15, 24, 54, 58; access to, 32; affect of, 19; bans and, 182–83; benefits of, 33, 183–84; call to, 11; Christian, 4, 5, 14, 17, 20–21, 63; colonial, 21, 83; as constructed dominance, 18; as emotional place, 13; as frontier aesthetic, 21; global, 27, 179, 180, 193; historical character of, 18; imperial, 31, 184; international, 26–31, 32, 183, 184, 186; making of, 5, 44; material, 40; Muslims and, 8, 14–35, 183; nonwhites and, 32; politics and, 26, 185–86; protection of, 37; psychic, 40; psychosexual structure of, 18; racism and, 6–7; subject and, 51; violence and, 21, 152–53

white supremacy, 4, 7, 37, 41, 46, 58, 69, 82, 89, 117, 121, 125, 133, 135, 196; anti-Muslim feeling and, 2; colonialism/imperialism and, 9–10; defining, 45; global, 5, 6, 26–31, 142, 178, 192, 193, 194, 197; legal process and, 132; Muslims and, 14–35, 88, 120; racial, 8

Williams, Eric, 192

Winant, Howard, 21

Winegard, Bo, 139

Winter, Jay, 146, 147

Winter Soldiers, 158, 160, 161

Women of Grace (blog), 78

women's rights, 2, 3, 10–11, 179

Wood, Caleigh, 71

Wood, John, 74, 80; suit by, 71–72, 73

Woods, James, 75

World Socialist website, 172

World Trade Center, 62, 71, 152

Wynter, Sylvia, 142

Wyrick, Christopher, 69, 70, 74

Wyrick, Kristy, 70

Xenakis, Stephen N., 122, 133–34

Xi Jinping, Uyghurs and, 189–90

Ximenes, Archbishop, 115

Xinjiang province, 28, 33, 188; cultural genocide in, 191; forced labor in, 190

Xu, Frank, 67–68

Yeğenoğlu, Meyda, 43, 85

Yemen, 29, 194; bombing of, 181, 183, 184

Yilmaz, Ferruh, 196

Zaimov, Stoyan, 76

Zayid, Mayzoon, 193

Zero Dark Thirty (film), 149

Ziff, Edward, 141

Zi Jinping, 33

Zionism, 17, 31, 46, 57, 58, 138, 214n5

Zionists, 53, 54, 65, 70, 76, 80, 82, 120; Muslims and, 55–60

Zubaydah, Abu, 150, 151

SHERENE H. RAZACK is Distinguished Professor and Penny Kanner Endowed Chair in the Department of Gender Studies at the University of California, Los Angeles. A feminist critical race scholar, she is author of six books, including *Casting Out: The Eviction of Muslims from Western Law and Politics.*

Lightning Source UK Ltd.
Milton Keynes UK
UKHW020943180522
403171UK00011B/1040